The Single Woman's Guide to Retirement

Jan Cullinane

WILEY

John Wiley & Sons, Inc.

Cover Design: Lesley Q. Palmer
Cover Illustration: Sarah Wilkins

Published by John Wiley & Sons, Inc., Hoboken, New Jersey.
Published simultaneously in Canada.

For general information on our other products and services or for technical support, please contact our Customer Care Department within the United States at (800) 762-2974, outside the United States at (317) 572-3993 or fax (317) 572-4002.

This and other AARP books are available in a variety of formats at AARP's online bookstore, aarp.org/bookstore, and through local and online bookstores.

Wiley publishes in a variety of print and electronic formats and by print-on-demand. Some material included with standard print versions of this book may not be included in e-books or in print-on-demand. If this book refers to media such as a CD or DVD that is not included in the version you purchased, you may download this material at http://booksupport.wiley.com. For more information about Wiley products, visit www.wiley.com.

Library of Congress Cataloging-in-Publication Data:

Cullinane, Jan, author.
    The single woman's guide to retirement / Jan Cullinane.
       pages cm
    Includes index.
    ISBN 978-1-118-22950-7 (pbk.); ISBN 978-1-118-28498-8 (ebk);
    ISBN 978-1-118-28401-8 (ebk); ISBN 978-1-118-28300-4 (ebk)
       1. Single women–Retirement–United States.   2. Women–Retirement–United
       States. 3. Retirement–United States–Planning.   4. Retirement income–United
       States–Planning.   I. Title.
    HQ1063.2.U6C853 2012
    306.3'808652—dc23

                                                              2012020176

Printed in the United States of America.

10 9 8 7 6 5 4 3 2

Contents

Preface

Why did I decide to write a book about single women and retirement? My previous book, *The New Retirement: The Ultimate Guide to the Rest of Your Life*, was primarily targeted to couples. Over the past decade, as I gave many talks about retirement, I noticed a curious phenomenon. Women would routinely come up after a presentation and say, "I've never married. All the ads for places to live are targeted to couples. Where should *I* move?" or "My ex handled the money. Now I'm on my own—help!" or "I may be getting divorced. What should I do to protect myself?" or "I was a stay-at-home mom and haven't worked in 30 years. How do I get back into the workplace?" or "I'm widowed, in my late 50s, and I'd like to date again. What about me?"

These are examples from an important and growing demographic: single women, whether they're thinking about retirement or already retired, women ranging in age from their 40s to decades beyond.

Even if you're happily married or have a significant other now, there's an 80 to 90 percent chance you'll be making all decisions, financial and otherwise, at some point. Retirement is an odyssey that can be exciting and liberating, scary and stressful, and often it is a cauldron of change and conflicting emotions.

Single women are the second-largest category of home-buyers; women surpass men in college graduation rates and are slowly catching up to men in salaries. But, we know all is not rosy. Single women are also the most likely to end up in poverty, have concerns about outliving their money, and worry about taking care of themselves—and their aging parents—as they age.

So, what's in this book? It addresses dating, divorce, death of a spouse, relocation, health, volunteering, working, boomerang children, caregiving, and money. It contains worksheets, the latest research about mature single women, contributions from other experts, references, and lots of anecdotes, examples, and suggestions from single women I know or have met personally or professionally, including some virtual acquaintances. Helpful hints, fun facts, and tantalizing tidbits are sprinkled throughout as well. The book is designed to be a guide for single women about all aspects of retirement and to provide a blueprint for a satisfying and successful retirement. It's also specific. If a place to relocate is recommended, there are specific communities referenced along with their Web sites, not just a city or state. If you're looking to find a single stateroom on a cruise ship, specific cruise ships are listed. Looking for legitimate work-at-home possibilities? You'll see companies, requirements, and contact info. I guess it's my science background, but I happen to like details as well as stories.

I mentioned that anecdotes from single women are woven throughout the book. A few examples: Joanne C. left her prestigious career to care for her ill parents; Marie V. is widowed and found a job homeshoring (working from home); Ann F. started her own business; Louise O. picked up stakes in the United States and moved to Boquete, Panama; Bonnie W. loves to travel with like-minded women and found an easy way to do so; Emily is a lesbian and found the perfect place to live; Jacque B. wanted a home of her own combined with the support of a cohousing community—and found it; Rebecca V. has two boomerang children and is struggling to save for retirement; Mary Pat R. pushes her comfort zone by volunteering in less-developed countries; Andrea C. was scammed through a dating site; and Patti K. met her soon-to-be husband through one. (To protect their privacy, women who contributed stories are mostly identified by their first or middle name and last initial, although a few requested that only their first name be used.)

What is the common thread among these women? They represent the 25 million single (divorced, widowed, never-married) women over the age of 45 in the United States. Real women sharing real challenges, solutions, exhilaration, fears, and ideas as they approach or begin this journey we call retirement. Jonathon

Brown, a social psychologist at the University of Washington, shares this analogy when it comes to grappling with life's twists and turns:

> It's like the difference between a dog and a duck. A duck goes in the water and doesn't get wet. That's a gift ducks get early in life. A dog goes in the water and it has to shake itself dry. Maybe you're never going to be a duck, but you can learn to be a better dog. You can learn to handle life better.

If you're a duck in all areas of your life, you're one lucky woman. But, if, like most of us, you're a dog, you can still adapt, embrace, learn, and thrive.

Acknowledgments

Many thanks to the many women who shared their fascinating stories, provided excellent advice, and demonstrate resilience, strength, and hope. And, to the professionals who provided insights about law, employment, aging, and finances. I'd also like to express gratitude to the wonderful people at John Wiley & Sons, especially Debra Englander, Kimberly Bernard, Claire New, Christina Verigan, and Tula Batanchiev; and to the AARP experts: Deb Briceland-Betts, Mary Liz Burns, Christina Smith FitzPatrick, Albert Hollenbeck, Gary Koenig, Amy Levner, Susan Lutz, George (Sandy) Mackenzie, Harry R. Moody, Leslie Nettleford, Cassandra D. Oshinnaiye, Jonathan Peterson, Matthew Phillips, Erin Scheithe, Amy Slonim, Lori A. Trawinski, Mikki Waid, Ryan Wilson, and Melissa Castro Wyatt. Finally, a huge shout-out to Jodi Lipson, the managing editor for the books program at AARP.

CHAPTER 1

Retirement and the Single Woman

Do one thing every day that scares you.

—Eleanor Roosevelt

■ ■ ■

Sex and the Single Girl, Helen Gurley Brown's 1962 blockbuster book, encouraged single women to become strong and independent and to live life to the fullest. More than 50 years later, that's still excellent advice. Let's substitute "retirement" for "sex" and "woman" for "girl." *Retirement and the Single Woman* doesn't sound quite as titillating, does it? The term "girl" no longer applies, and although sex is important, there are additional vital issues to discuss when it comes to this transition called retirement. But, as in Brown's book, strength, independence, and a satisfying life are still noble goals for single women.

In this chapter, we'll take a look at what makes this demographic important and growing. If you're not a numbers person, you'll at least be happy to note that a lot more research is now being done on women in general and single women in particular. This certainly has not been the case in the past.

What would you rather do, plan a two-week vacation or plan for retirement? It's easier and a lot more fun preparing to bask in the sun on a tropical island or to tour Tuscany than to look ahead to the next 30 or so years of your life. It's something that we can't

1

ignore and should be excited about doing, if we have the right tools and mind-set. That is the purpose of this book—to help you plan a fun, rewarding, and successful retirement, to give you specific thoughts and ideas on how to do this, and to hear from real single women about their real-life experiences.

We can now expect to live, on average, to the ripe old age of 81. Of course, longevity is affected by lifestyle, age, and genetic factors (I just completed a life-expectancy calculator that said I should plan to live to 97). The good news is that we can live a long time. The scary news is that we can live a long time, so we had better be prepared. And getting ready for retirement is a lot more than just about money, although being financially secure is an important consideration. It's also about what to do with 168 hours a week. It's about maybe working, maybe relocating, perhaps reinventing yourself, ideally deepening connections, possibly taking care of elderly parents, maybe about never-having-left-the-coop children or boomerang children, and about trying to stay as healthy as possible. It's a new life chapter, and one we should welcome.

You may be asking yourself if you *should* retire. How do you know when it's the right time to retire from a primary career? Think about your answers to these three questions: Do I have enough? Have I had enough? Do I have enough to do? If the response is a resounding and unqualified "yes" to all three, you're probably ready to retire. If you're unsure, or just for fun, take the "Are You Ready for Retirement Quiz" in Appendix 1 at the end of this chapter. The quiz addresses areas you should consider when deciding whether or not it's the right time for you to retire.

For More Information

To get an idea of your life expectancy, check out www.livingto100.com or http://apps.bluezones.com/vitality. Fun and easy, and you receive immediate feedback on your input.

A few years ago, TV and newspapers announced with much fanfare that a little more than half of all women (and 70 percent of African American women) in the United States were living in a home without a spouse. Although the U.S. Census data applied to women age 15 years and older and included a small number of husbands who were in jail, in the military, or out of town working, this reflects a big shift from previous decades. Married couples became a minority of all households in 2005, demonstrating that single women are a demographic to be seriously addressed.

By the way, I recognize that some women prefer the term "unmarried" to "single" because they may have children or a significant other, or they are widowed or divorced, but for simplicity's sake, we'll use "single" in this book to include all of the above.

The 5Ds

The number of mature single women is huge (more than 25 million over the age of 45) and growing. The reason for this increase can be attributed to what I call the 5Ds: **D**eath of a spouse (women outlive men by an average of five years); **D**ivorce (25 percent of all divorces are between couples over 50, according to the National Center for Marriage and Family Research); **D**elayed marriage (the median age for a woman's first marriage is 26 today, compared to the early 20s after World War II); **D**umped (in a relationship heading to the altar, but derailed by either side); and just **D**on't want to be married (never-married boomers—those born between 1946 and 1964—make up 10 percent of single women).

More women are taking longer to find their "soul mate," seeking more pleasure out of life, and emphasizing career and education over marriage. Single women are just as happy, productive, and socially engaged as their married counterparts. The 19th-century

Did You Know?

Among adults age 46–64, about a third are single (divorced, separated, never married, or widowed), according to Bowling Green State University demographers. And most of these single people are living alone.

Fun Fact

Did you know there's a "National Singles and Unmarried Americans Week"? It's celebrated the third full week in September and was started in Ohio in the 1980s.

---

stereotype of the severe, unattractive, hair-in-a-bun, glasses-on-a-chain spinster is at long last dead.

A *Time* magazine cover recently asked "Who Needs Marriage?" Among those who were unmarried, almost half of those surveyed agreed that the institution of marriage was no longer viable (reminds me of the famous quote attributed to Groucho Marx: "Marriage is a great institution . . . but who wants to live in an institution?").

What Makes Single Women Special?

As with any large group, it's impossible and foolhardy to make generalizations, but, there are some general characteristics of this demographic:

- **Economics.** Single women are now in a better position than ever to support themselves, although it is also true that more than half of all poor adult women are single. Women currently make $0.81 for every $1.00 a man makes, even when controlling for experience and education. This discrepancy is shrinking (it was $0.76 in 2000), but gender inequity persists. Women are overrepresented in lower-paying jobs such as those in sales, service, teaching, and nursing, and underrepresented in the more lucrative science, technology, engineering, and math (STEM) careers. Women are also more likely to take time out of the workforce for caregiving.

  As women continue to make gains in salary and education, they will be in a better position to choose the kind of life they want. And it's never too late. After 20 years of being married and a stay-at-home mom to her four children and being the "woman behind the man," Sylvia M. was divorced from her husband. She went back to school, got an accounting degree, and passed the CPA exam. She is now working for a small CPA firm, loving her life, and making more (a lot more!) than her ex-husband.

Presently, about 1 in 10 people over the age of 65 live in poverty. That's a big improvement from the 1970s, when it was about one in four. When we narrow those statistics from the U.S. Census, the numbers are disconcerting. The poverty rate for *single* women over 65 is 17 percent. Breaking that down in more detail, single African-American women over 65 have a poverty rate of 32 percent, single Hispanic women 44 percent, and white women 15 percent. Why? Lower-income jobs, fewer employee benefits, fewer pensions, lower Social Security payments, and smaller investment income all contribute. The "Dollars and Sense" chapter will help ensure you aren't part of these glum statistics.

The Million-Dollar Difference?

What if women were better negotiators? Fascinating research by Linda Babcock shows that "women who consistently negotiate their salary increases earn at least $1 million more during their careers than women who don't." She also found that "by not negotiating a first salary, an individual stands to lose more than $500,000 by age 60."

Women undervalue themselves, often feeling grateful to be offered a job, and underestimate their market value by up to 30 percent. We offer the asking price for a home about three times more frequently than men, and pay an average of $200 more for a car. We (along with our daughters and granddaughters) need to bone up on those negotiation skills. See the "More 411" section at the end of this chapter for help in this area.

- **Education.** On college campuses, women outnumber men by an almost 3:2 ratio. Women earn more high school diplomas, associate's degrees, bachelor's degrees, and master's degrees than do men, and are closing in on the number of doctorates. Though we still lag in STEM degrees, we earn almost half of law and medical degrees and represent almost 80 percent of veterinary school students. This increasing professionalism will propel women to a higher standard of living.

- **Psychology.** The paradigm of singlehood is changing. Being single is "a satisfying destination rather than an anxiety-ridden way station, a sign of independence rather than a mark of shame, an opportunity to develop a variety of relationships rather than a demand to stuff all one's emotional eggs into one basket" as Jillian Straus remarks in *Psychology Today.* The creative term "freemale" has been coined to describe this lifestyle. Single women can have children (with or without sex) without the stigma. "Single women can pick up the check at work and sperm at the bank," as Dr. Bella DePaulo, professor of psychology at the University of California, Santa Barbara, cleverly remarks. And what about happiness? The conventional wisdom is that married people are happier, but a Michigan State University study found that although there was a slight upward shift in happiness after getting married, it was temporary (two years), and people returned to their basic happiness set-point, which is determined by personality traits and genetics.

- **The Mind and Body.** As we age, we aren't losing our minds as soon as men are. At least that's what a recent study in *Neurology* reported. That should offer some consolation. Men are one and a half times more likely to suffer mild cognitive impairment (forgetting names and where they left things, not being able to follow a conversation easily) than are women. Men decline earlier but at a more gradual rate; since women tend to be older than men when they get dementia, their decline is more dramatic. It's true that women have higher rates of Alzheimer's disease; some researchers theorize that because we live longer, we're more apt to progress to this state.

One of the reasons women outlive men is our sex chromosomes; women have two X chromosomes, while men have an X and a Y chromosome. Having that additional X confers some significant advantages, including a stronger immune system and the higher likelihood of surviving sepsis (blood poisoning), injuries, and trauma.

- **"Marriage Advantage."** What about the studies that show marrieds are healthier than their unmarried counterparts? As the research has been refined (the first study about the "marriage advantage" is 150 years old!), it turns out that those who are not happy in their marriages are less healthy than those who have never married. Linda Waite, a sociologist at the University of Chicago, found that those who were divorced or widowed were worse off (more health and mobility problems) than the never-marrieds. And women who remarried after a divorce experienced more health and mobility problems than their married counterparts who remained with their original spouse. So, marriage per se is not an automatic prescription for happiness and health. Although a *happy* marriage does confer some health benefits, the subsequent loss of a spouse through divorce or death negates this "marriage advantage." It's interesting to note it was only 200 years ago that a strong link between love and marriage became common; originally, marriage was a way of pooling resources for the survival of children.

    One marriage "disadvantage" could be physical fitness. The Cooper Clinic in Dallas, Texas, found that women who remained single during a several-year fitness study had slightly higher cardiovascular fitness than their married sisters.

- **Feelings about Retirement and $$$.** Single women over 50 hold some important (and unsettling) attitudes about the financial aspects of retirement: Only 2 percent of single women are "very confident" that they can retire comfortably; 57 percent of single women cited Social Security as their primary source of income in retirement; single women estimated they would need $250,000 to retire comfortably, but only 8 percent have saved that much, according to the Transamerica Retirement Survey. Yes, a lot of statistics, but . . . more than three-fourths of women are still enthusiastic about retirement.

    Health care is another big expense in retirement that must be considered. Indefinite, long-term care isn't covered by Medicare, and there can be other out-of-pocket costs even after you reach the magic age of 65. Again, we have good news and bad news. The good news: If you are struggling with retirement planning, you are not alone. The bad news: Single women need to do better planning for their retirement. More good news: That is one of the topics this book addresses. The subsequent chapters lay out a specific road map to a successful retirement regarding all facets of this transition, both financial and nonfinancial.

- **Investing.** From the time we are young, women learn less about money from our parents than do men, and what we are taught is more about budgeting and saving rather than stocks, bonds, and estate planning, according to an expert on financial literacy, Dr. Tahira Hira, professor of Personal Finance and Consumer Economics at Iowa State University. (When I was growing up, talking about the cost of anything in our largely female family was taboo.) Even among women who make over $100,000 a year, about half still have fears about becoming "bag ladies" when they become older.

  Single women are the most prudent investors. One study showed single women earned 2.3 percent greater returns than did single men. Compared to men, women make fewer overall investing mistakes and are more likely to get help from a financial professional, save a bit more out of their paychecks, ask more questions, and do more research.

  Women are also generally more risk-averse investors than men. In surveys, more than half have compared investing to gambling, and they tend to miss those large, short-term returns; feel they have less experience and knowledge; generally invest less money (men jump in quickly, and women tend to teeter); and own fewer funds. Even though we know there are no guarantees, more than four out of five women want a product that provides guaranteed income for life, regardless of how the market is performing. Women also aren't as interested in the subject of money as men and would rather learn about finances up close and personal—either one-on-one or in a "safe" group setting with women in similar circumstances.

Women, more often than men, need the nudge of a life event to trigger investing, such as divorce, widowhood, or childbirth. Remember, at some point, 80 to 90 percent of *all* women will be solely responsible for their finances. See Chapter 8 for specifics on building and maintaining that nest egg.

- **Home Ownership.** Single women make up more than one-fifth of all home buyers; they are the second largest contingent of home purchasers, according to the National Board of Realtors. Single women see a home as a symbol of success, providing roots and security. Banks no longer balk at lending money for mortgages to single women (as was previously the case; that is, of course, if you can get a loan these days, which is getting more difficult). Almost half of mature single women are open to having a roommate, and they are more likely to purchase condos or a two-bedroom home. Some places are more desirable for single women; that will be discussed in Chapters 5 and 6.
- **Social Support.** Social support is critical for a successful retirement, and it's an area where many single women shine. The importance of friends on longevity has been repeatedly demonstrated. A 10-year study found those with the largest network of friends outlived those with the fewest friends by 22 percent (the study found that it was friends and not children or spouses who made the difference). A 13-year study found that those who were socially engaged lived two and a half years longer than those who weren't. In a third study, a group of heart attack victims was followed for one year, and those who were socially isolated had a lower survival rate than those who weren't. And a study in the journal *Cancer* reported that women with advanced ovarian cancer who had strong social support responded better to chemotherapy. Okay, you get the point—social support is important. In fact, social support is sometimes called Vitamin F—the "F" stands for friendship.

But *why* does social support result in a longer life span? It's thought that good friends help prevent depression, encourage healthy behavior, boost self-esteem, model coping

9

mechanisms, provide more resources, and play a role in lowering the stress hormone cortisol in their friends. Biologically (sorry, but I used to teach this stuff), scientists found that heart attack victims with higher levels of social support had lower levels of stress hormones, which resulted in less cell damage. We often have a richer and more varied support system than do men, and single women often work particularly hard at developing and maintaining these rich connections. Women "tend and befriend"—we protect and nurture, are more empathetic, and seek support from others. See Chapter 7 for a broader discussion of developing and deepening connections.

- **Work.** For the most part, single women will have to work longer than their married counterparts since they may not have another source of income. Compared to men, we live longer, make less money on average, are more likely to work (or have worked) part-time, have often left the workforce (an average of 15 years) to care for children and parents, and more often lack a pension. When we do receive a pension, it's generally about half as much as a man's. Our nest eggs end up being smaller than men's—about a third smaller. Interestingly, a Charles Schwab survey found that 95 percent of Americans said they are not willing to spend less in retirement, and almost half plan to delay the transition by working longer.

  Women now make up half of the nation's workforce, and more than half of professional and management positions, according to the U.S. Government Accountability Office. Men initially lost more jobs in the recent recession (that's why it's sometimes called a "mancession") because male-dominated construction and manufacturing jobs were disproportionately affected, but as job loss slowed, more women have been affected. In our so-called Great Recession, women lost one out of three jobs, but if you're divorced and relying on support from your ex, it's no comfort that men are out of more jobs than women. Women are more strongly represented in areas of job growth, such as health care and education. Single working females have a slight edge in income growth over their married counterparts over the last quarter century. See Chapter 3 for specifics on hot jobs and how to get them.

Fun Fact

Women control 60 percent of all wealth in the United States, according to Allianz Life Insurance.

- **Caregiving.** The majority of caregivers for older adults are women. Approximately one in four caregivers are single women, caring for sick or disabled family members an average of 20 hours a week, and 84 percent of never-married women provide some assistance to their parents. We often think of caregiving as something we do for our elders, but women 40 and older make up 39 percent of custodial single moms.

    Single women caring for elderly parents fare more poorly than their married counterparts in finances, well-being, and social support. About a fifth of women caregivers have to pass up promotions, decrease their number of working hours, switch from full- to part-time work, and take a leave of absence or retire early. Stress, health problems, and depression are reported. But on the positive side, women caregivers gain more purpose, personal growth, and self-acceptance.

    At the other end of the spectrum is boomerang kids. About 85 percent of 2011 college graduates had to move back home due to lack of a job and/or huge debt, and more than 1 in 10 parents with grown kids have seen one or more return to the (crowded) nest. While having your adult children live with you temporarily can be a good thing, you need to be careful that it doesn't derail your retirement planning. See Chapter 7 for an in-depth discussion of this topic.

- **Exercise.** New research demonstrates that women's bodies respond differently to exercise than do men's bodies. Maybe this explains why the weight seems to fall off a guy when he works out, but not for us. It seems reasonable that if we increase our activity level, we will burn more calories and lose weight. Pretty straightforward, right? Yet, research shows that for *women*, creating a calorie deficit through exercise increases the amount of acylated ghrelin, the hormone that increases appetite (no wonder I'm starving after I play three sets of tennis). For men, the hormone level changed very little or not at all. In fact, men reported a decrease in appetite during vigorous exercise and evidenced decreased levels of acylated ghrelin for two hours after.

Women's bodies are genetically programmed to maintain their fat levels for reproduction, even though we may be waaaaayyyy beyond that point. So, should we toss our hand weights and cancel our membership to the gym? Not so fast. Once weight is lost, working out seems to be the critical ingredient for keeping weight gain at bay. Research on rats found that active but obesity-prone rodents who slimmed down because of food restrictions and were then allowed to eat at will gained less weight, ate less, and metabolized food differently than did the sedentary group of rats. How much exercise is necessary? About an hour a day for women. What works best? And, are there any shortcuts? Sort of. See Chapter 4 for specifics.

- **Sex, Love, and Independence.** Single women don't want to compromise when it comes to relationships, according to a Match.com study that found only 23 percent of single women 60 and older are likely to "make a committed relationship with someone who offers everything you are looking for in a relationship but with whom you are not in love." Only 19 percent of this group would enter a committed relationship without sexual attraction. Across every age group in this study, women were more likely than men to want to continue to control their own bank account, cultivate their own interests, take vacations by themselves, and go out with their women friends on a regular basis.
- **Hormones.** Obviously, single women don't have a monopoly on menopause, but it's worth mentioning since it's a rite of passage for all women. Postmenopausal women tend to be less active and have a lower resting metabolic rate, burning about 200 fewer calories a day than premenopausal women. Does estrogen equal muscle strength? Studies show that estrogen has a favorable effect on skeletal muscle strength in women.

And, there is a lot of discussion about the Women's Health Initiative, a federal study that ended three years early because researchers decided that it would be injurious to women to continue the hormone replacement study. Read more about this study, and why some consider it flawed, in Chapter 4.

Single women have both opportunities and challenges when it comes to this transition we call retirement. The Holmes and Rahe Stress Scale lists 43 of life's biggest stressors. The death of a spouse or child is number 1; a minor parking violation is number 43. Retirement is listed at number 10. Let's reduce the stress and start exploring the ways to ensure a happy retirement.

If you're no longer working, you'll have the benefits of time and choice in retirement. On to Chapter 2 to see how you might enjoy these gifts.

My Life   Single and Satisfied—Jean L.'s take on being single:

"Yes, I'm single, have always been single, and I'm luvin' it," I have said countless times to the unbelieving American male, and to many girlfriends as well. What's not to love? Go where I want, say what I want, see what I want, be what I want . . . just my own choices, however difficult they may be at times. From my youth, saddled with a moderate amount of responsibility being the oldest of six, I set my sights early on exploring things near and far. This is not to say my path has been simple or easy, but it has been an adventure at every turn.

My background is theater, so "art, beauty, and truth" beckoned. My first tip to The Single Woman is to pursue that which you love. When you have a passion for something, joy is real, and if you're lucky enough to express yourself and find others who share your passion, you will never feel alone or lonely (and there is a difference). There is so much to discover, learn, experience, and enjoy, how can anyone ever be "alone" or "bored"? The hardest part is to select from all the options and forge ahead! A single woman has so many alternatives, and fortunately the choice is hers alone to make (of course, lots of input from confidantes is most important).

Another wonder-filled gift is time alone—to reflect, to regroup, to dream dreams, to venture into new arenas. Hooray for the pleasures of "time on our hands" (that is, if you are not a Type A personality and can manage it).

We have finally reached a stage in our lives where we can listen to the "inner child" and thumb our noses, quietly or overtly, at our peers, our colleagues, and our relatives; we can become our Own Person and enjoy every minute of every day. What better way to wake up in the morning than with a brand new day to greet us and go forward with a new project, or a list of things we want to accomplish.

Needless to say, responsibility comes with freedom. Because I've felt so blessed in so many areas of my life, I was able to take chances (No Risk = No Reward) and wanted to give back. I was able in semi-retirement to put my background and talents to work to establish and direct a Sunday School. Unsuspecting, I was hijacked for this project by my parish priest, and something I had never dreamed of doing became a contribution of some value for me, besides being extremely rewarding and providing me with a true sense of self worth. The moral of this story: If someone approaches you with a new idea, something you've never really seen yourself doing, give it a chance; perhaps you do have the right stuff to get to the goal.

Volunteerism also beckoned, and I found myself immersed in a new culture, teaching and lecturing in the Philippines, working in the rice paddies, feeding the goats! Italy is my favorite country, and I made my way to the mountains of Abruzzo to assist the victims of the 2009 earthquake. Making new friends, sharing ideas, living another kind of life altogether. Back to the motto: No Risk = No Reward. Dare to go outside your comfort zone; you'll find your mettle tested and a reason to explore.

Now you're wondering: how can I afford a single lifestyle? I believe in the adage, "Where there's a will, there's a way." Begin with what is important to you. If it is money, by all means continue working, especially if you enjoy your career. If it is the quality of life and relationships, money becomes secondary, but that is not to say it is not necessary. Budgeting is of prime importance at all times—and I would add to that list "creativity."

For instance, when I travel, which I do a lot, I believe in exchanging homes. It is terrifically economical and lots of fun, too. There are many ways to make life full of adventure and camaraderie without it costing a fortune. Start a book club, a film club, a salon . . . find a pen pal (or a husband!) Most importantly, select your living accommodations wisely. If you like to travel, is it wise to keep a grand home? A simple pied-a-terre sometimes will do later in life if you plan to be on the move.

I'm pretty frugal. When you are single, you need to provide for yourself and make sure all bases are covered, especially in the event of an unforeseen illness. My advice would be to begin saving and investing immediately during your prime years. I've watched my personal finances grow as the years have rolled by, counting my blessings all the way to the bank (although the blessings aren't quite as big these days).

Most of us have family, loved ones we cherish deeply, and so there is the issue of The Parents as we get on in years. Because I had no immediate family of my own, when my dear mother became ill, I was the one able to care for her. While caretaking is not an option for everyone, it gave me great solace to be able to give back something to this wonderful woman who had given me so much. I spent years caring for her and was only too happy to be able to assist her during those infirm years. This disconcerting event (sickness of a loved one) can even provide the opportunity for a full-time caretaker to take up some project or study she might never have put aside time for . . . a new language, finishing up that degree, learning to cook, writing a book of poetry! Those quiet hours can be a blessing as well as a burden.

Now is the time to take stock of your life—plan and live your dream!

More 411

Babcock, Linda. *Ask for It: How Women Can Use the Power of Negotiation to Get What They Really Want.* New York: Bantam, 2009.

Babcock, Linda. *Women Don't Ask: The High Cost of Avoiding Negotiation—and Positive Strategies for Change.* New York: Bantam, 2007.

Coontz, Stephanie. *Marriage: A History*. New York: Penguin, 2006.

DePaulo, Bella. *Singled Out: How Singles Are Stereotyped, Stigmatized, and Ignored, and Still Live Happily Ever After*. New York: St. Martin's Griffin, 2007.

DePaulo, Bella. *Singlism: What It Is, Why It Matters, and How to Stop It*. DoubleDoor Books, 2011.

Ivengar, Sheena. *The Art of Choosing*. New York: Twelve, 2011.

Milazzo, Vickie. *Wicked Success Is Inside Every Woman*. New York: Wiley, 2011.

Miller, Lee E. *A Woman's Guide to Successful Negotiating*. New York: McGraw-Hill, 2010.

Appendix 1: Are You Ready for Retirement Quiz*

You might be old enough to be retired and can't wait. Or you might have retirement foisted upon you. But the really big question is— are you ready for retirement? Take this fun quiz and find out. (Get your score at the end.)

Finances: Will you be able to live on your pension (if you're lucky enough to receive one), Social Security, and accumulated retirement savings?

1. Do you know how much all of your major income streams will amount to?

   ☐ Yes

   ☐ No

2. Have you estimated what your retirement spending requirements will be?

   ☐ Yes

   ☐ No

---

*Reprinted with permission of the publisher, TopRetirements.com.

3. Is your mortgage paid off?
   - ☐ Yes
   - ☐ No

4. Is your credit card debt retired?
   - ☐ Yes
   - ☐ No

5. Does your investment profile/portfolio match your new situation?
   - ☐ Yes
   - ☐ No

6. Do you have a qualified financial advisor?
   - ☐ Yes
   - ☐ No

7. Do you have an up-to-date will?
   - ☐ Yes
   - ☐ No

8. If your finances aren't up to snuff, have you thought about what kind of work or other adjustments you need to make?
   - ☐ Yes
   - ☐ No

Location: Do you know where you want to live in retirement?

1. Have you thought about where you want to live?
   - ☐ Yes
   - ☐ No

2. Will your family and friends be happy with your decision?
   ☐ Yes
   ☐ No

3. Is your retirement location compatible with your financial situation?
   ☐ Yes
   ☐ No

4. Have you thought about where you should be living in late retirement, if you are lucky enough to live that long?
   ☐ Yes
   ☐ No

Lifestyle: Are you prepared for what is going to be a major adjustment?

1. Have you thought about what you are going to do the day you retire?
   ☐ Yes
   ☐ No

2. How about what you will do every day, two years or more after your retirement?
   ☐ Yes
   ☐ No

3. Do you have a hobby, sport, or passion to keep you busy?
   ☐ Yes
   ☐ No

4. Will you continue to work in some fashion after retirement?
   ☐ Yes
   ☐ No

5. Do you know what kind of volunteering you want to do?
   ☐ Yes
   ☐ No

6. Do you have an Advanced Health Care Directive?
   ☐ Yes
   ☐ No

Scorecard: How well prepared are you?

15 or more Yes answers: Very well prepared—good job!

12–14 Yes answers: You've done a lot of work, but there's more to do.

8–11 Yes answers: Keep at it, you can be ready!

Fewer than 8: Yikes—you had better get busy if you want to enjoy retirement!

CHAPTER

Deciding What to Do with 168 Hours a Week

Live as if you were to die tomorrow. Learn as if you were to live forever.

—Mahatma Gandhi

Let's see: 24 hours a day × 7 days a week = 168 hours a week. It's basic math, but an important concept—how will you best use this newfound time? Okay, even if you take out 8 hours a day for sleep, that still leaves 112 hours a week. Pre-retired women age 40–75 want time with friends and family (77 percent), want to volunteer (31 percent), plan to work either full- or part-time (27 percent), and would like to travel (27 percent) when they retire, according to an Ameriprise Financial survey. Lifelong learning, becoming an entrepreneur, dipping into new adventures, and revisiting or exploring new hobbies are other frequently cited desires. You have decades to enjoy. Even if you're 65 and a woman, you can plan to live another 20 years. Alas, for men it's only 17.3 years more. Lots of delicious weeks stretch ahead. Of course, we want them to be healthy and we don't want to outlive our money. Those last two topics are addressed in subsequent chapters.

21

When deciding what to do with this bonus time, it's a good idea to think about both short- and long-term goals. This is true for all areas of life, including your personal and spiritual growth, health, finances, working, relationships, and community involvement. Although some women enjoy approaching each day with an open mind and seeing where the day takes them, most like some sort of structure. One acronym I like for goal setting is SMART: **S**pecific, **M**easureable, **A**ttainable, **R**ealistic, and **T**ime-sensitive. For example, "I will read three classics during the next 12 months" is much better than "I will read more." Better yet, write down your goals. If you do, you're much more likely to achieve them.

We will discuss working in Chapter 3 and we know this is necessary and desirable for many single women. But let's explore some of the other interests that single women want or plan to pursue in retirement. Note that I emphasize *experiences*, rather than accumulating *things*, since experiences generate more happiness than material purchases.

Travel

If you're planning to "play" in retirement, you're not alone. Travel is often at the top of many lists. The pleasure of deciding where you want to go and arranging your meals and activities according to your own schedule is appealing. But many single women have a huge gripe: the dreaded single supplement, which is a surcharge of 10 to 100 percent of double-occupancy rates for hotel rooms and cruise staterooms. We'll keep this in mind as we take a look at possibilities for travel.

Cruises

Cruising is popular among single women. Someone else is doing the cooking, serving, and cleaning, and even if you go solo, you

For More Information

For tons of information on travel-related content, including tips and links to member discounts, check out www.aarp.org/travel.

Fun Fact

Istanbul was the number one travel choice for *New York Times* readers in 2011.

---

can enjoy the camaraderie of others for three daily meals and excursions. Cruises also offer evening entertainment, lectures, and both structured and unstructured activities throughout the day. Gloria T., a widow, just returned from a cruise that included stops in Libya, Tunisia, Sardinia, and Spain. She chose the assigned late dining time, and by dining with the same people each evening, she established friendships over the month-long cruise. Some of her tablemates were single men and women; others were married but traveling by themselves because their spouses got seasick, were working, or were just not interested in cruising or the itinerary. A number of cruise lines or travel agencies have introduced themed sailings, from antiques to poker to politics to singles to wellness. Check out www.cruisecritic.com, www .frommers.com, www.themecruisefinder.com, or www.vacationstogo .com, and perhaps you'll find a passion near and dear to you.

Which cruise lines are most single-friendly? P&O's *Azura* has 18 solo staterooms. The *Norwegian Epic* (Norwegian Cruise Line) offers 128 single studios with access to a group meeting area, and the newest Norwegian Cruise Line ship, the *Breakaway*, has 59 staterooms for singles. The single rooms on the *Azura* and the *Epic* are wildly popular, so look for more ships offering the single stateroom.

The mv *Discovery* (Voyages of Discovery) and the British family-operated *Fred. Olsen* (yes, the period belongs there) offer single cabins. Royal Caribbean's retooled *Radiance of the Seas* has three single (interior) staterooms. Some cruise lines, including Princess (hey, this is the *Love Boat* cruise line, after all), don't have any single cabins, but Princess will help you find a "match" if you want a roommate (you must ask for the match at least 70 days prior to departure). Silversea Cruises reduces the single supplement to only 10 to 25 percent of the normal supplement on approximately 20 of its sailings; Crystal Cruises also has reduced single supplements. If you're an AARP member, MSC Cruises reduces the single supplement by 50 percent. Cruise lines sometimes suspend their single supplement during the low season.

Cruise lines offer "meet and greets" and parties for singles (some separate older singles from the 20- and 30-somethings, who may have a different agenda), and sometimes at the "welcome" show, the cruise director will ask all singles to stand, so you get a quick idea of who is single. There are several embarkation ports in Florida—Fort Lauderdale, Miami, Tampa, and Port Canaveral come to mind—and since there are many mature single women in Florida who like leaving from a convenient port (no flights to deal with), ships leaving from the Sunshine State often have an abundance of single cruisers. Of course, ships sail from other ports, too, in the United States and around the world. Keep in mind that there can be additional discounts if you're over 50; an active or retired police, military, or airline employee; or a past guest. There are even regional discounts. I received a discount on a recent cruise for being a Florida resident. Be sure to check all possible saving opportunities.

Cruise Critic (www.cruisecritic.com) has lots of single cruise reviews by ship, and it also offers its "Roll Call Forums," where you can virtually meet up with other people to arrange excursions. I did this on a cruise that stopped in St. Petersburg, Russia, and saved half the cost of the ship's excursion—with the same itinerary and caliber of guide. (Be careful, though. If you're on an independent excursion and miss the ship, you're responsible for getting back on.) Another good source for cruises is www.vacationstogo.com. I've booked last-minute travel through this site and was happy with the service and pricing, and it offers a helpful site for single cruisers and runs a "match" program if you'd like a roommate. Some of VacationsToGo's "hosted" trips are for singles over 40, so single cruises don't have to be wild, alcohol-fueled orgy-seeking parties . . . but maybe that's a good choice, too!

If you like to cruise outside the box (ship?), you could follow 63-year-old Jamie D.'s example. She recently returned from a Norwegian Coastal Voyage on Hurtigruten's MS *Polarlys*, a working ship that delivers mail and supplies to 34 ports along the Norwegian coast while also carrying tourists, locals, and cars. There is no single supplement in the winter. No TV, no lectures, no dancing, no casino, just the wild beauty of the coastline. And, if you're lucky, you'll see Nature's spectacular show, the northern lights, as did Jamie, on the last evening of the trip.

To save money, consider a repositioning cruise. When cruise lines need to move their ships from one place to another, such as from Europe to the Caribbean in the fall, you can often snag savings of 50 percent or more. Consider anything that is $100 a day a very good deal.

Women-Only Travel Sites

A fair number of the many online travel sites cater to women only, and some of those attach age restrictions to their trips. The travel companies may target active travelers in small groups with an eye to comfort, safety, and no planning on your part—you just have to show up; others are more relaxed and unstructured, offering participants more choices.

AdventureWomen (www.adventurewomen.com) is for women over 30, has been around for 30 years, and advertises that 70 percent of its clients are repeat customers. Bonnie W. is one of these repeat customers; she has enjoyed 15 trips in the last 18 years. "I've always had the desire to travel," explains Bonnie. "As a single, it's not always easy to find traveling partners to share those once-in-a-lifetime moments and memories. I discovered AdventureWomen when I was 33 (I'm 51 now). It's a great way to share your travels with an eclectic mix of women, to push my limits, and to continue on my journey of self-discovery. One of the greatest benefits is meeting women who become forever friends."

Gutsy Women Travel (www.gutsywomentravel.com)—don't you love the name?—has reasonably sized groups (maximum of 20) and activities including going to theater performances, shopping, hiking, visiting galleries, and seeing how other women live. Gusty Women Travel offers to cover the single supplement if you sign up to share a room, even if the company can't find you a roommate; a few restrictions go along with this "Guaranteed Share Program."

Specific sites cater to women over 50, such as Journeywoman (www.journeywoman.com), a fun (one quote: "Age is only important if you're cheese") and easy site that also offers tips for travel, and Senior Women's Travel (www.poshnosh.com), which reassures you that "your travel days are not over." There are sites for lesbian travel as well. Olivia (www.olivia.com) has a travel section on its site, offering room-sharing based on age as well as smoking and drinking preferences. A second example is Sweet (www.discoversweet .com), a lesbian travel company that is carbon-neutral and encourages community service projects on its trips. Purple Roofs (www .purpleroofs.com) is a site that lists gay-owned and gay-friendly bed and breakfasts, inns, hotels, travel agents, and tour operators.

Single-Travel Sites

If you'd like to book a trip with both male and female singles (keep in mind that single women often outnumber single men, sometimes by a 3:1 ratio), here are a few suggestions: O Solo Mio (www .osolomio.com) offers trips for those 35 and older, although not too many people over 60 sign up, with a room-sharing service based on factors including whether you snore or are a night owl. Singles Travel International (www.singlestravelintl.com), with average participants between the ages of 38 and 62, also will cover the single supplement if it can't find you a roommate; it's reassuring to note that 9 out of 10 people who sign up don't know another passenger— until they start the trip, that is!

Voluntourism

Paint a building, support the medical needs of a clinic, teach English, help at-risk children, care for animals rescued from industrialized farms. If you'd like to combine two goals in retirement, travel and volunteering, consider a volunteer vacation. Also called humanitours—although this sounds like the name of a dinosaur to me—you can make a difference while you travel. Heck, you might even be able to deduct the cost of the trip, assuming you itemize, if volunteering is the reason for the travel, and the sponsoring organization is a tax-exempt religious, charitable, educational, or similar entity. If you plan to deduct your volunteer vacation, it's better to travel with an established organization rather than go it alone. Keep detailed records of your expenses, consult your tax advisor, see whether the organization you're considering is listed with the

Internal Revenue Service in its Publication 78, and contact the IRS for additional information (www.irs.gov).

For example, Habitat for Humanity (www.habitat.org) offers a "hand up, not a handout" for almost two million people worldwide (of course, you can also volunteer within your own community). Owners of the homes must contribute to the build, help build other homes, and be able to repay an affordable loan. Jane K. has participated in five "Women Builds" homes built by—you guessed it—all women. As Jane says, "There is no greater reward for donating your time than when you are working alongside the future owners and see their excitement about having their own place in a few months."

Have a recreational vehicle? "Don't overlook the world of volunteer vacations available to women who have RVs," says Janet G., who lived full-time on the go for 10 years by boat and RV. "When housing must be provided for volunteers, things get more complicated, but RVers bring their own housing with them. Usually the volunteer is given a campsite, often with some or all hook-ups for the RV. Work may include building trails in a national park, guiding guests in a state park, or helping restore a National Historic Site. There are also several church-based groups in which RVers live and work at a project site, and Habitat for Humanity also has an RV group, the Care-A-Vanners."

How about building water purification systems in Urubamba, Peru? Mary Pat R., 52, signed up with ProWorld (www.proworldvolunteers .org) to fire and shape water filtration pots made from mud and sawdust, and she also helped out with an after-school program. Mary Pat explains that she "lived with a local family, doing the best I could to learn Spanish, exchange ideas and thoughts, and share our different cultures, life histories, and paths. I definitely pushed my comfort zone, and was thrilled with how fun it was and how happy and simple my weeks were. I also acquired some really good insights about what may and may not keep me happy as I explore an overwhelming freedom of choice in planning my next life stage. Insights about how alone I can be, how much contact with friends and family is important, how much I would need a peer group, a chance for meeting new men, for intellectual stimulation, for productivity and for physical beauty, and even physical comfort. . . . I learned a lot in the little bit of time I was with ProWorld."

Learn and Travel

"Senior" and "elder" are often considered dirty words in the United States. In fact, many "senior centers" have renamed themselves "community centers" or another moniker because people in their 50s, 60s, and sometimes even 70s wouldn't patronize them—because they don't consider themselves old, and "senior centers" are for "old" people. That's what happened with the venerable "Elderhostel" organization. The term "elderhostel" was coined in 1974, but it has been changed—twice—first to Exploritas in 2009, and then to Road Scholar (www.roadscholar.org, although if you enter www.elderhostel.org from habit you will be automatically redirected). With 8,000 tours to every state and 90 countries, this non-profit organization is a leader in the educational travel business.

Another learn-and-travel group is Senior Summer School (www.seniorsummerschool.com), which offers active adults "education vacations" to several college towns. Sometimes you stay right on campus, and the program includes lectures, sightseeing, and most meals. Courses last from one to six weeks, and costs range from $700 to $5,000.

Hire a Companion

If you'd rather not travel alone (independently or as part of a group), you can purchase the services of a travel companion. One such company that offers this service is Davis International LLC (www.davisinternationallllc.com). Companions are available for flying, taking cruises, navigating a foreign country, having company on a trip, or even relocating. If you're cruising and want a companion, you can also check out Cruise Critic (www.cruisecritic.com, click on "Boards"); for companions for land and sea, check out Lonely Planet (www.lonelyplanet.com, click on "Thorn Tree forum").

Travel with Grandchildren

About a third of grandparents who travel have taken a child on a vacation. Of course, a Disney cruise (www.disneycruise.disney.go.com) with your little princes and princesses might immediately come to mind, and it's a good option. Road Scholar (www.roadscholar.org), previously known as Elderhostel and Exploritas, offers a multitude of intergenerational trips both within the United States and internationally. Single Parent Travel (www.singleparenttravel.net) caters to any adult (grandmother, aunt, etc.) traveling alone with children. You'll need to bring a notarized letter from the parents authorizing medical care, copies of the children's insurance cards, and (for some foreign destinations) documentation that you have parental permission to travel with the children. Of course, you could also design your own trip. Claudia R. booked her own flights and took her two preteen grandchildren on the *Explorer II* to the Galapagos Islands during summer break. An active, wonderful trip was enjoyed by all. Lynne R. lives on the East Coast, has a son in Seattle and a daughter in Salt Lake City, and has five grandchildren. Lynne does a reverse kind of travel—she stays with her grandchildren so her own children can travel—sometimes for work, sometimes for pleasure. Good Grandma!

Cheap Travel

If you have an adventurous streak, you could do what Suzann R. has done for years: stay all over the world for free using no-cost sites such as CouchSurfing (www.couchsurfing.org), or Itamos (www.itamos .com). People host visitors in their homes—for free. I've used the word a lot, I know, but "free" is a powerful word. Of course, be careful because there are some not-so-honest people out there. Suzann also stays in youth hostels. As she emphatically states, "They are NOT just for the young!" Or do a swap through Craigslist (www .craigslist.com) or house-swapping companies, which you can find online. Whatever service you use, be sure to scrutinize photos and check references.

If You're Disabled

Have a service dog? Do you use a wheelchair or scooter or need dialysis? Are you deaf or vision impaired? Do you have special dietary requirements? Are you traveling with a companion with Alzheimer's? No matter what the disability, opportunities for travel abound, although you may need to do some advance planning.

Vacationing on a cruise ship can be smooth sailing. Ships have a number of accessible staterooms, and, if you have a service dog, provide a place for the dog to relieve itself, usually a 4-by-4 box filled with mulch or woodchips in an area lightly frequented by passengers. Pools and hot tubs may have lifts. The Access Department at a cruise line can help facilitate your needs for dialysis, Braille menus, under-the-pillow vibrating alarm clocks; you get the idea. Of course, you also need to check out your accessibility options when you get off the ship at ports; this is often more challenging and restrictive. Some cruise companies offer better accommodations than others, but most are improving their efforts to make sailing accessible. CruiseCritic (www.cruisecritic.com) has lots of specific reviews and recommendations for cruising if disabled.

If you'd like to explore terra firma as well as the seven seas and you're a slow walker, use a wheelchair, or want a travel companion, check out Accessible Journeys (www.disabilitytravel.com). This site is a rich resource for travel tips and travel tales. Access-Able Travel Source (www.access-able.com) is another company that specializes in travel for those with special needs. Have disability, will travel!

Travel Tips from Single Women Travelers

Yes, we know single women should walk confidently, keep valuables hidden (better yet, leave them at home), be aware of their surroundings and avoid dangerous situations, share their whereabouts with others, ensure that their hotel rooms are secure and located in safe areas, dress conservatively, and be familiar with the culture of the area. They may even need to say they're married and wear a fake ring or not look men in the eye, depending where they're traveling.

Here are a few additional tips from single women travelers:

- When purchasing luggage, Kris H. considers whether the pattern or look of it indicates that it's a woman's bag. If it is, it may be more attractive to thieves looking to find gems and jewelry.
- Bette L. carries a Platinum American Express card. Although it's pricey at $450 a year, Bette likes it because, she says,

"It admits me into almost all the airline clubs where you aren't at the mercy of customer service if you are stranded. It is a safe place to rest between flights, and you can work or just veg. I am 74 and travel a lot. I have been stranded due to weather and have had other problems with my reservations. The airline clubs have been very accommodating; they get me rescheduled and take care of me."

- "Buy medical insurance for that cruise or trip abroad, unless you know for a fact that your existing policy will cover such care or indeed, you have deep pockets," suggests Diane E., based on two medical emergencies she experienced while traveling. This is a hot topic for debate. Many people pass on insurance, putting it in the not-going-to-purchase-it category of extended warranties or service contracts.

- Tamara J. suggests books geared to the solo traveler, or guide books, such as the *Lonely Planet* or *Rough Guide* series, that include specific information for independent travelers.

- Becky R. never stays in a hotel. She uses sites such as www .homeaway.com and www.vacationroost.com to find lodging. Becky likes the homier atmosphere and space this option offers.

- Stephanie R. uses the Internet to search for trips without single supplements. She puts "no single supplement" or "single supplement waived" into her search bar along with her desired destination and sees what pops up.

- Francesca A. always asks for a discount on the single supplement, even if she doesn't see one offered. "The worst they can say is no; I've discovered just about everything is negotiable."

- Sally F. has been disabled for the last six years with transverse myelitis, similar to multiple sclerosis, but it hasn't slowed her down. She has visited Machu Picchu, Easter Island, Egypt, Petra, Glasgow, Costa Rica, and Bogota. "*Yes*, the wheelchair is for you!" says Sally. "My doctor said he would not allow me to travel unless I agreed to use a wheelchair in airports. I can use my cane elsewhere. I feel embarrassed and like a wimp, but I do it. It lets me avoid the long screening lines, which are physically stressful, and gets me on the airplane ahead of everyone else, and I get through customs quickly. In some countries being in a wheelchair means no exit tax. You do not need a doctor's note, but it helps if you have your handicapped hang-tag with you."

Lily V. summed it up well: "The best weapon for safe, fun, and affordable travel? Knowledge."

Giving Back

"The best way to find yourself is to lose yourself in the service of others." Wise man, that Mahatma Gandhi. I know I also used him for the introductory quote for this chapter, but with such sage words, why not?

Volunteer Activities

Perhaps not surprisingly, women volunteer more than men (30 percent compared to 24 percent) and singles volunteer more than marrieds, according to the Bureau of Labor Statistics. Both sexes volunteer an average of 50 hours a year. For the last five years, Utah holds the honor of having the largest volunteer rate, a whopping 45 percent of the population. People who volunteer often gain as much or more than those they are helping.

The opportunities for volunteering are legion. Most volunteers are involved in religious organizations, education and youth services, or social or community service organizations. Historically, women's volunteer activities primarily involve fundraising; serving, preparing, collecting, and distributing food; and tutoring or teaching. A few suggestions via online sites (note that voluntourism was addressed above):

- **Create the Good** (www.createthegood.org). Do you have "5 minutes/5 hours/5 days"? AARP's easy site (you don't have to be a member to use it) lets you peruse requests for volunteers based on your location. Put in your zip code and how far you're willing to travel, and it lists the needs of various organizations in your area. For example, the Thoughtful

Treasures Program would like small craft items for pediatric patients at the National Institutes of Health; the gifts will let the children know that people in the community are thinking about them as they go through their difficult medical treatment. The site also offers guides for putting together your own volunteer project, such as holding a coat drive or sending books to troops.

- **VolunteerMatch** (www.volunteermatch.org). You'll find onsite and at-home options. Click on "search for virtual opportunities" and be a one-on-one mentor with a South African child affected by poverty and HIV/AIDS. All you need is a webcam, high-speed Internet, and 30 minutes a week, after completing a short online training class. Or write a grant application for a community group trying to improve adult literacy. The site also offers tons of "real" opportunities based on zip code and skills (those you have or those you'd like to develop).
- **National Wildlife Federation** (www.nwf.org). Let's not forget our animal friends. Show others how to restore habitats, garden for wildlife, or provide administrative support from a local office or your home. You can also contact your local zoo or Humane Society.
- **Green Volunteers** (www.greenvolunteers.com). This site offers more than 500 nature conservatory volunteer projects, both within the United States and abroad. Two other possibilities are The Nature Conservancy (www.nature.org) and Conservation International (www.conservation.org).
- **United We Serve** (www.serve.gov). Are you a do-it-yourselfer? United We Serve is an initiative by President Barack Obama that provides you with online tool kits to create your own projects such as organizing a book or food drive, helping veterans access community services, or working on a problem facing your community.
- **Points of Light** (www.pointsoflight.org). So it doesn't seem that I'm favoring one political party: George H. W. Bush founded Points of Light in 1990. The emphasis of this volunteer organization is people driving change in their communities. "Make a Difference Day," created by *USA Weekend,* is one of Points of Light's signature events.

- **Free Rice** (www.freerice.com), Free Kibble (www.freekibble.com or www.freekibblekat.com), and Charitii (www.charitii.com). Get smarter and help others (including our furry friends) by using these three free (try saying that several times fast!) sites. Depending on the site, for each question you answer correctly, 10 grains of rice are donated to the World Food Programme or 10 pieces of kibble will be donated to animal shelters across the country, or you can solve multiple-choice crossword puzzles and choose among several charities where you can donate water, educational programming time, or square inches of rainforest to The Nature Conservancy. Warning: These sites can be addictive.

Charitable Giving

"Women at virtually every income level are more likely to give to charity and to give more money on average than their male counterparts, after controlling for education, income and other factors that influence giving," according to the Women's Philanthropy Institute. Single women are twice as likely to give as single men. I guess that more women than men subscribe to J. Paul Getty's belief that "Money is like manure. You have to spread it around or it smells."

Women give substantially more than men in the following charitable categories: international, community, religion, health care, youth, and family. Men contribute more than women to arts and culture, according to the Women's Philanthropy Institute.

Just Plain Fun

Developing new interests, honing an oft-ignored skill, or resurrecting abandoned hobbies or dreams is good for the mind and often good for the body. Although we'll look at exercise in more depth in Chapter 4, picking up that old tennis racket (actually, get a new one—they are vastly improved), bowling, walking, playing golf, swimming or biking (easy on the joints), lifting weights (build up bone density), or belly dancing (maybe those six-pack abs will finally materialize) are all great possibilities, but as the old disclaimer goes, check with your physician first. Or, learn a new skill.

Kathy F. bought a Mac, signed up for iMovie and iDVD classes at the local Apple store, and now creates fabulous DVDs of her travels. Jayne L. delved into her family's Irish ancestry at www.ancestry .com, traced her roots back to 1488, found a cousin she didn't know existed, and learned more about her grandfather's days in the coal mines of Nova Scotia. Like to read? Diane P. started a book club in her new neighborhood. With so many readers' guides online or in the backs of books, it's easy, it's social, and it's intellectually stimulating (unless the current choice is a bodice-ripper, but hey, get the juices flowing). There are also online book clubs you can join—check your library. Many will send you five-minute portions of a book to read. By the end of the week, if you're hooked, you can check it out or reserve it, buy it, or download it on your e-reader, and join in the discussions. Or, check out a site like www. onlinebookclub.org, with lots of good discussions about books (no big surprise), writing, and other topics, or www.sheknows.com, which includes a book club for women.

You might get bitten by the acting bug like Lucinda W. She loved her roles in *My Fair Lady, Our Town,* and *Sorry, Wrong Number* in high school, and now she has the time to indulge her love for performing in her used-to-be-a-church-but-is-now-a-community-theater. If you don't want the glare of the bright lights, there are tons of behind-the-scenes opportunities.

Are you a game lover? Marianne M., living in Texas, organizes a monthly game night, rotating among euchre, train dominoes, Bunco, and Pictionary. There are free online games as well—just type "free online games" into your search engine, and be prepared to be overwhelmed by AARP and scores of other sites. Roseanne K. dusted off her console piano and now relishes practicing an hour a day. Nikki G. sings in the choir at her place of worship.

With all the delicious possibilities to explore, this quote frequently attributed to Will Rogers may resonate with you: "Why not go out on a limb—that's where the fruit is."

Lifelong Learning

As both an undergraduate and graduate student (I'm 58 and for a number of years in a previous life I was an assistant professor of anatomy and physiology and microbiology at the community college level), I was taught that once nerve cells die, that's it—we can only lose them, not make them. It has been just in the last decade or so that scientists have discovered that this tenet, which was preached for 100 years or so, isn't true. Nerve cells (also called neurons) can regenerate, and probably more important, the connections that allow them to communicate with one another, called synapses, can also sprout. But this doesn't happen on its own. To stimulate growth of our brain, we need to introduce novelty, practice active learning, upend our routines, solve problems, have lots of social interactions, and be mentally engaged. We'll see later that being *physically* engaged also stimulates the growth of synapses. We've already mentioned some ways we can galvanize our brain cells: Travel to a new place, develop or dust off old hobbies, read books that cause us to really think, take on work projects or volunteer in areas outside of our comfort zone.

Let's look at ways to rev up our cognitive motor with lifelong learning. If it isn't important to you, it should be—it could be a matter of life or (brain) death. It can also be a lot of fun. Formal and informal lifelong learning opportunities abound. Here are several to consider.

Take College Classes or Pursue a Degree

I'm sure you've heard how popular college towns are for retirement— we'll look at some later—and it's not just because of the cheap beer. You can often audit a regular college class for free or very low cost, assuming you meet the age and residency requirements and space is available. What fun to not worry about exams or papers, just relish the sheer joy of learning. Or if you'd like to complete or pursue another degree, many colleges exempt older students from taking the ACT or SAT. The College Level Examination Program (CLEP) allows you to earn college credit by passing a 90-minute exam in a variety of subjects. At about $80 an exam, that's a lot cheaper and faster—assuming you pass—than paying tuition. Check out your closest community college or university to find out what bargains are available for you. If you're thinking about an online degree, consider an accredited program through a recognized institution;

employers look more kindly on these, unless you're just doing it for your own edification.

Adult Education

Many counties, colleges, school systems, and libraries offer inexpensive or free (love that word) classes for adults. Ann B. regularly attends free lectures sponsored by her local university on cutting-edge research ranging from the bacteria inhabiting our gut to the continuing effects of the Gulf oil spill. Leslie K. takes computer classes through her county's adult education classes, and she teaches a class on conversational Italian. Holly R. joins patrons in her library for the library book club—this month it's *The Paris Wife*. Road Scholar (www.roadscholar.org), mentioned earlier under travel, combines elements of both learning and travel.

If your idea of lifelong learning involves using your computer while you're sipping your tea or coffee and lounging in your jammies, these free resources might be just the ticket:

- **Learn a Language.** A number of libraries offer an opportunity to learn a language online through Rocket Languages (www.rocketlanguage.com), including American Sign Language, Japanese, Hindi, German, and Italian. If you purchased the Japanese program from Rocket Language rather than accessing the program through the library, it would cost $100 to $150.
- **Classes through the Massachusetts Institute of Technology and Yale.** Yes, *that* MIT and *that* Yale. No fees and no registration. Of course, no credit is given, no degree is conferred, and no contacting the professors with questions, but we mustn't be greedy. Go to www.mit.edu and click on "OpenCourseWare" under "education." For the Yale site, go to http://oyc.yale.edu/. Classes in English, engineering, science, philosophy, history, economics, art . . . it's a huge selection and a great way to make those 168 hours a week meaningful.
- **About U.** About U (http://u.about.com) sends you a mini-lesson weekly or daily from a large selection of classes. Yoga for back pain, anyone?

- **Business Training Courses.** The federal government, through the Small Business Administration (www.sba.gov), offers free training, including classes on starting, managing, and financing a business. Its Women's Business Centers offers assistance as well (click on "Counseling and Training").
- **Osher Lifelong Learning Institute.** The Bernard Osher Foundation is a 30-year-old philanthropic institution that supports lifelong learning for adults 50 and older. Osher is present on about 120 campuses across the United States, offering member-driven courses facilitated by peers and college faculty. Each campus runs its institute a bit differently. For example, at the University of Maryland in College Park (go Terps!—my alma mater) you'd pay $50 a semester for unlimited courses, free parking, use of the shuttle bus, library privileges, and discounts on other events. Sample courses include America's Role in the World, Islamic History and Civilization, Spanish, Oral Communication, and Writing Your Personal Memories Workshop. Scholarships are also available. Sign me up.
- **One Day University.** Were you the type of student who crammed? For about $150, you can attend live lectures by top professors from prestigious universities, such as Yale, Harvard, Cambridge, and Georgetown. Subjects cover diverse topics, and it's all in a single day. One Day U (www.onedayu.com) is offered in about a dozen cities throughout the country, including New York, Boston, Philadelphia, and Washington, DC. The average student age is 59.

Reinvention

Reinvention is a buzzword, and there are books, blogs, articles, and coaching services addressing the concept. The gift of time that is retirement can be the perfect time for reinventing ourselves. Moving to a new location, starting a new business, learning new skills, going back to school, and broadening travel horizons are all paths to reinvention. And, of course, change is also thrust upon us by difficult and unexpected circumstances. Our positive response to these challenges is a testament to the resiliency, determination, and inventiveness of single women. As an example, here is Ann F.'s story about her lifelong learning and reinvention(s):

My Life Ann F. is Sixty, Sexy, Sassy, and Free

I'm 65, but just before my 60th birthday, I took on a major life change. Let me digress, before moving forward.

In earlier years, I reinvented myself many times. I taught Special Ed in Miami, then moved to Japan, returned to the states, went to graduate school, and started a second career as a social worker. I married at 30, had my son at 32, and settled into mediocrity (sort of) for the next 20+ years. Don't get me wrong, I was an upstanding professional, a wife, a mother, involved in my community and my career. In 1987, I started working for myself as a psychotherapist and eventually as a speaker and coach. (By the way, I haven't ever worked for anyone else since.)

At 56 I divorced, after 26 years. Sept. 11 was the epiphany for me; it screamed, "Life is way too short to be unhappy!!" I hadn't been happy in that marriage for quite some time, don't think he was either, so decided to not "settle" any longer. At this point we'd been living in Austin, Texas, for 20 years.

So, there I was, ready to move forward, excited and fearful at the same time. I began getting the "itch"—the yearning for something different. Just before my 60th birthday, I realized that the work I do isn't dependent on where I live. As long as there is an airport, computer, and phone, I can work anywhere. What a revelation. So, six days after my 60th birthday, I boarded a flight to spend 10 days in New York City, exploring the possibility of a move there . . . a lifelong dream. I've always wanted to be in NYC, with Broadway, concerts, a walking city, lectures, etc.

Several weeks later, I was in my apartment in NYC on the Upper West Side. My son had rented a van. We stashed my two cats in a big travel home in the back, along with my computer, printer, some files, some clothes and he drove Mom to NY and dropped me off (sort of the reverse of the parent dropping the kid off at college). Before leaving Austin, I'd sold nearly everything and only sent up a few boxes of extra clothes, books, etc. It was, indeed, a starting over.

All was well, life was an adventure, I was having fun, making money, dating, having sex, very confident, had tons of friends . . . and then I was diagnosed with breast cancer, stage 2. I spent many months involved with this: two surgeries, chemotherapy, radiation, etc. I wasn't able to travel to speak or work much.

It's one year later, my hair has grown back, treatment is complete, I'm cancer free, *and* I learned that even though my earning capacity greatly slowed down, even though I adventured through cancer living alone, I am now able to nurture myself, appreciate the incredible help and contributions of others and am now thriving.

Yes, Virginia . . . there is life after cancer . . . and I'm *thriving*, not just surviving.

If you want to or need to continue working, or some combination of the two, the next chapter is for you.

More 411

www.independenttraveler.com (bargains, trips, and deals)

www.retiringsingles.com ("for nomad-footed singles with wanderlust on their minds")

www.womansviewtravel.com ("unique travel encounters with the world")

CHAPTER

Working in Retirement: An Oxymoron?

Behind every successful man is a woman waiting for his job.
— Anonymous

■ ■ ■

The previous chapter explored what you might do with those extra hours you'll have if you retire, and continuing to work might be on your list.

For many single women, working longer is a financial necessity, but there are additional reasons to consider as well: having structure, providing an identity, achieving goals, solving problems creatively, contributing to society, maintaining social interactions, staying active, and being intellectually challenged. And, of course, for many people, making money equates with self-worth. So some people continue to work indefinitely.

But it's instructive to compare what people *say* they want to happen and what *actually* happens to them regarding working; in other words, expectations versus reality. If we look at a recent Employee Benefit Research Institute (EBRI) survey, almost half of all people surveyed (45 percent) retired earlier than planned. What happened? Downsizing, rightsizing, or closing a company; becoming ill or disabled; having to care for a spouse, parent, or other family member; and changing skills necessary for the position all contribute to the expectation versus reality statistics. Did anyone in the survey report retiring because of a big inheritance, the lottery, or for some other good reason? Alas, only a few percent cited positive reasons for their unexpected retirement. It seems important to have a Plan B, or even a Plan C, just like my tennis pro says, to do if things aren't working out well on the court during a match.

What about working after leaving a primary career? There is much discussion about reinventing, retooling, pursuing new careers, starting businesses, and creating encore careers. Again, if we look at the EBRI survey, we find that although 74 percent of people say that they want to work in some capacity in retirement, only 23 percent actually are doing so. And, what does working in retirement really mean? The first several retirement years are usually the most costly retirement years, factoring in traveling, trying out new hobbies or sports (golf and skiing are not cheap), caring for elderly parents, (still) paying children's college tuitions, and relocating or remodeling. So, if you can work at a lower salary or even part-time during the first few years of retirement, and I know that sounds like an oxymoron, it can help prevent your nest egg from cracking. Having even half of your former salary, and hopefully half the stress, can go a long way toward making your retirement financially solvent. To see how having a transition job can affect your financial retirement planning, and it does have a pretty remarkable effect on your money, put "Merrill Lynch New Retirement Illustrator" into your computer's search bar, and try out this easy, customizable calculator.

Did You Know?

There's a potential silver lining to the trend of delaying retirement that began in the late 1990s and is expected to last another 20 years or so. Working longer results in larger Social Security payments for individuals. It will also help fund Social Security and Medicare coffers, according to the Rand Corporation.

Significant Statistic

What about an inheritance in lieu of working? About 20 percent of middle boomers, those born between 1952 and 1958, have received an inheritance, averaging about $120,000, according to MetLife. AARP reports that only about 15 percent of all boomers expect an inheritance. Another reason for Plans A, B, and C. Bottom line: Don't plan on Mom and Dad funding your retirement.

Are things really that dire for mature workers? If you're looking for employment, the median time it takes workers ages 55 to 64 to find another job is 44.6 weeks, according to the Bureau of Labor Statistics. Although the present job market is challenging, there are positive signs for those wishing to work. Northeastern University researchers predict that the United States will create almost 15 million jobs by 2018, with only 9 million new workers to fill them, even though the economy isn't currently sizzling. Demographics are on our side. By 2016, one-third of all workers will be 50 or older, so when employers are hiring, there will be more of us swimming in the employment pool. Boomers (born between 1946 and 1964) at 78 million strong outnumber Generation X (1965 and 1976) with Gen X's measly 46 million. But watch out for the upcoming Generation Y (1977 and 2002) at more than 70 million strong.

Many employers recognize the sterling attributes that mature employees bring to the workplace, including a strong work ethic, willingness to mentor, confidence, dependability, experience, wisdom, and punctuality. And don't forget less turnover; older workers stay with their employers three times longer than young'uns. Those reentering the working world may be happy to work more flexible hours, which is a boon to employers. CVS Caremark, for example, actively recruits older workers. About 20 percent of its employees are over 50, and it offers an innovative "snowbird program," which lets about 1,200 employees work seasonally in a different CVS for part of the year. One example is Carla T. She is a pharmacist, working part-time in a CVS in Florida during the winter (living at an

RV resort) and in her home state of Connecticut the rest of the year. Carla has been doing this for about four years and is delighted with the arrangement.

What about the costs of hiring an older worker? Cornell University found that companies with health care plans were less likely to hire an older worker because of increased costs. Hint: Let a potential employer know if you don't need health care coverage. A skilled, seasoned worker can be cost-effective when compared with the investment of time in a new employee. And, older employees usually don't need dependent coverage.

Research by Joanna Lahey at the National Bureau of Economic Research found that younger women were 40 percent more likely to be called for an interview than women over 50 years of age, when age was apparent from the resume. And, the U.S. Equal Employment Opportunity Commission (EEOC) reported that 23,465 charges of age discrimination were filed in 2011, comprising 24 percent of the total discrimination charges.

While we're on the topic of discrimination, what about weight? A poll of employers found that when asked, "Has someone's weight ever influenced your decision on whether to hire him or her?" 26 percent said "yes" and 28 percent said "maybe unconsciously." According to the U.S. Centers for Disease Control and Prevention (CDC), 64 percent of adult women are overweight or obese. It's scary to think that an unconscious or conscious bias against weight can affect getting a job, but you should be aware that it's out there. There is also the disturbing trend of hiring only those who currently have a job. So, think carefully about leaving a job without having another one lined up.

Let's get down to work (pun intended) and see what's out there and how to become successful job seekers.

Preparing for That New Job

Employers have a list of "soft skills," aside from the basic qualifications unique to the position, that they seek in an employee. These include verbal, listening, and written communication skills; initiative; creative thinking; problem solving; ability to cooperate, resolve conflicts, and negotiate with others; flexibility; technical literacy;

integrity; a positive attitude; reliability; loyalty; professionalism on and off the job; sensitivity to diversity; and a willingness to learn. Incorporating these traits into your resume, cover letter, and interviews will go a long way toward snagging that job, and they are traits anyone can cultivate, learn, or develop.

If you haven't interviewed recently, you may be surprised at some of the questions you might be asked to answer. One hot area is behavioral interview questions, such as, "Tell me about a time when you . . . used your persuasion skills to convince someone to see things your way; had a number of things to do and needed to prioritize; missed an obvious solution to a problem; tried to accomplish something and failed; set a goal and reached it (or failed to reach it); had to make a difficult decision." One way to approach this type of question is to use the SAR technique: S—describe the situation, A—recount the action you took, R—describe the results.

Another type of question is to test *how* you think, such as: How many ping pong balls fit into a bedroom? The interviewer isn't really looking for a concrete answer, but just an idea of how you process new information. I'm in my 50s and have never been asked these types of questions in an interview, but I can assure you that my three adult children have. What if you can't answer the question? Recent research from Harvard found that if you do an artful dodge, that is, answer a similar question eloquently, your answer will be viewed more favorably than an unpolished but truthful answer. (Personal confession: Years ago, I used this tactic unknowingly when answering one of the six questions on my written comprehensive exam to get my master's degree. I was asked a question that I couldn't address in depth—frankly, I really didn't know much about it. So, I did the best I could, writing about a paragraph in response to the real question, then writing another question in a related area and went to town answering it. Luckily for me, it worked.)

About half of employers are now administering personality assessments, where the goal is to see if you're a good culture fit for the company. Sometimes this is given, often online, to all applicants; other times it's given when the field is narrowed to several candidates. Biggest mistakes made during a face-to-face interview? According to a survey from Accountemps, they demonstrate little or no knowledge about the company; inability to discuss skills, goals, and career plans; lacking eye contact and enthusiasm; and arriving late. It's encouraging that these mistakes can be avoided.

Realize, too, that more and more companies do credit checks on potential hires, so don't let a bad credit report derail your chances for a job. Check your credit score to be sure it's accurate and healthy.

Tip

Check out www.aarpworksearch.org, AARP Foundation's WorkSearch Information Network, a resource that guides you through the entire job search process from start to finish, including free interest, ability, and skills assessments.

Where Are Women Working?

More than half of all working women (53 percent) were employed in just three industries, according to 2010 U.S. Bureau of Labor Statistics: education and health services; trade, transportation, and utilities; and local government. Single-women households make an average of $27,000. Only one in four Fortune 1000 CEO positions is held by a woman, according to Catalyst, but women are also less likely to be among the long-term unemployed.

What and Where Are the Jobs?

Every two years, the U.S. Bureau of Labor Statistics produces its *Occupational Outlook Handbook*, which contains all kinds of fascinating and useful information, including areas of job growth and demographics. You can download this free treasure trove of information online at www.bls.gov/OCO. The *Handbook* makes employment projections and provides information about salaries, the education or training required for each job, what the job entails, and the job market by state. The *Handbook* is updated as conditions change. It is worthwhile to spend time investigating this site if you plan to choose a new career and you want to know if it's a viable choice, to perhaps give you some new ideas for working in retirement, or to show you the job market in your present location or place you're considering relocating.

Many people may not have the time, desire, or finances to go back and pursue a medical degree or other type of advanced degree. For example, biomedical engineers are in demand, but such positions require an advanced degree; accountants must have a bachelor's degree, and to become a CPA you need 150 total college credits. Keep in mind that coursework and continuing education courses are compelling fillers for employment gaps in resumes; it's easy to become obsolete without them. The following list includes occupations with the fastest or largest increase in total number of jobs that do not require years of education, although some additional training or education may be necessary.

- **Fastest Growing.** When you combine an aging population with increased longevity, it's no wonder that health care is a growth area. Half of the top 20 fastest-growing jobs are in the health sector. Hot jobs include home health aides, personal care aides, physical therapist aides, biomedical engineers, physical therapy assistants, occupational therapist aides, medical secretaries. And—let's not forget our animal friends who need health care—veterinary technologists and technicians. One in four new jobs will be in the area of health care or the related social assistance positions of personal and home care aides. Most home health aides and social assistance workers are women 55 and older.

- **Biggest Numerical Growth.** Jobs with the biggest increase in raw numbers, again, not including those requiring a four-year degree or more, include registered nurses (although many nurses are expected to have their BSN, a bachelor's of science degree in nursing), retail salespeople, home health aides, customer service representatives, food preparers and servers, office clerks (e.g., bookkeepers), nursing aides/orderlies/attendants, truck drivers, receptionists, administrative assistants, and cashiers. Health care and social assistance are projected to account for about 28 percent of all new jobs.

- **Growth by Industry.** The construction industry will add jobs, but isn't expected to recover its pre-recession employment levels by 2020. In the service industry, we've already mentioned growth in health care, social assistance, admin support, retail, and food service. (For social assistance agencies where you help people but don't need a medical background, check out "More 411" at the end of this chapter.) Other growth industries, again, excluding jobs where a four-year degree is not necessarily required in the field, include some government positions, arts, entertainment, real estate, and information.

- **Bachelor's Degree and Beyond Growth Occupations.** This is for those of you who would love to go back to college for a new career, believing in Ann Landers's response to a letter from a 42-year-old woman struggling with the idea of returning to medical school to become a physician because of her age. "And how old will you be in four years if you don't go to medical school?" the sage advice columnist asked. Keep this in mind: Of the 18 million college students in the United States, almost 10 percent of them are single women with children. When a woman can't find employment in a tough job market, one of the largest drawbacks of going back to school—foregone income—is no longer an issue. Many colleges offer short-term certificate programs, such as completing six courses to receive a certificate in project management, or continuing education classes in a specific area. Be sure to pursue financial aid (see the tip on page 49) and meet with the college counselor. He or she can help you focus on your strengths and desires, and add helpful information on regional job demands and scholarships or loans. Remember, sometimes you can't choose to change careers; career change is foisted on you by circumstances beyond your control. Hot jobs needing a bachelor's degree or more: think accountants, engineers, computer analysts, financial analysts, physical therapists, pharmacists, and physicians.

Tip

Free money for school? Check out these organizations that provide scholarship money to women, which can range from a few hundred dollars to a full ride: the AARP Foundation Women's Scholarship Program (www .aarp.org and put "Women's Scholarship Program" into the AARP search bar); the American Association of University Women (AAUW) (www.aauw .org—click on "Learn" then "Scholarships and Awards"); Charlotte W. Newcombe Foundation for Mature Women Students (www.newcombefoun dation.org); Jeannette Rankin Foundation (www.rankinfoundation.org); and Talbots Scholarship Program (www.scholarshipamerica.org/talbotswomen /instructions.php).

Also, contact the financial aid office at individual colleges, and if you are working, ask your human resources department about tuition reimbursement for classes or coursework.

There is also FastWeb (www.fastweb.com), a free scholarship search site, but if you sign up you have to agree to be "reached by colleges or marketing partners." And, see Chapter 8 for advice on creating a 529 college savings plan for yourself.

- **Employment Growth by State.** The *Occupational Outlook Handbook* allows you to search, by state, the projected increase in jobs by numbers or by percentages for the next decade. For example, increases in employment in Utah are about double that of Oregon. You can narrow information down further by specific categories of job growth. For example, let's say you're interested in living in North Carolina and would like to be involved in adult literacy or perhaps teach a GED program. You'd find that over the next decade that specific employment sector in North Carolina is expected to grow by about 20 percent.
- **Salaries.** The nifty handbook can tell you the average salary for a particular job, as well as where the jobs are most plentiful and the range of salaries. Using our adult literacy/ GED teacher example, you'll see that the average salary for this position is about $50,000 a year, with the highest average salary found in schools and the lowest average found

in vocational rehab services. You could then find out which state employs the most people in this field, and at what average salary, and which pays the most for this type of work (California). Of course, California also has a higher cost of living, but you get the idea—you can gather a lot of info by exploring the *Occupational Outlook Handbook.*

Did You Know?

What does *she* make? Interested in finding out what people are being paid? Two free useful sites in addition to the *Occupational Outlook Handbook*: www.salary.com and www.glassdoor.com (employees self-report salaries by position/location).

Job-Hunting Resources, Strategies, and Ideas

Let's take a look at 15 specific suggestions that may help you find that perfect job.

AARP Best Employers for Workers over 50

Every two years, AARP publishes a list of employers that value workers 50 and older. Companies must apply for inclusion on this list; criteria for possible selection include benefits for retirees, opportunities for training and education, and forward-looking work practices such as phased retirement, job sharing, and flexibility in scheduling.

The top five employers (out of the 50 recognized) in 2011 were Scripps Health, Cornell University, First Horizon National Corporation, West Virginia University, and the YMCA of Greater Rochester. If you have any of AARP's best employers in your area (or in an area where you're considering relocating), it's worth knowing. AARP also has what it calls a National Employer Team, companies that "want to hire older workers." To access this list, go to www.aarp.org and put "National Employer Team" in the search bar. Finally, for those wanting to move abroad, check out the employers who are AARP International Winners.

The Water Cooler

AARP also offers "The Water Cooler." If you want to seek and share advice about finding a job, jump-starting a new career or business, returning to work after retiring, achieving work/life balance, or tackling age hangups, go to www.aarp.org and put "The Water Cooler" into the search bar, then click on "Online Community Group: The Water Cooler."

Online Job Sites

Where to begin? There are many (50,000!) job sites, including AARP's, but *Fortune* magazine recommends www.indeed.com and www.simplyhired.com because they "scrape thousands of job boards and employer sites for free. Both tell you what LinkedIn contacts you have at a company posting a job." Be sure to use relevant keywords from the job descriptions to increase your chances of getting through the company's scanning software. Generally, online job boards aren't as effective as networking or applying directly through a company's Web site. For a targeted search on sites directed to workers 50 and older, see the listings in the "More 411" section at the end of this chapter.

Networking

The technique of networking can't be overemphasized. Let *everyone* know you're looking for a job—friends, relatives, neighbors, former bosses, colleagues, your connections at places of worship (some religious institutions are getting into the act, with support groups and networking events), organizations that you belong to or where you volunteer, alumni events, associations and college career centers (many will assist alumni diving back into the labor pool), your dog groomer, or people you meet at a wedding. Or join or start a MeetUp (www.meetup.com) group. Search terms such as networking, job hunting, unemployed, or new career for MeetUps close to your zip code. You get the idea—cast a wide net.

Only half of adults 50 to 64 use social media sites, so creating a profile on LinkedIn (www.linkedin.com) demonstrates that you're technologically savvy and extends your network even farther. Need help with social media? Many college career centers, recognizing that alumni may be new at this game, help them create an online presence. Continuing ed classes and chambers of commerce often offer this type of assistance.

Informational Interview

A specific kind of networking, an informational interview can expand your network and help you determine what would be a good career fit. Find someone in a job you'd like to have; a person who has only been in the position for a few years would be better, and probably more likely to meet with you, than asking the CEO for a meeting. Ask around for recommendations to get a specific name, and if the person is an alum of your college, even better. After all, most people like to talk about themselves and what they do. Remember the thank-you note when it's over.

Temping

If you believe variety is the spice of life, consider temping. It can sometimes lead to a full-time position. You can try out a number of jobs, experience different corporate cultures, strengthen your resume, and meet a wide of range of people; it can be a stop-gap measure during a downturn (although the number of people applying for temp positions increases), and during heady economic times, temp agencies clamor for people. Some examples of temp agencies are Adecco, Kelly Services, Manpower, and Office Team. See the "More 411" section at the end of this chapter for temp agency contact information.

Volunteer

Perhaps you have a job, but you have a passion to pursue a different career. Keep working toward your goal and find a substitute that feeds your soul in the interim. Envision yourself as a lawyer who protects children? Volunteer as a guardian ad litem. Would you love to be a counselor but can't quit your day job right now? Volunteer for a crisis center. See more about volunteering in Chapter 2.

Homeshoring (Working from Home)

Yes, I know that this one sounds like a scam, with visions of stuffing envelopes, purchasing start-up kits, or buying work-at-home directories. But some legitimate companies exist. An up-to-date computer; a high-speed Internet connection; a feature-free landline phone (no call-waiting beeping while you're talking to a customer); a headset; free or paid online training; and a background, drug, and credit check may be required. Called "homeshoring," customer service agents can work out of their home. Some people hired for this type of work are independent contractors; others are employees of the company. Pay usually ranges from minimum wage to $15 an hour; some work is commission based.

There's an estimated demand for several hundred thousands of these jobs, according to International Data Corporation, a marketing research company. See "More 411" at the end of this chapter for specific company names, and see "Educational Opportunities" later in this chapter for a discussion of online tutoring.

Here's Marie V.'s story about her work-at-home job:

> Everyone loved my husband. He was one of those people who never knew a stranger and was always surrounded by old friends and making new ones wherever he went. But no one loved him more—or misses him more—than I do. Walt was a disabled vet, left a paraplegic from his time spent in Vietnam. When he died at the too-young age of 55, I thought my world had crumbled and would never be rebuilt. At just 48 years old myself, there were days I could barely bring myself to get out of bed, and I sure didn't know what the future held. As the widow of a veteran, I began receiving a small pension, but it didn't take long for me to realize that it wouldn't go far enough to make ends meet. By the time I got back on my feet emotionally, about a year after Walt's death, I was in desperate need of a more substantial income.
>
> Fortunately, I was able to turn to the Paralyzed Veterans of America, a great nonprofit organization that provides resources for veterans paralyzed in the line of duty as well as their immediate families. I explained that I needed to find a job to supplement my income, but I still wasn't ready to leave

the house each day for a typical office job. With so many work-at-home scams out there, I needed some guidance to find a legitimate work-at-home opportunity.

The Paralyzed Veterans of America directed me to Alpine Access, which turned out to be the life raft I was looking for. After researching the company, I applied for a home-based call center job and was hired right away. A couple of key things were important to me: One, I would be a true employee of the company, not an independent contractor; and two, I would be able to work part-time from the comfort of my own home.

Today, I work about 30 hours each week as a tech support representative for a cell phone company. I have the flexibility to create my own schedule, I save money because I can eat lunch at home and don't have to worry about wardrobe or commuting expenses, and I get to work in my own home, which is a great comfort to me as a widow. The job is demanding, but it turns out that's just what I needed. Helping others over the phone is a great distraction that helps take my mind off my own troubles. In my free time, I've returned to doing freelance Web design and helping friends troubleshoot computer problems, and I've even recently been able to care for ailing family members out of state. Although I still miss Walt every day, finding a job with Alpine Access was a big step toward returning to my life. Stay connected, earn money, and enjoy the comfort and security of working from home—would this work for you?

Seasonal Options

Like the great outdoors? Check out www.coolworks.com for jobs at national parks, ski resorts, theme parks, tour companies, and so on. There is even a link for the "Older and Bolder" under "Find a Job." Or, if you're an RVer, consider work camping or "workamping," earning wages and a free campsite in exchange for working at the camp (check out www.work-camping.com or www.workamper .com). An estimated 80,000 retirees are work campers, according to Kampgrounds of America, Inc.

A seasonal position can often become a full-time position, as it did for Melanie F., who began working during the holidays at a major department store and ultimately became a full-time employee. Or what about becoming a tour guide during the busy tourist season? Tawanda K. leads Segway tours in her hometown of Minneapolis during the summer.

Work Part Time with Health Benefits

Costco, FedEx, Home Depot, Trader Joe's, and UPS are examples of companies that provide benefits with part-time employment. Positions within a school system, such as a teacher's aide or a crossing guard, also often pay benefits to their part-time employees. For many people, health benefits, or a lack of them, are a big issue, especially if you're younger than 65 or not eligible for Medicare.

Opportunities in Education

If you have a master's degree or a special credential (such as CPA or law degree), consider an adjunct position at a college or community college. Stephanie D. is a retired lawyer and teaches courses on contracts and the legal aspects of business start-ups at a community college. Or you could substitute teach. When Vicki F.'s husband passed away at age 50, she substitute taught for a year while she assessed her work options. How about teaching English as a second language? Look into certification as a teacher of English to speakers of other languages (TESOL, www.tesol.org) or as a teacher of English as a foreign language (TEFL, www.tefl.com). Certification classes can be online, in-class, or a hybrid of the two. Brenda K. moved to Prague in the Czech Republic and has taught English for the last seven years.

Does tutoring or test prep interest you? If you have the right academic background, this can be done through a company such as Kaplan, Kumon, or Sylvan. Or consider companies that hire online tutors such as www.smarthinking.com, www.tutor.com, or www.tutorvista.com (this last one requires an advanced degree). Consider becoming a teacher's aide (usually you don't need a college degree—but patience and love of kids are a must). Or, become a teacher. Jobs in science and math are the most plentiful, and there are alternative routes to teaching without a degree in education. Kathy H. did this; she parlayed her psychology degree into a full-time fifth-grade teaching assignment in a Catholic school. She did go back to school part-time to get her teaching credential, and then she moved to a public school for a higher salary.

The Peace Corps

Here's a thought for those who want to do good for others. About 5 percent of Peace Corps volunteers are people 50 and older. Financial benefits include full health care coverage during the 27-month commitment; a living allowance that includes housing, food, and incidentals; and a transition payment when you return from overseas of $7,425 (pretax). Hmmm . . . living expenses—check; medical coverage (you do need to medically qualify)—check; a payment when you return to the United States—check. When you add in learning another language, developing new skills, and helping others help themselves, the Peace Corps sounds like a good idea, especially if you can rent or sublease your home while you're gone. Opportunities in health, education, youth and community development, agriculture, food security, and the environment are offered. To investigate further, go to www.peacecorps.gov and click on "Who Volunteers?" under "Learn about Volunteering" and then "50+ Volunteers."

Create Your Own Job and Be Your Own Boss

Women now make up more than 40 percent of entrepreneurs in the United States, according to the *Christian Science Monitor*. This is the catch-all category, where your imagination is the only limitation. Some examples: Carol B. started her own tutoring service after working for a test-prep company for several years. Barbara J. delivered the newspaper for supplemental income after her divorce. Kelly A. began a mobile pet-grooming service. Rebecca F. became a certified personal trainer and Zumba instructor (and many mature women are happy to see someone closer to their age, as opposed to some young hardbody). Pat M. established her own real-estate staging and interior design business. Paulette A. initiated her own dog-walking/dog-sitting service. This last one is a hot area; more than 60 percent of U.S. households have at least one pet, and we spend close to $50 billion on them each year! Marianne H. became a consultant for direct sales at in-home parties (check out the clothing lines of CAbi and Etcetera and the jewelry lines of Silpada and Premier, for example). Jody C. launched her own company doing tax consulting and tax-return preparation after working as a CPA for many years. Crafty? Gloria sells her handmade wristlets on www .etsy.com. Shop 'til you drop. Annie F. worked as a secret shopper for a few years (www.secretshopper.com). Connie A. and Janet C. share a position teaching high school French. Connie teaches three classes in the morning; Janet teaches in the afternoon.

For free help starting your own business, contact the U.S. Small Business Administration (www.sba.gov) for online training, info about business loans, and additional help. Since 2011, there has been a push for expanded access for women-owned small business and federal contracting opportunities.

Franchises

Franchise fees range from several thousand dollars (usually home-based businesses) to millions of dollars. Examples of franchises include H&R Block, Home Instead Senior Care, Jazzercise, Subway, and Supercuts. AARP also offers suggestions for good franchises for those over 50 at www.aarp.org/work/self-employment/info-03-2011/starting-a-business-over-50.2.html. Get input from a franchise lawyer and develop a solid business plan before going the franchise route. Check out "Franchising Pros and Cons: Is Franchising Right for You?" in Appendix 3. Several franchise sites are listed in the "More 411" section.

Did You Know?

Build it and they will come. To stimulate tourism and generate income, many states are turning to gambling. Florida, Maine, Massachusetts, New York, Ohio, and Pennsylvania are among the states considering, building, or expanding casinos, which generate lots of jobs. The new Horseshoe Casino Cincinnati, for example, will open up an estimated 1,700 jobs. Slots (yup, bad pun) for dealers, security guards, cashiers, and food and beverage workers need to be filled. Salaries range from $25,000 (plus tips) for cashiers to $40,000 a year (plus tips) for dealers. It's something to consider if you're betting you'll need a job.

As we know, things don't always get wrapped up perfectly like they do at the end of some 30-minute TV shows. Here's is Joanne C.'s story about her evolving life and career:

I've been told that my decision took courage. Right now, I think it was a rush of insanity!

I'm certain that my story mirrors that of thousands of other 50-ish people who are still wondering what they're going to be when they grow up.

I started college in the 1970s with great personal expectations of becoming a lawyer or a teacher. Neither of those paths was traveled as I found myself working on Wall Street instead. It was a fun, pressure-packed job, but after nine years, I realized that was not what I wanted to do for the rest of my life. I went to work for Dun & Bradstreet selling business information. I have a clear recollection of walking into their lobby in January of 1989 and saying to myself, "I'm going to retire from this company." Well, that didn't happen, either.

I enjoyed a successful sales career, moving up the food chain, winning awards, making good money. I liked the job and loved the customers. There was a lot of pressure, but success made that tolerable. Seventeen years into my career, my focus shifted dramatically. My mother's health began to decline. I wanted to do everything I could to help her, and my father, as their lives were changing. I also had a career to maintain.

As a sales professional, you live and die by your results, and mine were tanking. My time management skills were thrown by the wayside as I was spending all of my time with my mother: doctors, hospitals, rehab, nursing home, and then finally home to care for her through her last days. I'd taken a three-month, unpaid family leave of absence. Aside from needing to be with her, I was hoping to hide for a while and ignore my poor performance. But the damage was already done. After Mom died, I returned to work and found myself on probationary status with a small timeframe to improve. I needed to get out from under that weight and find a new home, hopefully within the company. The writing was on the wall.

Over the last three years, I've had four different jobs. I was successful in each and was asked to take on other responsibilities. During that stretch, my father's health declined and I cared for him. After his death, I was distracted, disenchanted, and discouraged. There was no meeting of the minds between the corporate aspiration and my need to feel better about myself. All I knew was that I was miserable. This "career" no longer provided any satisfaction. I needed to do something different—the question was *what?*

During my time as a caregiver, I felt as though I went through some form of discernment—head and heart struggling with each other: My head telling me I was good at what I was doing and could still make it work; my heart telling me it was empty and needed something else. What was it? What would make me feel good and whole? I just don't know and this is the stumbling block. It's easy to say, "I want to reinvent myself," but to do it, you need a plan. All I did know was that I'd had enough of corporate America and I wanted to, in such overplayed words—"give back."

I walked away from a 21-year career at a major corporation with no plan. Am I nuts?

Being single (never married) and over 50, I've had to rely on myself for most things. I've been frugal with money and, hopefully, somewhat savvy with investments. I've always contributed to my 401(k) and tried to save money. But how much is enough? That's the thought that wakes me in the middle of the night. At 52, I don't want to tap into my retirement fund. I know it's there; it's my safety net. I asked for, and my company afforded me, a severance package. That will give me six months to find direction.

I know that I never felt better about *me* than when I was caring for my parents. It was very difficult, on so many levels— but it gave me joy. My decision for the immediate future is to volunteer at the local medical center. I think that will help me determine if my caregiver role was reserved for my parents or if it will help me find a new direction.

I am a work in progress. I'm scared, but I need to find my way.

Tip

When job hunting, type your name into your search engine to see what shows up, review the social media sites that you're on (almost half of employers check out prospective employees on these sites), and e-mail your resume to yourself and a few trusted people prior to sending it to employers to be sure it looks like you want it to look.

Work on the Web

There are a number of opportunities to make money on the Internet. For example, if you're an expert and want to share your knowledge, check out www.justanswer.com; if you're an RN, you might be interested in www.fonemed.com; if you make jewelry, www.jewelrywonder.com and www.etsy.com might be good venues; if you have special expertise in the arts, home improvement, sports, travel, or other areas, check out http://voices.yahoo.com; and if you're willing to do something for $5, www.fiverr.com might be for you.

Resume, Cover Letter, and Interview Strategies for Older Workers[*]

Resumes

- Emphasize the most recent 15 years of your career in the experience section of your resume. Consider a "Previous Professional Experience" for experience older than 15 years, and list this older experience in a bare-bones fashion with few or no bullet points.
- Deemphasize dates. Certainly don't list your birthdate. Omit college-graduation dates that are more than 10 to 15 years old. A few experts even advise omitting dates from the listings of your jobs, instead just listing the number of years you were in each job.

---

[*]Copyright by Quintessential Careers. The original article can be found at: www.quintcareers.com/printable/older_worker_strategies.html. Reprinted with permission.

- Some experts suggest softening the job titles you list on your resume so you won't seem overqualified. For example, list "senior manager" instead of "vice president."
- Be sure to list all courses and professional-development activities that illustrate your willingness to learn and keep your skills updated.
- List all your computer and other technological skills that are relevant to the type of job you're applying for.
- Emphasize results, accomplishments, and achievements. List some accomplishments that set you apart from other job candidates. You will likely have a greater quantity and quality of achievements than will younger workers. In each job, what special things did you do to set yourself apart? How did you do the job better than anyone else or than anyone else could have done? What did you do to make it your own? What special things did you do to impress your boss so that you might be promoted? How did you leave your employers better off than before you worked for them? Accomplishments are the points that really help sell you to an employer—much more so than everyday job duties.
- If you are just entering the workforce after a career as a homemaker or volunteer or have large gaps of unpaid experience in your history, portray your skills on your resume as transferable and applicable to your next job.

Cover Letters

- Avoid cumulative experience statements. Older workers are justifiably proud of their work histories and have a tendency in cover letters to make statements such as this: "My 25+ years in management would enable me to make a significant contribution in the position you're advertising." With that much experience, it's probably best *not* to quantify in your cover letter. Stick to expressions such as "significant experience" or "extensive experience."
- Avoid an "autobiography letter" or one that rehashes the job history you've already laid out in your resume. It's never a good idea, but it's especially harmful for older

workers who will only call attention to their age with such a letter.

- Include language in your cover letter about flexibility, adaptability, and willingness to learn.
- Emphasize that you are a proven commodity (in unspoken counterpoint to a younger worker who may be untested).

Job Interviews

- Realize that you will probably be interviewed by someone younger than you, and don't be unnerved by that situation.
- Show yourself as a value-added employee. Overcoming the obstacles that may be inherent in your resume and cover letter is a major victory, but once you've gotten your foot in the door with an interview, you have to do more than younger workers would need to do to. "Despite your age, you've got to show that you're still very current in today's workplace, such as with your computer skills," says Deborah Russell, the former director of workforce issues at AARP, as quoted in the *Washington Post.* "Tell how flexible, adaptable, creative you can be, that you're a team player and able to work with multiple age generations."
- Stress your willingness to learn. One of the biggest obstacles to the hiring of older workers is the concern that their skills are outdated and they aren't willing to learn new skills. Writing in the *Milwaukee Journal Sentinel,* Margo Frey urges older workers to demonstrate their willingness to learn based on their past record and future commitment to keeping skills updated:
  - If you've taken courses and attended workshops, seminars, conferences, and other professional development events throughout your career, be sure the prospective employer knows that.
  - Especially ensure the employer knows your technology aptitude is up to date, particularly as it relates to the job you're interviewing for.
  - Telling the prospective employer that you sought out and paid for learning opportunities on your own can be especially impressive.

62

- ■ Convince the employer that you are more than willing to get up to speed on any skills that may be lagging.
- Subtly suggest that your work ethic is unsurpassed (in possible contrast to that of younger workers). Be sure prospective employers know that your references will vouch for your reliability and stable work record.
- Convince employers that your maturity is an advantage because your experience makes you wise in the ways of problem solving. "Wisdom involves using past experience to help solve a current situation," writes Margo Frey in the *Milwaukee Journal Sentinel.* "Having successfully survived difficult situations, older workers can apply their knowledge and experience to make better judgments than a young person might make. Wisdom also means keeping an open mind to better or more appropriate ways to solve a problem."
- Stress interpersonal skills, especially your delight in working with people of all ages. If you're interviewing for a job with client or customer interaction, AARP suggests you might want to mention your ability to identify with an aging customer base, where relevant.
- Be prepared for interview questions that are inappropriate, borderline illegal, or downright unlawful. If you are asked any question that suggests the employer wants to know how old you are or is concerned about your age, AARP recommends responding with a question such as: "How do you see my age affecting my ability to do the job?" Don't be defiant or confrontational as you ask the question; remain upbeat and positive. If you're asked whether you'd have a problem working for a younger manager, AARP suggests you respond with: "When I get to the point where I can't learn from someone younger or older than I am, I will stop working."

We had a 55-year-old correspondent who told us that she was asked what year she graduated from high school. At another interview, she was asked for a photo ID and presented with citizenship documentation clearly stating at the top of the page "To Be Completed by Employee on First Day of Employment." The consensus among career counselors

Tip

Not sure what you'd like to do? Check out www.vocationvacations.com where (for a fee) you can test drive a new career path, from actor or alpaca rancher to writer or yoga studio owner.

to whom we presented these situations was that they were clearly illegal. The counselors made these suggestions:

- Report the company and call the firm's president.
- Ask yourself if you would really want to work for such an unprofessional company.
- In response to the question about when a job applicant graduated from high school, say: "Can you tell me how this question applies to my ability to perform the job?" And when presented with the obviously post-offer forms, simply ask if the forms represent an offer of employment.
- Say: "I am sensing that there may be concerns about my age. Unless there is something I haven't been told, I can only assure you that there are no aspects of this position that I cannot handle, and I would be committed to bring you a wealth of education, training, and experience that few could equal."

(By the way, our correspondent's story has a happy ending; she e-mailed us a few weeks later to say that she has landed a promising job.)

Tip

Remember the all-important thank-you note after the interview. It demonstrates that you're a people person, it serves as a reminder, it's an opportunity to include any brilliant thoughts you remembered after the fact (and to restate your major points), and shows that you're organized.

If you're going to work, play, or do both in retirement, you'll want to be in top form both physically and mentally. That's the next chapter.

More 411

Finding a Job

Bolles, Richard. *What Color Is Your Parachute? 2012: A Practical Manual for Job Hunters and Career Changers.* Berkeley: Ten Speed Press, 2011.

Encore Careers (www.encore.org). Finding work that combines both passion and paychecks in the second half of life. Started by Marc Freedman, founder and CEO of Civic Ventures, a nonprofit think tank on boomers, work, and social purpose.

Hannon, Kerry. *Great Jobs for Everyone 50+: Finding Work That Keeps You Happy and Healthy . . . and Pays the Bills.* Hoboken: John Wiley & Sons, October 2012.

Hannon, Kerry. *What's Next? Follow Your Passion and Find Your Dream Job.* San Francisco: Chronicle Books, 2010.

Yate, Martin. *Knock 'Em Dead 2012: The Ultimate Job Search Guide.* Avon: Adams Media, 2011.

Homeshoring

Alpine Access. www.alpineaccess.com. 888-466-2749 (call center work from your home; $45 background/drug/credit check required)

Live Ops. www.liveops.com (call center work from your home; $50 background/credit check)

The Work at Home Gazette. www.theworkathomegazette.com (compilation of work-at-home opportunities)

Tigerfish. www.tigerfish.com (transcribing services; purchase of a $250 transcriber required)

West at Home. www.westathome.com (call center work from your home; $29.95 background check fee)

Working Solutions. www.workingsolutions.com or 866-857-4800 (call center work from your home; click on "Contact Us")

Senior Social Assistance Agencies

Comfort Keepers. www.comfortkeepers.com or 800-387-2415 (my sister worked for them for about a year; more than 600 franchises)

Home Instead Senior Care. www.homeinstead.com or 866-996-1087 (franchises in more than 800 cities worldwide)

Visiting Angels. www.visitingangels.com or 800-365-4189

Online Job Sites for Mature Workers (most sites have additional resources for finding/getting a job)

www.aarp.org (type "The Water Cooler" into the search bar and click on "Online Community Group: The Water Cooler" for its online networking community)

www.aarpworksearch.org (guides you through the job search process and offers free assessments)

www.jobsover50.com

www.primecb.com (a division of CareerBuilder.com)

www.retiredbrains.com

www.retirementjobs.com

www.seniorjobbank.org (sister site to Workforce50)

www.wiserworker.com

www.workforce50.com

Temp Agencies

Kelly Services. www.kellyservices.com (I worked for them during college breaks)

Manpower. www.manpower.com (also offers foreign assignments for those authorized to work in another country)

OfficeTeam. www.officeteam.com (specializes in administrative staffing)

Franchising

www.franchises.about.com
www.franchisesforwomen.com
www.womensfranchises.com

Appendix 3: Franchising Pros and Cons: Is Franchising Right for You?*

Pros of Franchise Businesses

- **Established Brand and Customer Base.** By far, the biggest advantage of buying into an established franchise is the strength of the brand and loyalty of its customers.
- **Marketing Support.** Franchises often have the support of a national campaign, as well as prepared marketing materials for a local campaign.
- **Reputable Suppliers.** Franchisors often have established relationships with suppliers for all the materials franchisees need.
- **Business Support.** There's a saying in franchising: "You're in business for yourself, but not by yourself" because you have a network of support.
- **Training.** Some of the better (and more expensive) franchise operations offer management and technical training.
- **Financial Assistance.** Some franchisors provide loans and other assistance to help franchisees.
- **Access to Proprietary Methods.** There's no need to reinvent the wheel as franchisees get access to all the trade secrets.
- **Ongoing Research and Development, New Products.** Franchisees can stick to improving their operations and let the franchisor spend the time and money developing products.
- **The Boss Is You.** As with any business that you own, you are in control of your destiny.
- **Reduced Risk.** For all of these reasons, starting a franchise of an established brand often has less risk than starting a business from nothing.

---

*By Randall S. Hansen, Ph.D. Copyright by Quintessential Careers. The original article can be found at www.quintcareers.com/franchising_pros_cons.html. Reprinted with permission.

Cons of Franchise Businesses

- **Initial Payout (Franchise Fee and Start-up Costs).** Some of the bigger franchise operations can involve very large initial costs, often more than what it would cost to start your own business.
- **Royalty Payments.** For as long as you are a franchisee, you will have to pay some percentage of the monthly gross back to the franchisor, reducing your profit potential.
- **Marketing/Advertising Fees.** To receive the wonderful marketing support from the franchisor, franchisees must pay these fees, according to some contracts.
- **Limited Creativity/Flexibility.** Most franchise contracts have very explicit standards, allowing little or no alterations or additions to the brand, stifling any creativity on the part of the franchisee. You must use their system, follow their rules.
- **Sole Sourcing.** Some franchise contracts stipulate that franchisees must buy supplies only from an approved list of suppliers, possibly at a higher cost.
- **Locked into Operation by Long-Term Contract.** If you don't do as much research as you should have and find yourself with the wrong franchise, you may be stuck for many years.
- **Dependent on Franchisor Success.** The reputation of your franchise is only as good as that of the franchisor, so any difficulties that the franchisor encounters will have a direct impact on you.
- **False Expectations.** Opening a franchise rather than starting your own business offers no guarantees of success. You still need to be a sharp businessperson to make it work.
- **Risk.** There's always risk in starting any new business.

Fitness in Body, Mind, and Spirit

The idea is to die young as late as possible.

—Ashley Montagu

■ ■ ■

"**D**on't trust anyone over 30." Remember that quote from the 1960s activist Jack Weinberg? Well, now we are them! Someone turns 50 every 8 seconds, and for the next 19 years, 10,000 people a day will be turning 65. The average lifespan for a woman is 81 years, and if you've reached that magic Medicare age of 65, expect to live another two decades. Of course, the goal is not just to have a long lifespan, but a healthy one, too, in body, mind, and spirit.

What Can the Nuns Teach Us?

One of my single women friends, Lorraine R., was waiting for an appointment to talk to a doctor about the results of her mammogram. She noticed several nuns of various orders in the waiting room, which she thought very odd. Well, it turns out that nuns have a higher incidence of breast cancer. Why is this so? When you're pregnant or breastfeeding, the levels of estrogen decline and/or fluctuate significantly, and estrogen is implicated in breast cancer.

So, if you've never had children or if you first became pregnant when you were 35 or older, you're more at risk for breast cancer.

Similarly, nuns have a lower incidence of cervical cancer. What's that about? It's now known that most cervical cancer is caused by a few strains of the human papillomaviruses (HPVs), which are sexually transmitted.

The point? Not to give a lesson on nuns and cancer incidence, but to point out that lifestyle factors can affect our health, and it's important to be aware of them.

Nature and Nurture

Both environment and genetics play a role in our mental and physical health and longevity. Scientists have tried to tease out how much each contributes to our health. One approach is by studying identical twins raised by different adoptive families from birth. The stories of these separated twins emphasize the effects of genetics. These separated twins often have similar tastes in food, beer, and cigarettes; suffer from the same health issues; and weigh the same. They often even drive the same kind of car, marry people with similar personalities, or name their children closely related names. An amazing testament to our genes.

Research has also found, however, that nature and nurture can overlap. Researchers have discovered that our genes (nature) can be shaped by our environment (nurture), beginning in the uterus. For example, if a fetus experiences a shortage of nutrients, the brain will get first dibs, perhaps resulting in a weaker heart when that person becomes an adult. Women who are depressed or anxious may also mold their children's brains through the effects of stress hormones such as cortisol.

Why bring this up? Certainly not as a way of blaming mothers for their children's problems (we get enough blame for that), but to reinforce that there are some things we can't change, some things we can influence, and some things we can control.

It's estimated that lifestyle choices affect more than three-fourths of the health care costs spent on diseases in the United States. One striking example is lung cancer; 80 percent of lung cancer in women is caused by smoking, according to the U.S. Centers for Disease Control and Prevention. Obesity and the lack of physical activity contribute to the incidence of heart disease, diabetes, and several types of cancer. It should be comforting to know that much of our health is within our control.

Women's Health Issues

Some diseases or conditions are more common in women than in men. These include Alzheimer's; obesity; mental health issues such as depression, anxiety, and eating disorders; osteoarthritis; breast cancer (men can get it, it's just much less common); and autoimmune diseases (including lupus and multiple sclerosis). Of course, women's reproductive cancers—such as ovarian, uterine (also called endometrial), cervical, and vulvar (external female genitalia)—are unique to women. Knowing which diseases you're more likely to get because of your gender can be helpful information, so you can take the appropriate steps to try to prevent them.

Women's Top 10 Threats

Of course, we realize the ultimate death rate is one per person, but let's try to postpone the inevitable. The top two killers of women, heart disease and cancer, account for almost 50 percent of all deaths. Women's 10 biggest killers (in order, with percentage of deaths in parentheses) are, according to the CDC:

1. Heart disease. It's the top killer of men and women in the United States. (accounts for 25 percent of all deaths)
2. Cancer. Lung is women's biggest cancer killer; colon and breast are major cancers, too. (22 percent)
3. Stroke. This is also called a "brain attack." Sixty percent of stroke deaths are among women. (7 percent)
4. COPD or chronic obstructive pulmonary disease. A lot of women are unfamiliar with this disease. It's our fourth biggest killer, affecting women more than men, mainly because of smoking, which accounts for approximately 90 percent of COPD (emphysema and chronic bronchitis are the two main forms of COPD). Experts believe tobacco affects

women more adversely than it does men, and women reportedly have a harder time quitting smoking. More women die from COPD than from breast cancer and diabetes combined, according to the COPD Foundation. (6 percent)

5. Alzheimer's disease. Women tend to get Alzheimer's later than men, and when we do get it, it comes on more forcefully. Women die from Alzheimer's almost twice as often as men, according to the U.S. Department of Health and Human Services. (4.3 percent)

6. Injuries. Car crashes account for most fatalities; one in seven adults doesn't use a seat belt. Falls and poisoning, such as from carbon monoxide, also contribute to this category. (3.6 percent)

7. Type 2 diabetes. This can affect heart, eyes, kidneys, and nerves. Although men and women are equally affected, women have more than three times the risk of developing heart disease as a result of diabetes. (2.9 percent)

8. Influenza and pneumonia. The flu is especially dangerous if you have a chronic health condition. (2.3 percent)

9. Kidney disease. This is often a result of high blood pressure or diabetes. (2 percent)

10. Septicemia. Blood poisoning is often the result of an infection in the body. (1.6 percent)

Did You Know?

An elephant sitting on your chest? Grabbing your left arm in pain? Only about 4 in 10 women experience the kind of acute chest pain typically described by men having a heart attack. Women's symptoms may include shortness of breath, weakness, fatigue, back pain, nausea, dizziness, and lower chest pain. Helene C. thought she had pulled a muscle in her upper back and delayed going to the doctor until the pain was severe. It was a heart attack, and Helene required five stents to open up her arteries.

What can we do to try to ensure we're not a statistic before our time? The list is the same list you see all the time: Don't smoke; stay active; eat a healthy diet; if you drink alcohol, do so in moderation; maintain a healthy weight; cultivate social connections; stay active mentally; avoid head injuries; avoid carcinogens (cancer-causing substances) and air pollution; and avoid too much sun (to prevent some types of cancer). It sounds like a simple list, but we know it's not always easy to implement.

Significant Statistic

We're on the right track. Smoking among women has dropped from 30 percent in 1974 to 18 percent today. That's critical, because the American Lung Association has identified cigarette smoking as *"the leading cause of preventable morbidity and premature mortality in the United States."* If you don't smoke, you've significantly lowered your chances of heart disease, several types of cancer, and COPD. Not to mention that smoking causes lower bone density in postmenopausal women and wrinkling of the skin. And think of the money you'll save if you give up cigarettes.

Besides the threats that can kill us, other issues affect our day-to-day quality of life. Getting hot flashes, experiencing creaky and achy joints, looking for that word we used to be able to pull from our long-term memory without effort, feeling tired or stressed, losing sexual desire, having trouble sleeping, gaining weight, suffering from urinary incontinence . . . this list can get pretty long. Some of this may be normal aging, but sometimes it can be an early warning sign as our bodies continue to change.

Okay, enough of the pity party. Let's explore what we can change, why it works, and some of the platitudes (and contradictions) we hear about becoming and staying healthy and living a long life.

How Can We Live Longer (and Healthier)?

It's estimated that there are about 125,000 centenarians, with women centenarians vastly outnumbering men. So we now have a new category, Supercentenarians. Supercentenarians are those 110 or older, with the worldwide number at 65 women and 5 men. Knowing their secrets to a long life is instructive. Commonalities for achieving their extreme longevity include: good genes—the majority of "Supers" have relatives who lived a long life, and their children are often in their 80s; they deal effectively with stress; they tend to live in nonindustrial areas with low pollution; they value spirituality; they don't smoke or abuse alcohol; they aren't obese; they have social support; they've largely escaped the typical mental and physical illnesses of "old age"; and they often have genetic mutations that favor long life. Again, some things we can control, some things we can't. That interplay of genes, environment, and individual behavior choices is a powerful cocktail.

Fun Fact

To drink or not to drink? A recent study from Harvard University found that middle-aged women who drank one alcoholic drink a day aged "more successfully" than nondrinkers or those who overindulge. That is, these women lowered their chances of diabetes, improved their cholesterol levels, reduced inflammation, and improved blood vessel function.

As part of a large National Institutes of Health–AARP Diet and Health Study, researchers looked at the effect of lifestyle factors, including moderate alcohol intake, on the incidence of diabetes. The researchers found that "participants with a low-risk lifestyle profile that included not smoking, engaging in regular physical activity, consuming a healthful diet, using alcohol in moderation, and having an optimal body weight had a dramatically lower risk for incident diabetes than those without such a profile."

But the American Medical Association announced that drinking only 3 to 6 glasses of alcohol a week can increase the risk of breast cancer by 15 percent. Bottoms up or not?

Mitochondria and Telomeres

Exercise, eat well, and keep stress in check. We've heard this advice before, but sometimes knowing how it actually works at the cellular level can drive a change in behavior and transform our bodies and lives. (I warned you earlier that I used to be an assistant professor of biology.) Let's take a look at two words you may or may not have heard of—mitochondria and telomeres—but they are inside us, and they are thought to play a powerful role in aging and longevity. We'll discuss mitochondria first.

You might remember from science classes that mitochondria are nicknamed "the powerhouses of the cell." Mitochondria turn food into energy through a series of complex chemical reactions. There are up to 2,000 tubular mitochondria per cell (some types of body cells don't have any), and in energy-intense cells, such as muscle and heart, which of course is also a muscle, mitochondria make up around half of the cell's volume. Research reveals that damage to our mitochondria might contribute to aging. A lifetime of insults to our mitochondria through free-radical damage can cause disease and slow down our body's processes.

Is there a way to protect, restore, or increase these mighty but misunderstood tubular structures? Research suggests the answer is yes—through exercise. Exercising 15 to 20 minutes a day three or four times a week (e.g., swimming, tennis, biking, and brisk walking) can actually increase the number of mitochondria per cell in about six weeks and make them more effective at burning fat. But, to maintain this benefit, you need to keep up the exercise regimen . . . as we know, use it or lose it. Strength training is also effective for increasing the number of mitochondria for inactive older adults, although the same effect hasn't been observed among younger people. Another fascinating study showed that with regular exercise, our mitochondria helped lower the risk of insulin resistance, thus helping prevent, or at least slow down, the onset of diabetes.

Now for telomeres. Remember again from your sciences classes that our genetic material is called DNA (deoxyribonucleic acid). At the end of our DNA strands (called chromosomes) there are little caps, like the plastic tips at the end of shoelaces, that protect our chromosomes from fraying and deteriorating. These are the telomeres. Every time a body cell divides, it needs to make another complete copy of its DNA, and when this happens, the telomeres shorten a bit. When telomeres become too short after a number of cell divisions, it affects the cell's ability to make more copies of its DNA, and the cell dies. This exciting information about telomeres has led to much study. It's thought that telomeres might be a big key to aging, and if we can make our telomeres longer and stronger, we'll have a lengthened lifespan and a healthier one. Research shows that shorter telomeres increase the risk of cancer. The 2009 Nobel Prize in Medicine was awarded to Elizabeth Blackburn, Jack Szostak, and Carol Greider for their research on telomeres.

Guess what? We can strengthen and lengthen our telomeres through exercise, lowering our stress levels, and proper eating. A study of twins found that those who exercised more had longer telomeres. And studies found that women who felt they were under stress had telomeres that were shorter than those who controlled their stress levels through exercise. Certain foods, such as those containing high levels of omega-3 fatty acids, including wild salmon, mackerel, and some nuts, also lengthen telomeres.

How Much, What, and When to Eat

More than 60 percent of adult women are overweight, and about a third of overweight women are considered obese. Obesity is linked to all kinds of health problems including postmenopausal breast cancer (even when our ovaries are kaput, our lovely fat cells pump out estrogen); colon, esophageal, kidney, and pancreatic cancers; diabetes; cardiovascular disease; gallstones; osteoarthritis; and sleep apnea. Why this epidemic of weight gain?

Proposed culprits include a slower metabolism as we age, inactivity due to too many sedentary activities such as watching TV and surfing the Internet, viruses, lack of sleep, easy availability of fast food, heavy friends, genetics, side effects of medicine, hormonal issues, car-dependent communities, air conditioning (it's too comfortable inside to go outside), and safety concerns that keep people within their homes. Other culprits may be companies that manipulate fat, salt, and sugar in foods that make us crave high-calorie food; diet drinks (artificial sweeteners prime our body for calories, and when they aren't forthcoming, our brain tells us we're hungry); and portion size. It's no wonder that the diet industry is a $60 billion bonanza. A weight loss of only 5 to 10 percent can make a difference, boosting self-confidence, lowering blood pressure and triglycerides, decreasing the risk of diabetes and heart disease, and lessening the wear and tear on our knee joints (and we already mentioned weight discrimination in Chapter 3).

How many calories per day do we need? To make it simple, a sedentary woman over 50 needs about 1,500 a day; an active woman up to 1,900 calories a day. Another easy way to calculate how many calories you need to reach a goal weight is to take the weight you'd like to be and multiply it by 12. So, if your goal is 140 pounds, consume about 1,680 calories per day. Most of us underestimate the number of calories we consume, so we need to be vigilant when keeping track. That leftover macaroni and cheese we eat off our grandchild's plate and that chocolate we pop into our mouth when we sit down to watch the evening news really do count. Many women swear by food journals to keep them honest. One study found that those who wrote down everything they ate lost twice as much weight as those who didn't. And how often to eat? The answer is: what works for you. Six small meals, three meals and two snacks, only three meals because you'll go wild if you eat more often? Experiment with different timings.

On a personal note, I like three meals along with two snacks, either high fiber like popcorn or nuts, or something with protein and produce, such as peanut butter with banana or celery. If I just *have* to eat some chocolate, and of course dark chocolate has flavonoids, which are healthy, I eat it later in the evening, since it makes me tired and I'll be going to bed soon. It took me a long time to figure out this is the best way for me to approach food. My friends who say they forgot to eat? I can't relate, that's for sure.

Studies on mice found that *when* they ate affected how much they weighed. Researchers who awakened mice and fed them when they would normally be asleep found this resulted in twice the weight gain compared to those mice fed the same diet during their normal waking hours. It's thought that their metabolic rate was lowered by changing their normal pattern. Studies are under way to see if this animal model holds for humans, too. So, those of us who are up late at night, when we'd normally be sleeping, should be watchful about eating. And we need to be careful when we eat out with friends, too. Brian Wansink, author of *Mindless Eating*, found that we eat 35 percent more when dining with one friend and 96 percent more when we're with a group of seven friends.

Of course, it's not only *how much* or *when*, but also, of course, *what* you eat. You may have seen the term "functional foods." These are foods that go beyond what food normally does for us, which is providing building blocks for growth, repair, and energy in order to run our bodies' vital processes such as digestion and respiration. Functional foods provide benefits beyond our basic nutritional needs. A few examples and what they do for us (note that they are all simple as well as super—in moderation):

- **Blueberries.** The color of blueberries is from pigments called anthocyanins, which may help reduce the incidence of cancer and stroke and improve memory and learning.
- **Walnuts.** The omega-3 fatty acids in walnuts have been found to reduce "bad" LDL cholesterol, lower blood pressure, and reduce inflammation. About 14 walnut halves is a good serving size. At close to 200 calories per serving, walnuts are an energy-dense food.
- **Broccoli.** We might all remember how George H. W. Bush declared he didn't like broccoli, but perhaps he didn't realize that the sulforophane in this veggie has anticancer properties that have been linked to the reduction of lung and stomach cancers.
- **Legumes.** This group includes kidney beans, lentils, green beans, soybeans, peanuts, and edamame (my favorite). Research indicates legumes have resistant starch, which lowers blood-sugar levels.
- **Avocados.** Like guacamole? You're in luck. The healthy monosaturated fats in this fruit help raise "good" HDL cholesterol, and the avocado's high level of potassium helps keep blood pressure in check.

How to Fool Ourselves or Change Our Environment to Eat Better and Less

How can we address our growing girth? I'm sure some readers are trying to pack on some pounds, but you're probably in the minority, so we'll ignore you—no offense. We know carrying around extra weight can contribute to a variety of illnesses, but we're human and it's much easier to be tempted in the present (we think about how good those peanut M&Ms taste *now*) than project into the future and do what's best for us. We're more into immediate gratification; behavioral economists call that approach "future discounting." We make approximately 200 decisions every day that influence our weight. With food easily available, many social events centered on food and alcohol, and fast and cheap food usually not as healthy, we need to actually fool ourselves or to manipulate our surroundings so that it's easier to eat better and to eat less. How to do this? Let's take a look at some "tricks" that can help:

- **Try the Volumetrics Plan.** Most of us like to eat, and some of us, such as yours truly, like to eat a lot—both frequently and in large amounts. The volumetrics plan, developed by Dr. Barbara Rolls of Penn State, focuses on eating food that is low in calories but filling, often because it contains a lot of water. **Tip:** Start your main meal with a broth-based soup chock full of low-calorie vegetables. This one trick allowed Gina C. to lose about 15 pounds this past year, because she felt fuller but consumed fewer calories. Other suggested foods that are low in energy density (calories) but high in volume include non-starchy veggies. Or, substitute grapes for raisins—you can eat two cups of grapes for the same 100 calories as a quarter-cup of raisins. *The Ultimate Volumetrics Diet* is listed in the "More 411" section.
- **Avoid Preposterous Portions.** Serving sizes have grown dramatically over the years. When combined with the psychology that we tend to eat more if it's in front of us and companies' increased profit margins when they charge a nominal fee of about 16 percent for a larger serving size, it's no wonder that we're becoming supersized.

  Here are some comparisons of serving sizes then and now:

	Then (1950s)	Now
French fries	2.5 ounces	7 ounces
Hershey bar	2 ounces	7 ounces
Movie popcorn	5 cups	11 cups
Soda	7 ounces	Up to 64 ounces

	Then (1950s)	Now
Muffin	3 ounces	6.5 ounces
Pasta	1.5 cups	3 cups
Hamburger patty	1.6 ounces	up to 8 ounces
Bagel	3-inch diameter	6-inch diameter
Chicken Caesar salad	1.5 cups	3.5 cups
Cheesecake	3 ounces	7 ounces
Cookie	1.5-inch diameter	3.5-inch diameter
Chicken stir-fry	2 cups	4.5 cups
Chips (individual bag)	1 ounce	3.5 ounces
Chocolate milk (bottle)	10 ounces	20 ounces

This increase in portion size (and calories) is an insidious change that we have grown accustomed to in everyday life. Being aware of this is a first step toward addressing one of the many causes of weight gain. **Tip:** Look at labels to see what a "serving size" actually is; for example, a box of candy that could easily be wolfed down during the previews at the movie theater may actually be several servings. Look at the serving size as well as the calories.

Healthy Tip

Simpler is often healthier. Try to avoid foods with a long list of ingredients, most of which you don't know or can't pronounce. In general, the less processed the better. Five or fewer ingredients is a goal some people subscribe to . . . so they aren't eating a science project.

- **Use a Smaller Plate and a Tall, Skinny Glass.** Look at the sizes of the plates and glasses that are now sold. My 35-year-old Waterford Lismore wineglasses look positively tiny next to my recently purchased wineglasses, and my new salad plates are about the same size as my 35-year-old Noritake Blue Hill dinner plates. My new dishes have a lot more space that "needs" to be filled up with food. So, when you eat at home (or when you're out, if possible), use a small plate—it will help trick your mind into thinking you're eating more. Mentally divide your plate in half, and fill one half with veggies and/or fruit. Then, take the other half and divide it into two. Put protein in one of those halves (we're now really talking about a fourth of the plate), and some type of starch into the other half (or fourth). If you add in a small amount of dairy, you're actually implementing the 2011 "My Plate" guidelines, the update to the U.S. government's old food pyramid.

In terms of starch, research suggests that eating "resistant starch," which resists being digested in the small intestine (e.g., bananas, legumes, and oatmeal), means that you will feel full longer and perhaps lose weight.

And drink your liquid calories out of a tall, skinny glass. It *appears* to have more in it than a short, fat glass containing the same amount of liquid.

- **Choose Your Friends Wisely.** I'm certainly not advocating that you get rid of friends who love to eat, but researchers have found that obesity is socially contagious. Are you more likely to eat bigger portions or order dessert if you have friends who routinely do so? Less likely to exercise if your friends would rather watch TV or surf the Internet than take a long walk or go to the gym? Turns out we double our chances of becoming obese if we have four friends who are obese, according to Harvard researchers. And we tend to order and eat what a thin friend eats, even if it's a large amount or unhealthy selection. So be aware of this social bias when it comes to eating.

Fun Fact

Is coffee a health food? If the caffeine doesn't make you jumpy or you don't mind the temporary rise in blood pressure (you can always drink decaf) or you don't get heartburn or need to run to the bathroom too often or you're pregnant (probably not too many of you reading this book will fall into *that* category), think about upping your intake of java. The

NIH-AARP Diet and Health Study found that people who drank one to six cups of coffee a day reduced their risk of early mortality from all causes. Women coffee drinkers have a lower incidence of stroke, and women and men have a lower incidence of Parkinson's, dementia and Alzheimer's, diabetes, gallstones, abnormal heart rhythms, heart attack, and liver cancer. And, there's no doubt that coffee improves short-term mental and physical performance. "Yes, thanks, I'd love a refill."

- **Eat Mindfully.** I grew up with five siblings, I'm the third oldest, and if we didn't eat fast, we might not have gotten enough to eat. I devoured my food, and it's something I still struggle to change. Sometimes I'm literally out of breath from eating too fast. Try to eat slowly. It gives us more time for the brain to tell us we're full. Chew food thoroughly, put down your utensils between bites, focus and enjoy what you're eating without distractions such as TV. When you're sipping that glass of wine as you cook dinner, keep in mind that alcohol not only has calories, but it also lowers our inhibitions and we tend to eat more.

  Two interesting studies related to eating mindfully: Men (sorry, they used only men) were told to chew either 40 or 15 times before swallowing each bite during an unlimited meal. Those who chewed each bite 40 times ate 12 percent few calories than those who chewed 15 times. The 40-bite chewers also had lower levels of a hormone that tells us we're hungry. The other study involved eating pistachios with or without the shell. Study participants, both male and female, ate about 40 percent fewer calories when they had to open the pistachios themselves. More work = less eating.
- **Chill Out.** Stress increases cortisol production, which can increase appetite as well as cause the deposition of fat in the abdominal area. Consider meditation, deep-breathing, or exercise. These can lower cortisol levels.
- **Be Reasonable with Your Expectations.** Slow and steady does it. Don't expect to get back into the jeans you wore in tenth

grade. Or, if you do, don't expect to look the same in them. As one friend said defensively, "At least I can still fit into the same earrings I wore in high school." Plan on losing a half pound to two pounds per week. To lose two pounds a week, create a net loss of 7,000 calories through what you eat or how much you move or a combination of the two. (This is actually a simplification, since you tend to lose fat, lean muscle, and water and not just fat.) Food is more important than exercise for weight loss.

- **Get Your ZZZs.** Not getting sufficient sleep can be a triple whammy. Sleep-deprived women lose more muscle mass and lose less fat. Also, their leptin and ghrelin levels (hormones that influence appetite) are knocked out of whack. Sleep-deprived women (those who get four hours or less a night) ate more calories (329) per day and more fat grams (31) compared to those with sufficient sleep, according to a recent study. Try to get 7 to 9 hours a night. Easier said than done, of course. If you wake up tired and feel sleepy all day, even though you think you get enough sleep, you might have sleep apnea. If so, it's a good idea to get it checked out with your doctor, who might recommend lifestyle changes (such as avoiding certain foods, changing medicines, or sleeping in a different position), or mouthpieces or continuous positive airway devices (CPAPs) that help keep your airways open, or surgery. Good news: If you sleep alone or sleep with someone who doesn't snore, you get about an hour more sleep a night than those with snoring partners, according to Dr. Michael Roizen of the Cleveland Clinic.
- **Avoid Liquid Poison.** Obesity, type 2 diabetes, osteoporosis, metabolic syndrome (including high blood pressure and high cholesterol), kidney stones . . . all these have been associated with drinking too many soft drinks, according to the Mayo Clinic. And, unfortunately, our brain doesn't process calories from liquids like it does from solids. It's much easier to ingest more when a lot of our calories are in liquid form. Drinking diet drinks may not be much better. The phosphoric acid and caffeine may leech calcium out of bones

(true for non-diet soft drinks as well), and the artificial sweeteners (even though they are artificial) may make us crave sugar.

- **Eat More Fiber.** This is worth mentioning for a few reasons. Fiber can fill us up, so we are likely to eat less. And eating fiber helps prevent constipation, hemorrhoids, and diverticular disease. Diverticuli are pouches that develop in the colon that can become infected. Half of people over 60 have these pouches or diverticuli; women over 70 have surgery three times as often as men because of infected diverticuli. Fiber may also lower the incidence of some cancers, heart disease, diabetes, gallstones, and kidney stones. Women should get 20 to 35 grams of fiber a day; most of us get about half that. Good fiber sources: beans, fruit, veggies, whole grains, and nuts. Raise your fiber over three to four weeks; it may take time for your body to adjust (i.e., you may experience bloating or gas).

- **Drink Water, Water Everywhere.** We've heard that our brain sometimes interprets thirst as hunger; thus, drink water before reaching for those chips. Although the "eight glasses a day" mantra is no longer gospel, recent research from Virginia Tech has shown drinking two glasses of water before a meal really does help people lose weight. The study involved adults aged 55 to 75. All were on a restricted calorie diet, but the group that drank two glasses of water prior to eating lost 4.5 pounds more over the 12 weeks of the study. Why? The zero calories certainly help, and the water activates stretch receptors in your stomach that tell your brain you're getting fed and thus decreases feelings of hunger.

- **Know Which Fats Are Good or Bad.** For a long time, "fats" was a four-letter word, and for many women, it still is. But, keep in mind that you need fat to absorb fat-soluble vitamins (vitamins A, D, E, and K) as well as carotenoids, which are plant pigments that are antioxidants, from food. So having a salad with fat-free dressing or severely limiting your fat intake prevents you from getting the most from what you're eating.

Fat also makes you feel full (something called satiety), so you're not tempted to eat again as quickly.

But don't overdo it. The NIH-AARP Diet and Health Study found that "as the amount of fat a woman consumes increases, so does her risk of developing breast cancer. And this seems to be more pronounced in women not taking menopausal hormones." The study found that higher breast cancer incidence is linked to higher body fat as well.

Fat has 9 calories per gram, while protein and carbs only have 4 (if you were wondering, alcohol has 7), so you need to be mindful of the amount and type of fats you eat. Let's look at the types of fats:

- Unsaturated fats are either monounsaturated fats (olive, sesame, and canola oil) or polyunsaturated fats (corn, safflower, and sunflower seed oil). Unsaturated fats tend to be from plant sources and are usually liquid at room temperature.
- Trans fat is an unsaturated fat that has had hydrogen pumped into it to make it more solid. Most trans fats are created industrially (foods will have a longer shelf-life if they contain trans fats), although there are a few naturally occurring trans fats.
- Saturated fats—found in lard, cream, and butter—tend to be animal-based and solid at room temperature, although there are some exceptions, such as palm and coconut oil. A mini chemistry lesson: Whether a fat is saturated or not has to do with the kind and number of bonds between hydrogen and carbon atoms in the fat.

Virtually all scientists and nutritionists agree that monounsaturated fats, the kind found in the Mediterranean diet, are good and that trans fats are bad. The good fats tend to lower our LDL (low-density lipoprotein or "bad cholesterol"); the created trans fats have been shown to lower our HDL (high-density lipoprotein) and raise our LDL. Recent research from Massachusetts General Hospital suggests that raising levels of HDL may not directly lower the

Did You Know?

There are two kinds of HDL—one acts like an "industrial vacuum cleaner" and the other one like a DustBuster, as described by Berkeley Lab (part of the U.S. government). So, even if your HDL number is high, if it's predominantly in the form of the DustBuster HDL, it's not as effective at removing cholesterol from the arteries and transferring it to the liver for removal. There are two types of LDL (bad) as well, but turns out that the smaller LDL particle sizes are a bigger predictor of heart disease than the larger LDL particles. In the case of LDL cholesterol, bigger is better, and good things do not come in small packages. When we get our cholesterol levels checked, size is usually not measured. You'd need to ask your doctor for these additional tests, and most likely pay for them as well.

risk/incidence of heart disease, as has been believed for so many years.

- **Remember Out of Sight, Out of Mind.** Sometimes it's not so much willpower but more a matter of habit when it comes to eating. After Diana W.'s divorce, she got rid of all the junk food that her ex always wanted on hand. Her only choices, when the urge to snack struck, were healthy. She found it was much easier to resist eating unhealthy foods if she had to drive to the store to buy them. Twenty-seven pounds lighter, she has more energy, looks better, and has lowered her blood pressure. The down side, if you can call it that, is that Diana has to buy new clothes . . .

Women who had candy in a clear container on their desk ate more than twice as much as when the candy was in an opaque bowl several feet away, according to a Cornell University study. And Eileen K. found that she needed to change her route to work slightly to avoid the fast food restaurant that beckoned her with its small (12-ounce) mocha coffee (250 calories). Recall that a pound of fat equals 3,500 calories. Removing this one item from her daily intake (Eileen's average coffee stop was three times a week) and keeping the rest of her eating pattern the same,

Eileen lost about 11 pounds in a year, not to mention saving $$$.

- **Be Mindful When Eating Out.** If your job involves a lot of travel or you don't like to cook (that would be me), eating out can be a challenge. Eleanor O. travels a lot for her job and eats out frequently. She asks the waiter to put half of her meal in a to-go box at the beginning of her meal. In addition to fewer calories, she gets a second meal and saves money (she usually gets hotel rooms with a fridge). Daria R. uses the book *Eat This, Not That!* for food swaps, and also likes http://eatthis.menshealth.com/home, its corresponding Web site, for making better food choices. For example, at Red Lobster, Grilled Arctic Char with Spicy Glaze will set you back 730 calories, 29 grams of fat, and 1,020 mg of sodium; if you choose Blackened Sea Bass with Fresh Broccoli instead, it's 410 calories, 12 grams of fat, and 700 mg of sodium. A women's site, www.womenshealthmag.com, has a lot of info, but Daria prefers the layout of the men's site because it has more specifics. Many restaurants provide the nutritional content on the menu, in brochures (you may have to ask), or on their Web sites.
- *Remove* **Weight, Don't** *Lose* **Weight.** Dr. Pamela Peeke, an expert in nutrition science, suggests using the word "remove." "Remove" sounds like something permanent and something that is gone forever, while "lose" makes you think it might be found again. It's a good psychological ploy when thinking about weight loss (er . . . removal).
- **Try The Behaviors of Those Who Have Been Successful Losing Weight and Keeping It Off.** A group of about 5,000 people (80 percent of whom are women) have lost 30 or more pounds and kept it off for a year or more. (The average of the group is actually closer to 70 pounds and six years.) The group is called the National Weight Control Registry, run by Brown Medical School and the University of Colorado since 1994, and the goal is to find what these people do that works as far as weight removal, since the sobering statistic is that only 5 percent of people maintain their weight loss.

Their secrets? Forty-five percent did it on their own and 55 percent used a weight-loss program. Ninety-eight percent changed their eating habits in some way. Some pared down their choices to a few healthy options (novelty makes us eat more); 94 percent increased their activities and exercise about an hour a day (the most popular exercise is walking); about three-fourths ate breakfast every day and weighed themselves at least once a week; about half kept themselves honest by writing down everything they ate. Eat better, move more, monitor your weight—nothing really that magical about it, although it's not a piece of cake to do, pun intended.

- **Consider a Weight-Loss Company.** If we're going to pay a company to help us slim down, we should look for a program that fosters lifelong healthy dietary changes, promotes exercise, advocates slow and steady weight loss, offers support during weight loss and after we reach our goal, and is affordable. Weight Watchers International (www.weightwatchers .com) meets these criteria (although the fees can add up over time). With its new point system, Weight Watchers considers not only the calories, but also their source. Healthier foods (rich in protein and fiber) have fewer points than those with simple carbs and unhealthy fat, and fruits and non-starchy veggies have zero points. You can do Weight Watchers online or in person. Plan to spend about $13/week in person, or $18/month online, not including the food.

  If you want to take the decision making out of the equation, but also pay more, consider a company like Jenny Craig (www.jennycraig.com) or Nutrisystem (www.nutrisystem .com). In both cases, you get packaged meals delivered to your home, and support (online with both companies; Jenny Craig also has brick-and-mortar locations). Nutrisystem bases its food on the glycemic index, so there is an emphasis on foods that cause a slower rise in insulin. Jenny Craig has added an armband that will monitor your calorie intake and calorie burn (you upload your data). Jenny Craig and Nutrisystem both charge about $300 a month for food; Jenny Craig also has membership fees (about $30 a month).

- **Ask Your Doctor about the Knife.** Surgical procedures to sculpt the body and to lose weight are another (albeit drastic) option. Tummy tucks, liposuction, gastric banding, gastric bypass, gastric plication, and sleeve gastrectomy are examples of surgeries that shape the body and/or facilitate weight loss, but we'll leave that for another book. (And you may have heard the recent findings that gastric bypass may fuel alcoholism.) Do your research, and consult your doctor.
- **Take Advantage of Free Programs.** Programs such as Overeaters Anonymous, based on the 12 steps of Alcoholics Anonymous, are another option. Check online (www.oa.org) or your phone book for local meetings.

Preventive Health Screenings/Shots

An ounce of prevention . . . you know the old saying. Routine screenings should include blood pressure, cholesterol, diabetes, thyroid, mammograms, colonoscopies, bone density (when you're 65; earlier if you have risk factors), optical, dental, gynecological, and dermatological exams. Don't neglect your emotional health. Depression affects women twice as often as men, and one in four women will experience severe depression at some point, according to the National Institutes of Mental Health. Up to 8 percent of older women abuse alcohol; as we age we become less efficient at metabolizing alcohol and our lower muscle mass makes us feel the effects more quickly.

Thought your days of getting shots were over? Nope. Here's what we need:

- Every year: Flu shot.
- Every 10 years: Td/Tdap (tentanus, diphtheria, pertussis). Pertussis is whooping cough, and if you are around babies and young children, it's important to get this shot to protect them.
- If you're 60 (or earlier if you have a weakened immune system; it's approved by the FDA for adults 50 and older):

Shingles vaccine. One in three people in the United States gets shingles. The shot significantly decreases your risk of getting shingles and reduces the pain and complications if you do get it.

- If you're 65 (or earlier if you're a smoker or have asthma or certain other conditions): Pneumococcal (pneumonia) vaccine.
- If you travel: Talk to your health provider or contact the Health Department for specifics, depending on where you're going.
- If you're sexually active and you or your partner aren't monogamous: Get checked for sexually transmitted diseases (we used to call these venereal diseases). Rates of STDs such as chlamydia, syphilis, and HIV are going up, up, up among mature adults.

Menopause and Hormone Therapy

Many of us remember that day in 2002 (kind of like remembering where we were when Neil Armstrong walked on the moon), when the National Institute of Health's Women's Health Initiative prematurely halted its clinical trial on postmenopausal hormone therapy. Problems associated with hormone therapy (HT), it was discovered, outweighed the risks. Women with a uterus receiving both estrogen and progesterone (in the form of Premarin) had a higher risk of breast cancer, coronary heart disease, and pulmonary embolisms (blood clots in the lung) than those not taking HT (though those taking the drugs did have a lower incidence of hip fracture and colorectal cancer). Prescriptions for HT plummeted. Reports in the media were confusing. The media emphasized *relative* risks (reporting an increase of 26 percent in breast cancer) versus absolute risks (8 more cases of breast cancer in a group of 100,000 women taking both drugs). In addition, little attention was paid to quality-of-life issues and symptom relief (like those (*&@^!(%# hot flashes, sleep interruptions, and vaginal dryness). And the average age of women in the Women's Health Initiative was 63, so many had gone through menopause years earlier.

A new study called KEEPS, for Kronos Early Estrogen Prevention Study, is looking at women with an average age of 53. The study will try to determine whether taking estrogen earlier and closer to menopause will lower the risk of heart disease. So more studies are on the way, involving women of various ages and using HT for varying lengths of time. This is very important, since some effects, such as an increase in dementia, have been found, but only in women 65 and older who have taken HT for four years or more.

Until additional studies are completed and analyzed, what's a woman to do? As is usually advised, discuss your individual circumstances with your doctor. But here are the prevailing thoughts: If you are susceptible to blood clots or have cancer or heart disease, you should probably skip HT.

For some women, starting HT early and for a short period of time and at the lowest dosage to achieve your goals (such as to manage hot flashes, sleep better, or prevent osteoporosis) could be the way to go. If hot flashes are manageable but you have vaginal dryness, consider a vaginal tablet such as Vagifem, or an estrogen-free vaginal moisturizer such as Replens. If you choose to take HT, it can also be delivered via a patch or cream; the delivery method of HT is worth discussing with your doctor, since HT patches or cream go directly into the bloodstream, rather than from the gut to the liver, as do oral medications. Avoiding the liver can be preferable since estrogen passing through the liver can produce substances that promote atherosclerosis, according to Harvard Medical School.

Did You Know?

"Is it hot in here?" How often have we heard that? About 75 percent of women have hot flashes, and African Americans tend to have more hot flashes than do other ethnic groups. It's thought that reduced estrogen as we approach menopause is the culprit. It signals a part of our brain, the hypothalamus, which acts as a thermostat, and it's believed these lower estrogen levels cause our "power surges."

If you're not a candidate or don't want to consider HT, use trial and error to see if any of these make a difference: Avoid caffeine, alcohol, and spicy foods; reduce stress; dress lightly; don't smoke; employ deep breathing, especially when a hot flash begins; lose excess weight; exercise; try antidepressants, soy, black cohosh, and red clover. And, if all else fails, go see "Menopause the Musical." You won't notice you're "flashing" because you'll be laughing too hard.

The Fountain of Youth—Exercise

We've mentioned that exercise can lengthen our telomeres and increase our mitochondria and that this can contribute to living longer and healthier. Exercise has such a profound effect on so many aspects of our health that's it difficult to mention all the benefits, but here is a partial list:

- Twenty minutes of aerobic exercise a day can ease the pain from rheumatoid arthritis, which strikes more women than men.
- Exercise enables synapses to make better connections between nerve cells, thus improving decision-making skills.
- Weight-bearing exercise builds bone, and increased bone density decreases the risk of osteoporosis.
- Exercise strengthens muscles, and our heart is a muscle.
- Exercise increases our nitric oxide level, which keeps our endothelial cells supple. (Endothelial cells line our 60,000 miles of blood vessels.)
- Exercise decreases LDL (bad cholesterol) and increases HDL.
- Exercise improves our range of motion, endurance, and flexibility, and decreases the incidence of falls.
- Exercise elevates mood, endorphins, and energy levels (which can result in better or more sex) and decreases stress.
- Exercise lowers our chances of getting high blood pressure, strokes, heart disease, colon cancer, gallstones, and diabetes.
- Exercise improves our appearance and feelings of self-worth.

- Exercise lowers level of body fat, including visceral fat, which is linked to disease.
- Exercise is an effective treatment for moderate to mild depression.
- When we sweat, we produce dermicidin, a natural antimicrobial.
- Exercise enhances the immune function.
- Exercise improves sleep (results seem to be better if the exercise is in the morning rather than in the evening).
- Exercise improves breathing and increases lung capacity by strengthening respiratory muscles.
- Exercise increases lean body mass, which increases calorie burn.
- Kegel exercises (contracting and relaxing the muscles you use to control the flow of urine) improve bladder control.
- Exercise helps relieve symptoms of menopause (including the menopot—the lovely additional fat that accumulates around our middle after the age of 40).

The Best Exercise

As you've probably heard, the best exercise is the kind you'll actually do. After you've checked with your doctor, try to mix it up, including weight-bearing exercises 2 to 3 times a week for 30 minutes and high-intensity exercise, such as running for one minute, alternating with longer periods of less-strenuous exercise, such as brisk walking for two minutes, for a total of 15 minutes. This interval exercising might provide better results than a longer, moderate exercise period in which we don't challenge ourselves as much. (Competitive tennis and spinning classes are two examples of interval exercise.) Consider Pilates or yoga to strengthen the core and improve balance (falls are one of the biggest contributors to death and disability for older adults), and work on flexibility. Pilates can help prevent and relieve back pain. If you like to stretch, do it after you exercise, when your muscles are warm and more pliable.

If you hate the idea of exercise, think about activities you like to do such as biking, walking (including your dog, unless he's like mine and insists on stopping to pee on every bush), dancing, swimming, hiking, rock climbing, skiing, and Wii Fit Plus.

There's also a concept called NEAT (non-exercise activity thermogenesis), which includes behaviors like standing instead of sitting while talking on the phone, tapping your feet or strumming your fingers, turning down the heat (you burn more calories trying to warm yourself), and to use texting vernacular, LOL (laughing out loud), which also burns about 20 percent more calories than not laughing. Adding NEAT to your daily life can burn up to 350 calories a day.

Think friends. The social support aspect can make moving more fun, and it's harder to not exercise if you've made a commitment to someone else or a group. Personally, I need extrinsic motivators, which is why I play tennis and go to exercise classes. I wouldn't work out on my own if I didn't have to report to certain places at certain times. Jenny G. joins some friends at one of their homes where a personal trainer comes to work with their small group. Anne Marie A. is part of a group of mall walkers. Call the mall's management company or customer service and ask about programs, or organize your own—there's no excuse not to walk if it's raining outside. Another motivator can be a pedometer. If you're like most people and find that walking is your favorite exercise, and you want to get feedback, get a pedometer and aim for 10,000 steps a day (roughly 5 miles, depending on your stride).

Fun Fact

It's good to have a walking partner, but is it better to walk with dogs or people? It turns out if you have a commitment to walk a dog, you're even more likely to follow through. Researchers divided walkers into two groups: those who would go to an animal shelter to walk dogs, and those paired with a friend or spouse. The dogs were always ready and eager for their walk, and very few humans backed out on their responsibility to walk them; people paired with another human, however, frequently tried to talk one another out of exercising—and often succeeded in doing so. So, if you own a dog, you're more likely to exercise, not to mention receive the comfort and companionship of our "four-footed children."

Being Sedentary Is Evil

It's not just that exercising is good; being sedentary is bad. Even if you exercise several times a week, or even daily, the way you spend the rest of your day plays a role in how healthy you are. Women who spent six or more hours a day sitting had a death rate almost 35 percent higher than those who sat for three hours or less a day. This shocking research (I'm feeling guilty right now plopped in a chair typing on my computer) from the American Cancer Society found that while sitting you burn only a third as many calories as when you are up and walking, insulin is less effective getting glucose into your cells, the body has more trouble breaking down fats, and the risk of obesity increases. We need to move it or GAIN it.

Our Brain and Exercise

We mentioned earlier how *mental* gymnastics "exercise" the mind, causing the growth of new connections among our brain cells. Novel experiences and a change of routine not only help stimulate this neuron growth, but they also help us to become more resilient and deal with problems more effectively. Physical exercise, which increases blood flow to the brain, also causes growth in the area of the brain having to do with learning and memory. Particularly good exercises are those that make us think while we work out. Perhaps a vigorous game of table tennis (as crazy as it might sound, it's said to be one of the fastest growing sports in the United States), tennis (you can probably tell by now I'm addicted), rock climbing, golf (walk the course instead of driving a cart), martial arts, basketball, and volleyball. The focus and complex sequences involved in tai chi, yoga, qigong, and Pilates are also good for revving up brain connections, and the movements can be adapted for many fitness levels. If Title IX (the 1972 law prohibiting sex discrimination in education programs, including sports) came too late and you missed out on sports opportunities growing up, now's your chance to join in the fun.

Lori S.'s daily exercise regimen is not for the faint of heart:

I'm divorced and in my sixties; my 95-year old mother (who is still learning new pieces on the piano!) lives with me. I was a music teacher in New York and now reside in northeast Florida. I exercise to stay in shape and because I enjoy it. My pattern of exercise is usually the same every day. I just get up and go. I don't have to push myself—I am energized and committed. I have maintained a program of exercise for many years. Having a lifelong habit of physical activity and working out on my own schedule is key.

Basically, I start each day at 6 A.M. and spend about four hours a day in exercise of some sort, every day of the week. My get-fit strategy consists of my own personal plan. Having access to parks and beaches, I pick a destination, and walk or bike for at least an hour, five days a week, using music as a mood-setter. "Part II" of my fitness plan consists of classes (I belong to a club that includes classes as part of my membership fee), rotating among Pilates, step, yoga, weight training, and resist-a-ball. I'll often take two of these classes a day. "Part III" consists of additional daily biking or walking, and the elliptical machine.

Working out is really, for me, a competition against myself. The best way for me to know if I am working hard is to track my progress. As an example, since I do the elliptical and bike daily, I try to track my resistance level and miles, always trying to beat my previous day's record.

I've received comments from my friends about my so-called extreme exercise, but I enjoy it, I'm strong, fit, healthy, happy, and it keeps my brain in great working order, so I say, "Just do it."

Spirituality and Health

I'm using the word "spirituality" to refer to feelings or beliefs about our purpose, the meaning of life, sense of peace, and our connections to others, whether or not these feelings and beliefs are part of a formal religion. A number of research studies have attempted to pinpoint the role spirituality plays in our health. Consider longevity: Studies cited by Baylor University suggest that "those who have regular spiritual practices live longer." Why? It turns out that those who engage in regular spiritual practices have a lower level of a substance called interleukin-6, probably because of greater social support and the ability to cope. Since elevated inter-leukin-6 can increase your chances of disease, you're likely to live longer with lower levels of this substance coursing through your body. Spirituality seems to lower pain levels, and spiritual people with advanced cancer reported feeling less pain than those who did not consider themselves spiritual. In fact, prayer is often used as a non-pharmaceutical way of dealing with pain. Coping with disease (their own or that of loved ones) and a lessened fear of death are also cited as positives of those who consider themselves spiritual.

Spiritual beliefs may also aid in recovery from disease. Heart transplant patients who were spiritual had better functioning a year later than those who were not spiritual. It's thought this could be part of the "mind-body" connection: Our beliefs can certainly affect our body (we've all heard of the "placebo effect"). Sometimes, our beliefs can be destructive. We "deserve to be punished" if we get sick, for example, or we're angry and bitter when we pray to God to cure us but we don't get well.

So if you've decided to eat well, exercise, and use your spiritual-ity to help you cope with health issues, it's time to look at the best place for you to live. That's what the next two chapters will explore.

More 411

Health-Related Web Sites

AARP recommended health screenings (www.aarp.org /healthscreenings)

Cleveland Clinic (www.clevelandclinic.org)

Mayo Clinic (www.mayoclinic.com)

MedlinePlus (www.medlineplus.gov)

National Institutes of Health (www.nih.gov)—includes info on clinical trials

U.S. Centers for Disease Control and Prevention (www.cdc.gov)

Books

Amen, Daniel. *Change Your Brain, Change Your Body: Use Your Brain to Get and Keep the Body You Have Always Wanted.* New York: Three Rivers Press, 2010.

Campbell, Adam. *The Women's Health Big Book of Exercises.* New York: Rodale, 2009.

Phillips, Bill. *Body for Life.* New York: HarperCollins, 1999.

Roizen, Michael F., and Oz, Mehmet. *You: The Owner's Manual, Updated and Expanded Edition.* New York: William Morrow, 2008.

Rolls, Barbara. *The Ultimate Volumetrics Diet.* New York: William Morrow, 2012.

Roth, Geneen. *Women Food and God: An Unexpected Path to Almost Everything.* New York: Scribner, 2011.

Taubes, Gary. *Why We Get Fat: And What to Do About It.* New York: Knopf, 2010.

Wansink, Brian. *Mindless Eating: Why We Eat More Than We Think.* New York: Bantam, 2010.

Whyte, John. *AARP New American Diet: Lose Weight, Live Longer,* New York: John Wiley & Sons, 2012.

Whyte, John. *Is This Normal? The Essential Guide to Middle Age and Beyond.* New York: Rodale, 2011.

Yonan, Joe. *Serve Yourself: Nightly Adventures in Cooking for One.* Berkeley: Ten Speed Press, 2011.

Zinczenko, David. (He has written many, many good books about eating at home or in restaurants, food swaps, and exercise.)

CHAPTER

Where Is Your Heart? Exploring Options for Living

Where you live affects how you live.

—Anonymous

How did you end up where you're living now? For many people, it's because that's where their parents live or lived, where they attended college, or where they or someone else landed a job—in other words, mostly extrinsic factors dictate where you call home. But now that "You are free to move about the country," as Southwest Airlines says, you might find the choices for relocation daunting; you can choose to relocate to almost any place in the world. The purpose of this chapter is to reflect on the broader considerations about moving. The next chapter will get into specifics, with stories from single women about why they chose specific communities.

Before we start talking about relocating, let's acknowledge the obvious: The housing market, like the job market, isn't exactly sizzling. If you own, you might sell your home for less money than you'd like, but at least you can purchase a residence for less money in another part of the country, and many builders and sellers are offering attractive incentives. If you presently rent, it's even easier to relocate, whether you plan to continue to rent or to purchase a residence. During the heady days of the always-rising stock market, crazed real estate sales, and easier job-finding and -switching, it was a piece of cake to recommend many places for relocation. That is no longer the case. Some newer communities have been unable to build promised amenities or attract a viable number of residents, so potential purchasers have to be careful.

Fun Fact

Single women represent 21 percent of homebuyers and are responsible for more than 30 percent of the growth in home ownership in the United States since 1994, according to the National Association of Realtors.

How Many Boomers Really Are Moving?

Many surveys, interviews, and studies try to pinpoint who is staying put and who's going to relocate, since the immigration or emigration of the 78-million-large cohort of boomers has such huge consequences for many segments of the economy, including construction, health, retail, and local and state governments. Here's what three research studies show. Keep in mind, however, that as mentioned in Chapter 3, what people say they plan to do and what they actually do (expectations versus reality) can be quite different.

- A 2011 Associated Press/Life Goes Strong Poll found about a quarter of boomers "very likely" to move from their current location, and 60 percent believe they will live in at least one other residence during their retirement.
- The 2010 Del Webb Baby Boomer Survey found that more than one-third of respondents planned to move, and half of them think they will move to another state. (The states most frequently cited were Florida, North Carolina, South Carolina, and Tennessee.) A full 34 percent of those who are retired or semiretired actually did move. Even in these challenging economic times, moving vans are still rumbling down the road.

- The Center for Retirement Research at Boston College found that 30 percent of U.S. homeowners between the ages of 51 and 73 moved at least once over a 12-year period. The majority of moves were fewer than 20 miles; those who moved long distances favored the South Atlantic states, Arizona, and New Mexico.

Did You Know?

If you're 65, there's a 70 percent chance you'll live in the same place for the rest of your life, according to www.seniorresource.com.

Why Do People Move in Retirement?

Del Webb, a company that builds active-adult communities, found the most compelling reasons for moving, in order of importance, are: cost of living, access to preferred health care, cultural and recreational amenities, favorable climate, community and networking opportunities, desire to be close to children and grandchildren, and desire to be close to parents or in-laws. When polled, the majority of adults say they want to "age in place." But over time, people often find their support system has moved away (sometimes to the great unknown); their home no longer "works" for them because, for instance, they can no longer walk up and down the steps to their bedroom or washer and dryer; they live in the suburbs and would rather walk to do their basic errands than drive; they tire of inclement weather (as Lydia K., who moved to Arizona, said, "At least you don't have to shovel heat"); they are now widowed or divorced or no longer have a significant other or their previous home is too much or too large for them; they are looking for new experiences; or they want to "reinvent" themselves. In many cases, a combination of these factors precipitates the desire to relocate. If you're happy where you live, can afford it, have a large support group and good medical care, and have a reason to wake up every morning, there may indeed be no place like your current home.

Are some places better for single women to relocate to than others? The general answer is yes. Consider locations with a vibrant or relatively strong economy if you want or need to go back to work; lots of opportunities for involvement, including cultural, recreational, volunteer, and lifelong learning; and a large influx of people from other areas, since it's easier to meet new people if cliques aren't established. Then, too, think about transportation, walkability, health care, proximity to family, safety, and climate. Another thought: Consider taking your single friends or your "tribe" with you!

Tip

How walkable is your neighborhood or a community you're considering for relocation? Check out Walk Score (www.walkscore.com) to see how far it is to the nearest library, bank, restaurant, bookstore, grocery store, or park. Walk Score assigns an accessibility number of 0 to 100; the closer to 100, the less car-dependent the location. For example, Washington, DC, considered very walkable, has a Walk Score of 73.

What to avoid as a single woman? Suburbia and exurbia, unless you're really into driving and not concerned with social support; places that picture only couples in their ads; and any place that you haven't checked out first—but more about that later. Of course, with 25 million single women over the age of 45, there is no one-size-fits-all description. As you'll see in the real single women's examples in the next chapter, relocation choices range from the beauty and remoteness of the western North Carolina mountains to the social support of cohousing to the vitality of big-city living to retiring abroad.

For More Information

Whether you decide to move or stay, it's good to know about "universal design" principles—ways to make your home easy to access no matter your age, size, or abilities. Examples include comfort-height toilets (your thighs will thank you when you're older); rocker switches, which are kinder on arthritic hands; a first-floor master bedroom or an elevator or the ability to add an elevator; non-skid flooring; and curbless showers. All these make it easier to live longer in your residence. For an excellent list of interior and exterior universal design ideas, many of them very inexpensive to implement, see the Aging-in-Place Design Checklists in Appendix 5 at the end of this chapter. And check out the "Home Fit Guide" from AARP at www.aarp. org (type "Home Fit Guide" into the AARP search bar, then click on "Make Your House a Home—for Life").

What Single Women Want in a Home

Builders, increasingly aware that single women are the second-largest home-buying market, have started building more "women-centric" residences.

Carla F. is fairly representative of single women when it comes to home buying. She purchased a two-bedroom residence that cost about $200,000. She felt a smaller home was OK as long as there was ample kitchen and bathroom space, walk-in closets, and a gas fireplace, which is easier to light than a wood-burning one. Smaller means cheaper to buy, rent, cool, heat, insure, maintain, and furnish. She also wanted low maintenance, a reason why condos are also popular with single women.

Ramona W. chose to rent a home that also typifies what single women want: universal design principles incorporated into the home; a kitchen island facing a great room; plenty of storage; high-speed Internet capability; a first-floor master bedroom; and a laundry room, with a long counter, close to the master bedroom.

Single women express interest in green building, as long as it doesn't affect the price much, and residences that are designed to be "zero net," meaning they can produce as much energy as they consume. Through passive solar design, heavy-duty insulation, high-efficiency windows and appliances, and home systems that control and monitor the use of energy, energy use can be lowered by as much as 50 percent in many homes.

Security and safety are important to single women, as is a welcoming community that is heavy on activities and amenities with proximity to shopping and fitness centers. Dog parks; walking paths; health programs; events targeted to singles; and activities involving books, wine-tasting, travel, tennis, golf, and cards are also cited as important.

Let's take a look at some issues to think about if you're contemplating relocating.

Figuring Out What You Want and Need

What is it you must have in your retirement location? Is it good medical care, lots of culture, the ability to walk to stores and restaurants, easy access to airports, a short distance to mountains or lakes or the ocean, good employment opportunities, lack of snow, strong security, proximity to friends and family, the ability to meet others?

Are you in the position to have a second or even a third home? Do you want multiple homes even if you can afford one? Where do you vacation? What is it you *need* versus *want?* Sometimes, this gives you insight into what you're really looking for when you choose a place, or at least the desirable attributes. Thinking about your answers to these questions will narrow your choices.

Make a list of your priorities. My non-negotiables included an area with three seasons with the missing one being winter, proximity to the Atlantic Ocean, good medical care within a reasonable distance, a major airport within a tolerable drive to travel for business and to visit children and grandchildren or have them visit me, a newer development because it's easier to make friends when there are lots of new people, and an active tennis program.

Tip

When looking at a new location, find out whether your current health plan will still cover you and whether you'll be able to find doctors and specialists who accept your insurance.

Personality

Are you extroverted? Do you enjoy new adventures, embrace change, and make friends fairly easily? Are you ready to find a new doctor, dentist, hair salon, dog sitter, and support group (unless you take your friends with you)? If you move to a resort area, are you prepared to entertain a lot of visitors?

If you are anxious about making new friends and aren't super-outgoing, consider a master-planned or active-adult community. Activities are arranged by a lifestyle director, which makes it much simpler to meet others. And, be sure to check out what, if any, single groups are available, although you'll be able to institute your own group if one doesn't exist. A newer community is a good idea, too, since it's easier to find people looking to connect with others.

Cost

A lower cost of living is now the number one reason people want to relocate in retirement, replacing a desirable climate. An index called the Cost of Living Index, published by the Council for Community and Economic Research (C2ER), takes into account consumer goods and services. It's based on a national average of 100. How do you find the Cost of Living Index for an area? C2ER (www.coli.org) charges you for the information, but you can often find it for free. For example, let's say you're considering moving to St. George, Utah. If you put "St. George Utah cost of living 2012 first quarter" into your search engine, you'll see that the Cost of Living Index for St. George in 2012 is 92.2 for the first quarter (the C2ER does quarterly ratings). Remember, 100 is the average, so St. George's score would be below the average cost of living in the United States. Contrast that to New York City (Manhattan), which has a Cost of Living Index of 228.3 for the first quarter of 2012, more than twice the national average cost of living.

Web sites can also help calculate the cost (or savings) of moving from one area to another. Again, this can't take into consideration all the subtleties a relocation entails, such as association fees, additional travel, or even things like pest control (where I live in Florida, pest control is a necessity), but these calculators can be useful. Two examples: Go to www.bestplaces.net and click on "Compare Cost of Living" or try www.cityrating.com. If you type in that you're moving from Chicago, Illinois, to Gainesville, Florida, you'll see that Gainesville is cheaper than Chicago; an income of $28,000 in Gainesville will go as far as a $50,000 income in Chicago.

Of course, the cost of living is just one factor in deciding how much it will cost to live in a new location or remain in your present location. You need to know how your retirement income will be taxed. Would the lack of a state income tax make a difference? And you need to consider other taxes such as sales, property, inheritance, and estate taxes. Will you be paying condo fees and community fees?

As you can see, there are a lot of elements to consider, but more about this appears in Chapter 8. Begin with determining the lifestyle you want. Then see which places offer that lifestyle at a comfortable cost.

Did You Know?

How much should you pay for a house? Assuming you don't have a lot of debt, experts recommend that your monthly payment—including the mortgage payment, property taxes, and homeowner's insurance—take up 25 percent to 33 percent of your gross monthly income.

Often, we get bogged down trying to find that one "perfect" place we think is out there. But once we know what we must have in a community, many locations could fit our needs. Be wary of making no decision because it seems overwhelming; even not deciding is deciding.

Geography

It's important to sample all the seasons in a potential retirement location, or at least know what you'll be dealing with year-round. Clogged roads during the winter from the snowbirds escaping the cold north? Gorgeous weather in the fall, but unbearable humidity in the summer? Beautiful springs, but icy conditions in the dead of winter?

And, yes, we should all be one happy universal family, but sometimes people feel more comfortable living in one area than in another. Consider your politics, education level, religion, differences in food tastes, whether you're laid back or not, and even accents (will you be viewed as an outsider?) when deciding where to live. Nancy G. loves to hike, but she also loves to shop. Nancy realized her move to a small, scenic mountain town with shopping more than an hour's drive was a big mistake.

Locations with an influx of people from many areas, such as new communities or even certain states and cities such as Florida and Las Vegas, are often easier to adapt to than moving to smaller towns or even cities where there is less diversity.

Size and Downsize

If you're downsizing and moving into an apartment-style building, beware of the changes you'll have to get used to. If you've never lived in a place where your neighbors are very close, be sure to try it out before committing. Some people have a problem with sounds from adjacent condos, odors that might waft into your residence, or noisy pets. Or people find they miss walking outdoors directly into their own yard.

For More Information

Wondering about an area's air quality? Enter a zip code or state into www.airnow.gov and get information about the Air Quality Index. The index is determined from local, state, and federal sources.

Community Associations

Many planned communities have homeowner associations, sometimes called HOAs. According to the Community Associations Institute, more than 60 million Americans live in a community where there is some kind of an association that maintains common areas and enforces deed restrictions, perhaps including regulations about the number of dogs you can have or when you can set out your trash. Although some people love their associations (and I like mine) and other people hate theirs, about half of associations report some difficulty collecting assessments during the current housing slump and slowed economy. So, you have to think not only about whether you want to live in a community with an association, but also about whether it's financially sound.

Read the association's covenants, conditions, and restrictions (CC&Rs), available from the builder or developer, and be sure you're OK with the provisions, since you'll be expected to abide by them. Also ask a real estate agent or neighbor in the community to introduce you to members of the board so you can ask them directly about the viability of the association. And read the minutes of meetings; you'll get a sense of what's going on the community.

Condos

Condos used to be the easy way to go—low maintenance and simple to lock up and leave for a long trip or another home. Now, the world of condos is becoming more difficult. It's harder to get a loan because lenders are concerned about too many vacancies, too many rentals, too many people behind on their condo dues, developers too overextended, or prices too low. But condos still are worth considering, since pricing can be very attractive these days.

If you're considering a condo, be sure that the occupancy rate is high or many units have been sold. Also check the financial stability of the association governing the condo and find out if people are paying their dues. Sometimes condo fees can be very pricey, so factor that into the cost as well. Zero-lot-line homes, where the home is often right on the property line, and townhomes are other possibilities for lower maintenance.

Is Renting Allowed?

Many resort-type communities, especially those that are rich in amenities, have CC&Rs that allow rentals—some short-term, others a 30-day or more minimum. Some homebuyers are unhappy to find they have moved into a community where many of the people aren't full-time residents; other people want to rent out their second home in a community until they retire; and some people purchase a home as an investment and want to rent it out and never live there. Although it's not easy to do, rental policies can be changed by a vote of the membership. Be sure you're OK with any rental rules, whether you plan to rent or buy.

Developer Solvency

In this difficult housing environment, some communities have gone under, or they don't have a critical mass of residents, or the promised amenities never materialize. Exercise caution if the community is still developing. Barbara G. bought a second vacation home in a new master-planned community close to the ocean in Delaware, but many of the promised amenities were never built. Soon after, her job as an interior designer in Wilmington, Delaware, slowed due to the economy. Barbara was forced to sell her primary home in Wilmington because she couldn't afford both, and she can't sell the home in the master-planned community because of the lack of amenities.

Check out the developer and any builders you're considering with the Better Business Bureau and with the local builders association. Search the builder's name online to see if anything raises a warning flag, and ask neighbors what they think of the community and the builders. Other ways to find out about a community: Walk around on a weekend (if it's not gated) and introduce yourself to neighbors as a prospective resident; talk to residents at the pool, fitness center, or clubhouse; ask residents questions when a real estate agent shows you around; and go on a "discovery tour" (see the "Try It Out" section for an explanation). Be wary of being "first in" to a community, and really think hard about buying a place as an investment.

Problems Lurking in the Area?

Are there paper plants, Superfund sites, nuclear power plants, dog pounds (lots of barking), airplane flight paths, headlights that would shine into your main living area in a home or lot you're thinking about purchasing? Could that nearby undeveloped piece of land end up becoming a strip mall? These are all examples of unpleasant experiences others have had. Check with the city zoning and development office and see what's planned, what's being discussed, and what's close by.

Storage Facilities

If you have an RV, boat, or other items that need to be stored, is there a facility? If you live in a community that regulates RVs and boats, you won't be able to keep them in your driveway. Be sure there's a place for them onsite or close by.

New Home, Resale, or Rental?

Should you buy a new home, purchase an existing home, or rent? As with most things in life, the answer is that "it depends." With aggressive sales pricing, a resale in a community that is only partially built out could be a wonderful deal, but again, be sure promised amenities will be forthcoming. On the other hand, if you want to design your own home, new construction costs are lower than during the days of wildly escalating prices. An existing home in a well-established neighborhood might have more mature landscaping and perhaps other upgrades, but it may be more difficult to meet people, and new homes often have the most up-to-date energy-saving appliances and design elements. And right now interest rates are low, but you need to be able to get a loan and sell your house if you have one.

What about renting? A *Time* magazine had a provocative cover line: "Rethinking Homeownership: Why owning a home may no longer make economic sense." Renting is certainly something to consider.

Some single women don't like having to maintain a home, think they might relocate within a few years and won't be able to recoup their investment if they have to sell their house, or fear the stability of their current job. On the one hand, when you rent, you know the amount from month to month and if you can afford it; you're not borrowing money and hoping to pay it back; you have more mobility; and you could potentially invest the money not spent on maintaining a home and earn more money instead. On the other hand, because of the housing collapse, more people than ever are renting, causing rents to rise and rental incentives to disappear.

One way to decide whether to own or rent is to calculate the price-to-rent ratio: Divide the price of the home by the amount you would pay for a yearly rental of that home. If the number you get is much over 9, it usually means it's better to rent. For example, Olivia R. could purchase a home for $210,000 in Tennessee or rent it for $24,000 a year ($2,000/month), so the price-to-rent-ratio ($210,000 divided by $24,000) is less than 9. Factoring in equity and the tax benefits of being an owner, it's probably a better idea for Olivia to buy, assuming she plans to stay awhile. Homeownership as an ideal runs deep in the American psyche. Besides some financial benefits, there is the pride of ownership and increased sense of community and commitment as well as living in your investment. The days of wild speculation in real estate are pretty much over, at least for the foreseeable future.

Fun Fact

It's less expensive to buy than rent in 74 percent of the 50 largest U.S. cities, according to the real estate site Trulia (www.trulia.com).

Something else to consider is a rent-to-own option, an opportunity to try a specific home you like in a community you're considering. Of course, there are lots of details to iron out—who is responsible for what, such as a leaking hot water heater and the property taxes; how will you determine the sales price; and how long you can rent before deciding whether or not to purchase. Everything needs to be clear and in writing. If you type "rent-to-own contracts" in your search bar, you'll see a number of examples of sample contracts; some are free and some are not.

Is the Larger Community Ready?

Look to the future. Whether you move or stay where you are, think about your lifestyle when you get "old" (by the way, older adults say "old age" begins at 74, according to a Pew Research Center study). What does your community offer for an aging population? One-stop shopping for age-related services? Larger street signage, longer yellow lights, brighter street lighting, advanced stop lines (moving the vehicle stop line back from a pedestrian crossing for better visibility), grooved lane dividers, increased crossing times for crosswalks, dedicated left-turn lanes, pedestrian/bike/car-friendly roads (called "complete streets"), recessed bus stops, wide raised sidewalks with benches, and walking trails? How about age-appropriate fitness and recreation centers, free shuttle service, or top-notch public transportation? Even though you might think you'll be like Peter Pan and "never grow up," these are all things to consider. Check www.eldercare.gov to see what services are offered in the communities you're considering.

Try It Out

Now that you've thought about some factors that might affect your relocation decision, here are a few low- or no-cost ways to explore or try out locations:

- Retirement Ranger at www.topretirements.com/retirement ranger/ranger_login is free (although you do have to register), and it asks quick and easy questions that will generate a list of potential places to live.
- FindYourSpot at www.findyourspot.com is a quiz that helps clarify your priorities and instantly provides you with a suggested list of places based on your responses.
- Ideal Living Resort and Retirement Expo at www.livesouth .com holds free real estate shows mainly in the northeastern United States (in hotels) and promotes properties in about a dozen states and the Caribbean and Mexico. Disclosure: I presented seminars for them.
- BestPlaces at www.BestPlaces.net offers the "Find Your Best Place" quiz. Prioritize what you're looking for, and it'll generate a list of possible places.
- *Where to Retire* magazine (www.wheretoretire.com) has lots of articles and ads about you-know-what. Subscription is

$18 per year for six issues, and it's also available in many libraries.

- Discovery tours are offered by many large master-planned communities. Discounted rates are offered for a few-days visit, which might include lodging, food, a round of golf, and of course a tour. For example, the Landings at Skidaway Island in Savannah, Georgia (www.thelandings.com), offers lodging for one night, a tour, and access to the fitness center, tennis courts, pool, and clubhouse for $99. It's a great opportunity to sample the goods and talk to residents.
- Southeast Discovery, at www.southeastdiscovery.com, specializes in retirement, second homes, and vacation properties throughout the Southeast. There is no cost to you; the firm is paid a referral fee from the selling agent or developer upon a purchase. I know Marian Shaffer, who runs it, and she does an excellent job.
- Foreclosure tours are a way to view foreclosed properties in the way you can tour the stars' homes in LA. Tours usually last two to four hours, viewing up to about a dozen homes, and are free or nominally priced; some include a box lunch. Put "foreclosure tours" into your search engine and look for tours offered in areas you're interested in pursuing. Be very wary of purchasing foreclosures or short sales, though. The home could be in terrible disrepair and in a location experiencing a downward spiral. If you go this route, it is always good to get professional input, including legal assistance.
- Free land is possible. Yes, you read that correctly. Some rural small towns, looking to bulk up their dwindling populations, are offering free land. Try www.kansasfreeland.com to check out about a dozen communities offering building lots; you would need to move and live there for at least five years. Or, if Nebraska appeals to you, check out http://nebraskaccess .ne.gov/freeland.asp. Be sure to check it out in person before packing up your things.
- Home exchanges let you try out a possible retirement location while you live like a native. Stay in a home, apartment, condo, or other type of residence and try out your possible retirement location by using a site such as www.homeaway.com,

www.digsville.com, or www.singleshomeexchange.com (primarily but not exclusively for singles). If you're brave, you can stay for free at people's homes; just be sure you're willing to offer your home as well. Try www.globalfreeloaders.com, www.itamos.com, or www.exchangezones.com.

- Local newspapers can provide insight into a community you're considering, and you can find out what issues are being debated. For example, in our community there are discussions about building a new city hall, and there is hot debate about whether or not a play should be presented at the high school, since some view the particular play as too controversial.

- Chambers of commerce can provide useful information, too, but of course their purpose is to promote businesses and advocate for the community. One good Internet site that allows you to access all chambers of commerce is www.touristinformationdirectory.com.

If You Decide to Move

We know that these are not the days of yore when you could name a price, get multiple offers beyond the asking price, and move out in a week if you'd like. Socialite Candy Spelling's asking price for her Los Angeles mansion was $150 million, and after 28 months she sold it for a reported $85 million. OK, that price is not typical, but you get the idea. If you're selling your home, let's take a look at some ways to maximize your chances:

- **Find a Good Real Estate Agent.** You can sell a home yourself, and many have done so, using sites such as ForSalebyOwner (www.forsalebyowner.com) or www.craigslist.org. But most people still use an agent (by the way, I am not an agent). Choose a professional who knows your area well. When Regina A. moved from her home in Arlington Heights, Illinois, her agent knew the area so well and had so many contacts that her home was sold before the sale sign went up.

- **Ask Your Friends and Neighbors for Recommendations.** See who has the "for sale" signs posted in your area, and use an agent who sells homes in your price range. Consider using a big company, since bigger companies often mean larger advertising budgets, longer office hours, and more agents who will familiarize themselves with your home in an "open house." Interview several agents. The percentage of homes sold is more important than the amount of sales generated. An agent could have sold a very few expensive homes versus many homes at a lower cost. You should have a good gut feeling about the person as well, although do check references and choose someone who will be frank with you, which is not necessarily the person who suggests the highest listing price.

- **Price It Competitively.** With a lot of homes on the market, pricing your home appropriately is vital. Getting the comps (comparative prices, or the recent sale prices of similar homes, which your agent can provide), visiting open houses in your community, and surfing similar homes online in your area are all ways to figure out a price at which your home is most likely to sell quickly. And be aware of "attachment bias," the psychological trap of thinking that what we own is intrinsically worth more than something similar that someone else owns. Attachment bias is one of the big stumbling blocks in recognizing that, in the end, our home is worth what someone else is willing to pay for it, not what we think it is worth. Many people pass up reasonable offers because of attachment bias.

- **Use the Power of the Internet.** For 80 percent to 90 percent of people, looking to purchase a home begins on the Internet, according to the National Association of Realtors. So, be sure the pictures online look good. It's kind of like dating sites, where the pictures are so important. If a home you are trying to sell is vacant, consider "virtual staging." Alongside the pictures of your empty rooms, show virtual rooms decked out with furniture. They should be clearly labeled to let the prospective buyer know they are virtual pictures. Many people can't envision how an empty place would look furnished, and the scale of a room gets lost without furniture in the picture. Virtual staging can help sell your home. It's also a heck of a lot cheaper than actual staging, by potentially thousands of dollars. Check out a site such as

www.virtualstagingsolutions.com and www.virtuallystaging
properties.com to see how this works. Besides photos, consider
a professional video of your home; it can work wonders.
Patricia P. generated a lot of interest in her home through a
video available on her real estate agent's Web site. Her home
was in North Carolina, and the ultimate buyer was from New
Jersey. The buyer traveled to North Carolina to see the home
solely because of the video.

- **Consider Staging.** Arrange (real) furniture to make your
  home look as roomy as possible, floating it away from the
  walls; less is better. You can get tons of tips on the Internet.
  Type "HGTV staging your home" into your search bar to
  get some easy, good, and free advice about painting, lighting, arranging, and accessorizing. Or consider a professional
  stager who may use all or some of your own stuff or bring in
  his or her own furniture and accessories. The cost of professional staging can range from hundreds to thousands of
  dollars, but research shows that professionally staged homes
  sell more than three times faster than unstaged homes. Most
  agents know a good stager or decorator who can do this.
  You can also ask your friends, or find staging professionals at
  www.stagedhomes.com and www.iahsp.com.
- **Be Sure There Is Curb Appeal.** You don't want your home
  to be a "drive-by," but it very well could be if people aren't
  attracted to the house from the outside. Ensure that the
  house has sparkling windows and gleaming outdoor lights,
  weed-free (and poop-free, if you have a pet) grass, trimmed
  landscaping, fresh mulch and paint (remember the mail-
  box), seasonal flowers, and a new welcome mat.
- **Don't Forget the Adjoining Neighbors' Homes.** If you're on
  good terms with your neighbors and their homes could use
  spiffing up, approach them diplomatically, even offering to
  do the work, although I admit that's not an easy thing to do.
  If it's a true eyesore, you may be able to contact your local
  planning department, or the homeowners association, if
  there is one, for help.
- **Clean and Create.** Scrub until it shines and create space by
  underusing those closets, cabinets, and drawers. Now is the

time to donate and downsize and let the light flood in. Paint when necessary; neutrals are best. Remove pictures of your grandchildren and pets, adorable though they are, and other personal items. Prospective buyers want to feel the house is theirs and not yours. Do relatively simple updates such as replacing knobs and hanging framed mirrors in the bathrooms; Krista C. is convinced the framed mirrors are what sold her home. And replace old-fashioned hanging lights. My own pet peeve? A messy garage. If the garage looks pristine, I feel that the homeowners cared for the rest of the house as well.

- **Have It Inspected.** Get a home inspection before putting your home on the market. And, be sure your home passes the "smell test." One home I looked at, although very attractive, was so infused with the smell of cigarette smoke that it was no longer a contender. Ask a friend or your agent about your home's smell. We become so acclimated we might not notice. Of course, you can also use fresh flowers, scented candles, air fresheners, fresh-baked cookies, and Febreze.

- **Be Ready to Run.** You need to keep your home show-ready and be able to leave the house on demand; prospective buyers don't feel comfortable poking around if the owner is following them and telling them how wonderful the house is. One trick I used when I had to depart quickly when my house was on the market: Before leaving for work each morning, I put my piles of pesky papers into the dryer. I thought the odds of anyone looking in there were slim, and it kept the kitchen counter and area around the computer uncluttered. Try to get rid of any evidence of a pet when you're selling your home. Even if people consider their own pets "children with fur coats," the presence of a pet can be a turnoff. If you have a neighbor who will take your dog when a home is being shown and you're not there, that's a plus.

- **Get Help with Moving.** If you can't or don't want to organize a move on your own, "certified senior moving managers" can help facilitate the entire process. A moving manager can be a godsend if you're disabled, recently divorced, still grieving from a death, or unwilling to deal with the stress of moving.

(This is something to consider for your parents' move as well.) With the aging population, it's no big surprise that the use of senior moving managers has increased by almost 70 percent over the past few years. To find a moving manager, contact the National Association of Senior Move Managers (www.nasmm.org). Services can be priced by the hour or the job. Count on approximately $50 an hour or a few thousand dollars for a move.

OK, let's say you've decided to relocate. The next chapter provides specific suggestions and locations and the reasons why single women chose them.

More 411

Dana, Julie. *The Complete Idiot's Guide to Staging Your Home to Sell.* New York: Alpha, 2007.

Hall, Julie. *The Boomer Burden: Dealing with Your Parents' Lifetime Accumulation of Stuff.* Nashville: Thomas Nelson, 2008.

Klinenberg, Eric. *Going Solo: The Extraordinary Rise and Surprising Appeal of Living Alone.* New York: Penguin Press HC, 2012.

Ware, Ciji. *Rightsizing Your Life: Simplifying Your Surroundings while Keeping What Matters Most.* New York: Springboard Press, 2007.

Appendix 5: Aging-in-Place Design Checklists*

Exterior

- Low-maintenance exterior (vinyl, brick)
- Low-maintenance shrubs and plants
- Deck, patio, or balcony surfaces are no more than ½ inch below interior floor level if made of wood

---

*Source: National Association of Home Builders' Research Center's ToolBase .org, technical Web site for the home building industry (www.toolbase.org/ AgingInPlaceChecklists). Reprinted with permission.

Overall Floor Plan

- Option for main living on a single story, including bedroom and full bath
- No steps between rooms/areas on the same level
- 5-foot by 5-foot clear/turn space in living area, kitchen, a bedroom, and a bathroom

Hallways

- Minimum of 36 inches wide, wider preferred
- Well lit

Entry

- Accessible path of travel to the home
- At least one no-step entry with a cover
- Sensor light at exterior no-step entry focusing on the front-door lock
- 32 inches of clear width, which requires a 36-inch door
- Nonslip flooring in foyer
- Entry door sidelight or high/low peephole viewer; sidelight provides both privacy and safety
- Doorbell in accessible location
- Surface to place packages on when opening door

Thresholds

- Flush preferable
- Exterior maximum of ½ inch beveled
- Interior maximum of ¼ inch

Interior Doors

- 32 inches of clear width, which requires a 36-inch door
- Levered door hardware

Windows

- Plenty of windows for natural light
- Lowered windows or taller windows with lower sill height

- Low-maintenance exterior and interior finishes
- Easy-to-operate hardware

Garage or Carport

- Covered carports and boarding spaces
- Wider than average carports to accommodate lifts on vans
- Door heights may need to be 9 feet to accommodate some raised-roof vans
- 5-foot minimum access aisle between accessible van and car in garage
- If code requires floor to be several inches below entrance to house for fume protection, can slope entire floor from front to back to eliminate need for ramp or step
- Ramp to doorway if needed
- Handrail if steps

Faucets

- Lever or pedal-controlled handles
- Thermostatic or anti-scald controls
- Pressure-balanced faucets

Counters

- Wall support and provision for adjustable and/or varied height counters and removable base cabinets
- Upper wall cabinetry 3 inches lower than conventional height
- Accented stripes on edge of countertops to provide visual orientation to the workspace
- Counter space for dish landing adjacent to or opposite all appliances
- Base cabinet with roll-out trays and lazy susans
- Pull-down shelving
- Glass-front cabinet doors
- Open shelving for easy access to frequently used items

Appliances

- Easy-to-read controls
- Washing machine and dryer raised 12 to 15 inches above floor

- Front-loading laundry machines
- Microwave oven at counter height or in wall
- Side-by-side refrigerator/freezer
- Side-swing or wall oven
- Raised dishwasher with pushbutton controls
- Electric cooktop with level burners for safety in transferring between the burners, front controls and downdraft feature to pull heat away from user; light to indicate when surface is hot

Miscellaneous

- 30-inch by 48-inch clear space at appliances or 60-inch diameter clear space for turns
- Multilevel work areas to accommodate cooks of different heights
- Open undercounter seated work areas
- Placement of task lighting in appropriate work areas
- Loop handles for easy grip and pull
- Pull-out spray faucet; levered handles
- In multistory homes, laundry chute or laundry facilities in master bedroom

Bathroom

- Wall support and provision for adjustable and/or varied-height counters and removable base cabinets
- Contrasting color edge border at countertops
- At least one wheelchair-maneuverable bath on main level with 60-inch turning radius or acceptable T-turn space and 36-inch by 36-inch or 30-inch by 48-inch clear space
- Bracing in walls around tub, shower, shower seat, and toilet for installation of grab bars to support 250 to 300 pounds
- If stand-up shower is used in main bath, it is curbless and minimum of 36 inches wide
- Bathtub—lower for easier access
- Fold-down seat in the shower
- Adjustable/handheld showerheads, 6-foot hose
- Tub/shower controls offset from center
- Shower stall with built-in antibacterial protection

- Light in shower stall
- Toilet 2½ inches higher than standard toilet (17 to 19 inches) or height-adjustable
- Design of the toilet paper holder allows rolls to be changed with one hand
- Wall-hung sink with knee space and panel to protect user from pipes
- Slip-resistant flooring in bathroom and shower

Stairways, Lifts, and Elevators

- Adequate handrails on both sides of stairway, 1¼-inch diameter
- Increased visibility of stairs through contrast strip on top and bottom stairs, color contrast between treads and risers on stairs and use of lighting
- Multistory homes may provide either preframed shaft (i.e., stacked closets) for future elevator, or stairway width must be minimum of 4 feet to allow space for lift
- Residential elevator or lift

Ramps

- Slope no greater than 1-inch rise for each 12 inches in length, adequate handrails
- 5-foot landing provided at entrance
- 2-inch curbs for safety
- If feasible, consider a sloped front walkway instead of a ramp, or a walkway to a side or rear entrance, or through a garage

Storage

- Adjustable closet rods and shelves
- Lighting in closets
- Easy open doors that do not obstruct access

Electrical, Lighting, Safety, and Security

- Light switches by each entrance to halls and rooms
- Light receptacles with at least 2 bulbs in vital places (exits, bathroom)

- Light switches, thermostats, and other environmental controls placed in accessible locations no higher than 48 inches from floor
- Electrical outlets 15 inches on center from floor; may need to be closer than 12 feet apart
- Clear access space of 30 inches by 48 inches in front of switches and controls
- Rocker or touch light switches
- Audible and visual strobe light system to indicate when the doorbell, telephone, or smoke or CO_2 detectors have been activated
- High-tech security/intercom system that can be monitored, with the heating, air conditioning, and lighting, from any TV in the house
- Thermostats that are easy to see and read
- Preprogrammed thermostats
- Flashing porch light or 911 switch
- Direct wired to police, fire, and EMS (as option)
- Home wired for security
- Home wired for computers

Flooring

- Smooth, nonglare, slip-resistant surfaces, interior and exterior
- If carpeted, use low (less than ½-inch high pile) density, with firm pad
- Color/texture contrast to indicate change in surface levels

Heating, Ventilation, and Air Conditioning

- HVAC should be designed so filters are easily accessible
- Energy-efficient units
- Windows that can be opened for cross ventilation, fresh air

Energy Efficient Features

- In-line framing with 2-by-6 studs spaced 24 inches on center
- Air-barrier installation and sealing of duct work with mastic
- Reduced-size air conditioning units with gas furnaces

- Mechanical fresh air ventilation, installation of air returns in all bedrooms, and use of carbon monoxide detectors
- Installation of energy-efficient windows with low-e glass

Reduced Maintenance/Convenience Features

- Easy-to-clean surfaces
- Central vacuum
- Built-in pet-feeding system
- Built-in recycling system
- Videophones
- Intercom system

Other Ideas

- Separate apartment for rental income or future caregiver
- Flex room that can used as a nursery or playroom when the children are young and as a home office later; if combined with a full bath, room could also be used for an aging parent/aging in place

CHAPTER 6

A Place to Call Home: What Are Your Choices?

The ache for home lives in all of us, the safe place where we can go as we are and not be questioned.

—Maya Angelou

■ ■ ■

The previous chapter provided some points to ponder if you're thinking about relocating, including defining your non-negotiables, moving to reduce your cost of living (more about this in Chapter 8), separating wants from needs, and considering your personality traits. The end of a job, a new relationship status, a health problem, the need to downsize or leave a home that no longer works for you, or the allure of starting a new life or career—all of these can trigger a move.

Let's examine lifestyle choices that might appeal to you, and some specific suggestions. I love specifics.

Active-Adult Communities

Also called age-restricted, age-qualified, or age-targeted communities, active-adult communities have been around for more than 50 years and are a popular option for single women. Although in many communities you must be at least 55, this has been changing; in some communities residents can be as young as 45, so be sure to check the particular age restrictions of any community that interests you.

While most consumers 55 and over "were generally happy with their current homes, residents of age-restricted active-adult communities had the highest satisfaction rates," according to the MetLife Mature Market Institute. Low maintenance, lots to do, like-minded neighbors, security through restricted access, social support, clubs that specifically target singles, covenants that dictate the rules of the community, a wide range of housing, fantastic amenities gathered in one place, free of children and teenagers, and usually a full-time lifestyle director are some reasons for their appeal.

Some of the negatives typically associated with active-adult communities are being addressed. More home customization is now available, and more activities are scheduled in the mornings and evenings to accommodate the many working residents. In some active-adult communities, only about 10 percent of the residents are totally retired, and residents are often starting their own businesses. Newer communities are often built closer to cities, rather than out in the middle of nowhere, where land costs less. Developers need lots of room for tennis courts, pools, fitness centers, golf courses, hiking trails, pickleball courts, demo kitchens, and computer rooms, but in many instances, the level of amenities is ratcheting down. Most cities and towns welcome active-adult communities since residents pay property taxes but don't use as many services (kids are expensive to educate). Older adults patronize restaurants and shops, and they are more likely to volunteer; perhaps they will tutor the children they themselves don't have in the school system.

According to *Builder* magazine, the three biggest players in the active-adult field, by recent home sales, are Del Webb/Pulte, with more than 50 communities in 20 states; The Villages, located one hour north of Orlando, Florida, and nestled between the Gulf and Atlantic coasts, so big with its 80,000 residents that it has its own zip code; and K. Hovnanian, the largest active-adult home builder in the Northeast, with about 15 communities. If you're interested in Arizona or Texas, another active-adult builder is Robson, with six communities in Arizona and one in Denton, Texas.

Hint: When people move into an active-adult community, they tend to stay there. So, if you're younger, choose a newer active-adult community. It will have a lower average age than those that have been built out or that have been around for a number of years. And, it helps avoid the difficulty of breaking into cliques. If it's a new community, be sure that the developer is solvent and that the amenities are already in place or will be in place.

Some specifics? Carolyn K. chose Del Webb Orlando for her retirement location. Originally from the Midwest and never married (well, she said she was married to her career), Carolyn shopped around and ultimately looked at Del Webb Orlando, which is close to her sister's home. Carolyn's thoughts:

> The minute I walked into the model of my home, I knew it was the home for me. I was impressed with the various activities and events that the activity director plans for the residents such as weekly bridge games, a book club, dominoes, shopping excursions, beach outings, and various holiday parties (including a Super Bowl Party). The people in the community do outreach work, providing school supplies to one of the nearby schools for the children whose families cannot afford to buy some of the basic supplies. Del Webb neighbors provide holiday gifts to residents of a local nursing home who may not have any family. It didn't seem to matter whether you were single or married, there is something for everyone. People in the community are encouraged to make suggestions for events and activities as well.
>
> This is a newer Del Webb community and has a just-completed 31,000-square-foot amenity center with an indoor and outdoor pool, indoor walking track, bocce ball courts, tennis courts, fitness center, business center, etc. I have met wonderful people here who are living their retirement dream. Every month we have a Meet and Greet Breakfast that gives us the opportunity to meet any newcomers. We have a Welcome Committee that visits new residents and provides them with a variety of information such as how to get your Florida driver's license, your car registered, medical services in the community, or repair services. And, the Welcome Committee works to find out what the new residents' interests are and what types of activities

they would like to join or see added. This is a wonderful community of both married and single people who enjoy having fun together. My only regret is that I did not do this sooner.

Mimi V. moved to the active-adult community of Victoria Gardens in DeLand, Florida. She was 62 and working full-time in Longwood, Florida, when her husband, Dick, passed away. She moved to the Washington, DC, area and rented an apartment, "ready for a lifestyle change and to be near children and grandchildren." After four years in an apartment, she decided to investigate active-adult communities since she "liked the built-in activities, amenities, and opportunities to meet new friends." Mimi knew she wanted to move to Florida because she liked the climate and wanted be close to the ocean, which is about 20 miles away from her home.

Mimi also chose Victoria Park specifically for these reasons:

- *College town.* DeLand, home to Stetson University, is a cute college town with lots of restaurants and shops oozing small-town charm. The big-box stores are either in nearby Sanford or Daytona.
- *Appearance.* Victoria Gardens offers total landscape maintenance as part of the homeowner's association responsibilities. All the homes and common areas are beautifully kept at all times.
- *Active lifestyle.* The overall feeling here is one of active adults enjoying tennis, biking, walking, etc. Having worked for many years, I like to keep busy. There is always a card game or group meeting at the Clubhouse or Café. The professors from Stetson give lectures in our Clubhouse during the academic year, and we attend events on campus.
- *Support.* Recently, one of my friends who moved here about two years after I did passed away after a one-year battle with cancer. She had told me how amazed she was that so many neighbors wanted to help. There was a group of us who drove her to chemo; people cared for her on bad days etc. There was a memorial service at our Clubhouse. The ballroom was filled—standing room only. She was a special lady, but I thought it spoke well of the people here.

"I have found just what I was looking for here. I have a single family home for peace and quiet, a built-in social life when I feel like a party, and supportive, caring friends," Mimi said.

For contact information for these and other active-adult communities, see "More 411" at the end of this chapter.

New Urbanism or Traditional Neighborhood Developments

These communities are also called neotraditional communities, traditional neighborhoods, and smart-growth communities. You've heard about the book and movie *Eat, Pray, Love.* Well, in new urbanism communities you can eat, pray, love, and work, shop, live, learn, and walk everywhere as well. New urbanism is an alternative to suburban sprawl, where you need a car to get to basic services. A 10- or 15-minute walk allows you to get to where you need to go. The communities are distinguished by high-density housing, narrow roads to slow traffic, the absence of gates, a mix of housing styles that are close to the street, sidewalks, front porches to encourage the meeting and greeting of neighbors, garages accessed via alleys in the back of the homes, and parks and schools integrated into or close by the community.

Sound familiar? The original models are places like Annapolis, Maryland; Charleston, South Carolina; the Georgetown district of Washington, DC; Reston and Old Town Alexandria, Virginia; and Capri, Venice, and Florence, Italy. Because new urbanism communities deemphasize the car, an issue for many as we get older, and foster a sense of community, this is also an attractive option for single women. Since our environment shapes the way we live, anything that encourages walking or bike riding and increases social support is a plus.

Fun Fact

If you're a movie buff, you may have seen *The Truman Show* with Jim Carrey. It was filmed in Seaside, Florida, one of the first neotraditional communities.

A core principle of new urbanism is that a variety of home styles and prices are offered to accommodate a diverse group of people with a variety of economic backgrounds. In reality, many of these communities cater to a white, affluent clientele. Remember that everything—homes, shops, and so forth—starts off as brand new in these planned communities. This is appealing to some, a turn-off for others. For example, when I visited Celebration, Florida, I loved the look and feel of the community. Kids were riding bikes and eating ice cream cones at the town center, several women were talking on a front porch; small groups of young moms with babies in tow were eating lunch at an outside café. My friend thought it looked and felt contrived, as though it was laboring for a nostalgic feel. Different strokes . . .

Kathryn W. lives in the new urbanism community of NorthWest Crossing in Bend, Oregon. Her story:

As I sit here and look at the spectacular snow-covered mountains, the biggest decision that I have to make today is should I go cross-country skiing, ride my bike, or walk to the neighborhood café, sip wine, and read a good book. How did I get so lucky to live in this place I call home?

I am from Toledo, Ohio. After graduating from The Ohio State University, my girlfriend and I took off for San Francisco. We were both nurses and accepted jobs at Stanford University Hospital. I met my husband and decided that living in the West was for me. Had two fabulous kids but through life's twists and turns, I found myself single again at age 50, living in Arizona. I went back to work, not only because I had to but because I had a passion for helping others, specifically in health education. I was climbing the ladder, living frugally, and finding out about 401(k)s.

I was able to retire a bit early. I met my significant other, thanks to Match.com, and we were dividing our time between Washington and Arizona. In addition, we were frequently visiting Bend, as my daughter and her family live here. Sadly, my partner died. After that I decided that I wanted to live here permanently. Sooo, here I am! If you love the outdoors, Bend is the place for you. There is so much to do, including hiking, cycling, kayaking, rafting, fishing, golf, camping, snowshoeing, and skiing. There are many lakes within an hour of Bend, so if you enjoy the water, you've got it. Bend is high desert so there is little humidity, a great downtown with lovely shops, art galleries, several live theaters and numerous wonderful restaurants. Plus, there is an amphitheater, which is a great venue for outdoor concerts, festivals, and other year-round art and cultural events. And, the people are so nice.

I feel very healthy living here as the air is crisp and clean and there is a big emphasis on a healthy lifestyle. I believe that people move to Bend for a better quality of life and I think most of them find just that. And, a bonus, Bend has 300-plus days of sunshine a year.

My community, NorthWest Crossing, is designed to provide residents with conveniences like restaurants, shops, parks, school, and trails. I am fortunate to live across the street from one of the parks, which is great for my grandchildren and me. There are play areas, bike paths, picnic areas, and natural places to walk and explore. And, during the summer there are concerts, outdoor family movies, and even bike races for the children. Also, there's a fun farmer's market every week.

Financially, I am fortunate. I don't have tons of money but I have enough. My grandchildren are my volunteering for now. I am with them frequently and that is precious time for me. I am dating, thanks again to Match.com, and definitely would like another partner. I am very grateful for my wonderful circle of family and friends, my health, and my life here. It is the best!

Carol M. chose the traditional neighborhood development (TND) community of Daniel Island, near Charleston, South Carolina. Carol's story:

My initial decision was easy. I knew I needed to move. Nine years ago, I was a divorced woman living in San Francisco. My daughters, Megan and Susan, weren't committed to remaining in the San Francisco area. Most of my friends were still living in Connecticut, many commuting to Florida and points south for the winter. Although I loved San Francisco, leaving the crowded streets, the inclement weather, and the extremely high cost of living was beginning to look like a good idea.

My search for a new address was very calculated. I spent one week a month for six months, visiting places I thought could become my new home . . . Naples, Ponte Vedra Beach, Orlando, and West Palm Beach, Florida; Wilmington, North Carolina; and finally, Charleston, South Carolina.

I settled on Charleston because it met my criteria. It's a college town, on the water, with a variety of cultural activities including the symphony, ballet, and plenty of pretty decent theater. I arrived in Charleston on a Thursday. I found a house that had actually appeared to me in a dream, bought it on Friday, and returned to San Francisco on Saturday to get things in order to move. I knew not one soul in Charleston, but I did know in my heart that I was making the right decision. I landed on Daniel Island, a new urbanism community with a fabulous club offering golf, tennis, and croquet, and all within biking distance of my new home, and unlike San Francisco, year-round access. I joined the club and immediately found my way. The best thing about being a part of a newer community is that everyone is from another place and everyone is looking for new friends. So, not only did I find plenty of new friends but I've been able to "reconnect" with many of my Connecticut friends who've been conveniently "stopping by" on their way to points south!

Cohousing

The living style of cohousing originated in Denmark and migrated to the United States in the 1980s. Also called collaborative housing, this type of community is unique because of resident involvement in planning the community. People own their private homes, although of course there could be more than one person in a home. At the community level, residents don't comingle money, and social support is emphasized. Communities can contain from as few as 7 to as many as 70 residences. There is shared decision making without a hierarchy, management by residents, and communal open space and facilities including some group meals, but homes do have their own kitchens, and residents usually contribute to the community without any compensation.

There are more than 225 of these communities in the United States, listed on a cohousing Web site (www.cohousing.org). Some are completed, some are forming, and some have options on building sites. In addition, there are "elder cohousing communities" with a minimum age of 55 (www.abrahampaiss.com/ElderCohousing). Several are completed and others are under development or in the planning stages. As its Web site says, elder cohousing provides adults "the opportunity to live interdependently and 'age in community' within a close-knit group of neighbors." The characteristics of cohousing could make it an attractive option for single women.

Jacque B. chose Wolf Creek Lodge (www.wolfcreeklodge.org), a cohousing community in California. In Jacque's own words:

> I am a fan of the author Virginia Woolf and have especially enjoyed her extended essay, *A Room of One's Own*. The title alone piqued my interest, not only because of the reference to gender equality, a major theme of Woolf's, but also because, for most of my life, I never had a room of my own. My living situations have always been immersed in estrogen from growing up one of three sisters to parenting two daughters. Even my pets have been female. Growing up as the middle sister, I either shared a room with my older sister, or when it was decided she needed her own room, I shared a room with my younger sister. At one time, I even shared a room with my sister *and* grandfather. When I went to college, like my fellow classmates, I shared a room in the dorms, and upon graduating I found myself married and once again sharing a room, this time with my messiest roommate yet. Our first room as newlyweds was my mother-in-law's laundry room, which was used by the whole household, as my ex-husband had eight siblings.
>
> When I found myself devastatingly divorced after 30 years of marriage and desperately looking for some kind of silver lining, I remembered Virginia Woolf and *A Room of One's Own*. The silver lining being a house of my own! And I found a charming, historical Victorian house, with which I fell madly in love, and owning

133

it was definitely the salvation I was searching for at that time of my life. I was so proud of being an independent homeowner and enjoyed living in the beautiful foothills of the Sierra Nevada Mountains. My job in special education as a speech and language pathologist provided a very rewarding career, but I looked forward to retiring, which I did after teaching for 33 years.

Just before retirement, I survived a bout with cancer. Realizing the fragility of life, once I retired, I embarked on adventure traveling to the ends of the earth; I was literally checking off places in the book *1,000 Places to See Before You Die*. The trips distracted me from a downside of retirement: Once I found myself at home without a busy daily routine, I realized I did not like living by myself. When I heard about an upcoming slideshow on Senior Cohousing, my curiosity led me to attend. Senior Cohousing really does incorporate the best of two worlds: a house of my own *and* a built-in community! In an age influenced by the green movement, cohousing also helps create a more sustainable society. Shortly after my introduction to Senior Cohousing, I became a member of one—Wolf Creek Lodge in Grass Valley, California.

In addition to striking a balance between shared and private space, our beautiful Wolf Creek Lodge has many green amenities. I am excited to be a part of this vibrant community of physically active single men, women, and married couples and have become an advocate of cohousing in general. Another benefit: My fellow members helped me train for an annual triathlon. My life is now a team sport! As we age at Wolf Creek Lodge, we will have built-in support, which is one of the best recommendations for anyone, let alone for older adults.

So, I have come to see Virginia Woolf's argument in a new light: I embrace having a community at the doorstep of my private residence as a way to reconcile the benefits offered by a room of one's own and those offered by the community interactions we crave as social creatures. I agree with those futurists who suggest that cohousing is a new response to the 21st century's social, economic, and environmental challenges. I'm still into adventure at 61 years of age and aging is possibly our last, great adventure in life.

Cities and Small Towns

Sometimes it is true that bigger is better. Cities or towns provide opportunities to meet others and become an integral part of a place, have lots of cultural opportunities, and are often very walkable, all qualities that many single women find desirable. Of course, as with any choice, it's up to you to get involved and make the most of your location. SingleMindedWomen.com's "2012: Top Ten Cities for Single Women," determined by factors including cost of living, singles ratios, job growth, financial stability, beauty, culture, and social options, are: Austin, Houston, Nashville, Washington DC, Dallas, Charleston, Phoenix, Chicago, New York, and Raleigh. With three of the 10 cities in Texas, it may be time to invest in a 10-gallon hat.

Susan M., in her 60s, ultimately chose the mile-high city of Denver (in the top 10 list for 2010), after living in Pittsburgh (following a guy), London (the guy was a thing of the past), and Washington, DC. She has lived in Denver for the past four years. Luckily, she can do her consulting work from any location. She has this to say about Denver:

> The best word that I can think of to describe life in Denver is "easy." It's easy to make friends, even when you're single. People are open to newcomers because a lot of them are new, too. It's easy to get around town. Once you learn the street grid, you can't get too lost, and there's a good public transit system, including light rail. There are plenty of single-friendly activities, a great public library system that offers free programs of all sorts, a wonderful botanic garden for those of us with a love of gardens, lots of little theatre groups and other moderately priced entertainment for those of us on a budget. For me, it's important to be able to fly directly to London and other cities where the friends that I have made over a lifetime live now, so a city with a sizable airport is a plus.
>
> When it comes to recreation, Coloradans are a very health-conscious bunch and take recreational activities seriously. Denver has a great system of bike paths; the Highline Canal path, for instance, goes for about 60 miles. The mountains are always a presence in Denver; skiing, hiking, and camping

are an hour or two away. Name your favorite sport or pastime and you can probably find someone to do it with here.

What do I miss in Denver? A few things, I must confess. First of all, water! Oh, for the Chesapeake Bay or the Jersey Shore. Second, spring. Here in Denver we have what I call "sprinter"— spring one day, winter the next.

When I start to see people in the grocery store that I know, I know that I'm part of a community. Here in Denver, it's become a regular occurrence. There's no question I'm here to stay. I'm part of a family and I'm part of the community, too. I feel that I belong, and how important is that!

Looking for small town living? Barbara R. shares her story of finding serenity and "living juicy" in St. Marys, Georgia.

I've been single for 20 years now after discovering that you didn't have to marry somebody just because it made them happy. It did take four marriages, however, to finally convince me. In addition to that epiphany, I've also discovered that the ultimate best mate for life is yourself. And the best way to get to know yourself is to land in a place where serenity and peace soothe your soul, stir your spirit, and settle you to the point that you can become the person you were meant to be.

The first time I came to St. Marys, Georgia, I was drawn— not by the magic that I was only later to discover, but by a writing assignment for the local railroad. On a chilly, damp February morning, I stood in the middle of the median strip in front of a bed and breakfast and something truly astonishing happened. The most astounding sense of peace, something I had never felt in my life, washed over me. For the first time that I can remember in my entire life, I was totally still. Being the kind of person who has a 5-year plan and a 10-year plan, I always felt like I was moving, even when I was sitting still. This was a totally foreign feeling for me. I sloughed it off.

The second time I came to St. Marys to write a follow-up piece about the railroad, I stayed overnight at the Goodbread House Inn, the same B&B I had stood in front of in my moment of peace during my previous visit. For the first time in

25 years, I slept the entire night without awakening. The house (or was it the town?) embraced me with a sense of comfort I had never known.

The third time I came to St. Marys I bought the bed and breakfast with my best friend since forever. She too felt the serenity of the town and the enchantment of its people. That was in 2004.

Before I moved to St. Marys, I had spent 25 years in the fast lane as a successful advertising executive in Fort Lauderdale, first working at one of the area's largest agencies, and then opening up my own company. I was thriving as never before—in success, in money, in local fame, even in love. So at the time, even I didn't understand the siren call of the little town of St. Marys that pulled me out of glitzy Fort Lauderdale and the lifestyle I had enjoyed for two decades.

I suppose I did retire in a fashion when I moved to St. Marys. Though running the Goodbread House with my partner was time consuming, for the first time in my life I did stop and smell the roses. Long strolls on a moonlit night immersed in the seductive scents of gardenias and honeysuckle. Lazy times on a waterfront park swing, reading a trashy novel and marveling at the stunning sunsets that rivaled Key West's best evening skies. Lingering over a cool glass of Chardonnay at the local saloon where everybody really does "know your name." My life went from fast lane to crawl speed, and I loved every minute of it.

The first Christmas season I was in St. Marys, I went around pinching myself because it was like living inside a Norman Rockwell postcard—carolers on the streets, children on horse-drawn carriages, Santa lighting up the town, and everyone filled with the holiday spirit. That's about the time we put a sign on the front door of the B&B that said, "Enter as strangers. Leave as friends." It was so right. And so true.

Slowly, I dwindled my ad agency client list down to my most lucrative clients and having a little more time on my hands, I started the *St. Marys Magazine* because I wanted to share this little bit of Heaven on Earth with the world. From its first publication, the town seized it as if it was their own making, and with pride the entire town continues to celebrate each new issue.

Alas, my boyfriend of six years, a marvelously handsome and fun Englishman, opted to stay in Fort Lauderdale, which, to him, was Nirvana compared to his hometown of Liverpool. But even in a small town, it didn't take long for me to find an equally enjoyable companion whose intellect I admired. We continue to share nights of Scrabble and two dogs that we both adore. But I have no overwhelming desire to marry, and am completely sated in my single life. Because, you see, I found me. And I'm a pretty cool mate.

I no longer make $300,000 a year. But I do make enough. I love nothing more than taking my dogs on a golf cart ride to the river and meeting friends for good wine and good times. I live by the creed that's artistically painted on my kitchen walls: "Walk softly. Play happily. Dream sweetly. Love deeply. Live juicy."

My emphasis these days is on the "live juicy" part. So many people die with their music still inside. That's not on my bucket list. I'm involved in so many different aspects of our community—chair of the Convention & Visitors Bureau, founder of Coastal Georgia Film Alliance, founder of St. Marys EarthKeepers, on the Downtown Development Board . . . and the list goes on. I love helping make my adopted hometown the best that it can be. And I love telling people about it.

So here are my thoughts about being a single woman and retired: Find what you love to do, and live your life in a way that shows it. Find a place that soothes your soul and stirs your spirit. And move there. Give, give, give, because it is in the giving that you will find the most joy. And above all, live juicy.

Naturally Occurring Retirement Communities/Villages

A naturally occurring retirement community (NORC) is one that develops because people live in a place for a long time and age along with their neighbors. These aren't communities that are planned, they just evolve that way, although more people are finding out about this "village movement" and are purposefully moving to one of them. Sometimes "villages" and "NORCs" are used interchangeably. Usually, though, it's called a NORC when the aging happens by default, and it's called a village when the residents organize services by themselves (or at least start out that way). Strong social support makes NORCs/villages an attractive lifestyle option.

There is no strict definition of a NORC. It may be defined as a community where more than half the residents are 50 or over, or it's a NORC if there are at least 200 people and 40 percent of residents are over 65. Beacon Hill Village in Boston is a famous NORC; residents in apartment buildings in New York City may make up a NORC; Toco Hills NORC in Decatur, Georgia, is composed of residents in six zip codes; Capitol Hill Village in Washington, DC, has about 350 residents.

NORCs can have loosely organized groups of residents and volunteers who help residents stay in their homes, and more formal services such as home delivered meals, in-home counseling, preventative health programs, and home sharing. In some of these communities, you pay annual dues for services; in others, government programs or philanthropy might provide operating funds.

If you live in a NORC or think you do, and you are interested in services for your community, contact the NORC Supportive Services Program (www.norcs.org). To find out more about the village concept, check out the Village to Village Network (www.vtvnetwork .org).

Master-Planned Communities

When is a master-planned community not an ordinary subdivision? Scale and amenities are generally the defining characteristics. The emphasis is on amenities and activities such as golf, tennis, hiking trails, pools, fitness centers, and clubhouses with restaurants and meeting rooms. There is often more than one builder or developer in the community. Because of these communities' large size, there is usually a wide range of housing styles and prices, and many developers will be building for decades to come.

For example, one of the largest master-planned communities in the country, The Woodlands, near Houston, has 27,000 acres with six golf courses, 100 miles of trails, parks, a spa, a 200-acre lake, schools, medical facilities, an amphitheater, and a conference center.

When you combine amenities and size with a full-time lifestyle director and many resident-driven activities, master-planned communities, especially those that provide extra security because they are gated, can be an attractive option for single women. Like active-adult communities, master-planned communities also have home-owners associations (HOAs) that enforce rules and regulations, from the color of residential exteriors to what you can plant in your yard. As mentioned in the previous chapter, some people feel that HOAs maintain the value of their community; others chafe at the enforcement of the covenants. It's important to read the rules that govern your HOA prior to purchase. Keep in mind that all these fun things to do come with a price tag, so you'll be paying dues and fees to support this lifestyle. That being said, master-planned communities are a popular lifestyle choice. They offer a wide assortment of activities, lots of opportunities to get involved and meet people, and an environment that encourages physical fitness.

Linda W. moved to the master-planned community of Woodside Plantation in Aiken, South Carolina, as a married woman, but now is living there as a single woman:

> You think you are going to have a wonderful, long life when you retire but things do not always work out that way. It started out great. My husband, Jim, and I were able to retire at the young ages of 50 and 53, and found a place to live that was paradise—a pretty strong word, but just ask anyone living in Woodside and they will agree. In 2005, Jim was diagnosed with cancer and did not win his battle. He died on July 3, 2007.
>
> I wasn't sure how being single in a primarily couples' community would work out for me. Well, it has worked out better than anyone could imagine. Of course, I have all my couple friends who include me in almost everything. Without their friendship and support I would not have survived. But now, I have met some very interesting, friendly, funny, and just downright terrific single women who have either moved to Woodside as a single, or are widows like me.
>
> The Singles Group at Woodside has something for everyone. Activities include going to plays, the movies, dinner, lunch, cruises, overnight trips, and races. I join in when I can

but my life as president of the Women of Woodside has kept me very busy. It is an organization of 740 women with a mission of fundraising and volunteering for our local charities and for member enjoyment. Talk about neat women. They come from all over the United States, and many have had great jobs or raised families, and all give so much back to our community here in Aiken, South Carolina. Besides that, I play golf, bridge, and poker, and love to travel, cook, and entertain. Speaking of entertaining, I probably have friends, both couples and singles, over for dinner at least 4 to 5 times a month. This is one way I thank everyone who has invited me for dinner.

I know I found a home here at Woodside. I cannot imagine living anywhere else. I miss my husband every day, but getting involved in the community has been my saving grace. It has had a positive impact on me and I thank God every day for all my blessings.

Did You Know?

The 10 Best Selling Master-Planned Communities according to RCLCO, a real estate consulting firm: The Villages (central Florida); Villages of Irvine (Orange County, California); Cinco Ranch (Houston); The Woodlands (Houston); Mountain's Edge (Las Vegas); Telfair (Houston); Providence (Las Vegas); Brambleton (Ashburn, Virginia); Sienna Plantation (Houston); and Stapleton (Denver). What makes these communities successful? Ingredients include proximity to services and jobs (think oil for Houston), established and viable places to live (Woodlands has been around for 35 years), good schools, and great amenities.

Some established master-planned developments have just about everything rolled into one, including businesses, retail, medical services, schools, restaurants, houses of worship, amenities, and a variety of housing styles. Sometimes these communities are entirely active-adult; others may have an active-adult section in an otherwise multi-generational setting.

As one attractive example, here is Connie G.'s story about living in Fairfield Glade, Tennessee:

I'm a 61-year-old widowed, happily retired half-back. No, no, no we're not talking football here. You see, I lived my first 21 years of life in central Illinois, then married and lived the next 37 years in Sarasota, Florida, with a couple of years in the Portland, Oregon, area thrown in. Well, here I am halfway back, living up here in Fairfield Glade, Tennessee.

If it's beautiful scenery and kind and friendly people you want to have around you in retirement, by all means investigate Fairfield Glade. This is a place that has all sorts of clubs, activities, churches, entertainment, plays, golf courses, fishing lakes, and most importantly a wonderful wellness complex. If this is not enough to keep you busy, there are over 15 different volunteer groups as well.

What I love most is the fact I have four seasons again. Here are some other wonderful things about moving here: My car and home insurance rates dropped, as did my property tax. Homes are reasonably priced, and I feel safe. My son found a very comfortable two-bedroom/two-bath condo for me.

I am living in a place where people take their time and enjoy their days. Today, I was in yoga at 10:00 a.m. and at 11:45 a.m. I was taking my very first fly-fishing lesson! Here in Fairfield Glade I can rest or be as busy as I want . . . I am on my very own personal retirement adventure.

Continuing Care Retirement Communities

If you know you will need to take responsibility for your own care for the rest of your life, a continuing care retirement community may be something to consider. CCRCs allow you to age in place, moving from independent living to assisted living to skilled nursing care all on the same "campus." Many CCRCs also include Alzheimer's care.

Residences may be in the form of apartments, condos, duplexes, townhomes, or single-family homes. There are a variety of ways the approximately 2,000 CCRCs across the United States are structured. You could pay an entry fee and then monthly fees that cover all services, even though you may not need all services at first; you could perhaps purchase or rent your residence and pay monthly fees that cover certain services but pay more if your situation changes; you may pay for services a la carte depending on your needs. What happens to your residence if you decide to move or if you die? In some cases, your (purchased) residence can be passed on to your heirs; sometimes a portion or the entire amount of the entry fee will be refunded or will go to your estate; sometimes there are no refunds.

What happens if you run out of money? Because CCRC contracts can be fairly complex, it's a good idea to review them with a financial planner, an accountant, or an attorney. Remember to have your money person look at the financial statements of the CCRC, too. With people experiencing more difficulty selling their homes, some CCRCs, which often had waiting lists in the past, are having a harder time filling their communities and often are reducing some of their fees, and offering other incentives, or are open to negotiation. If you're in poor health when you enter a CCRC, you could be paying a lot of money for a little time. But for those with the financial means, a CCRC can provide great peace of mind.

Hazel R., for example, is a 78-year-old widow who retired from the Howard County, Maryland, school system and has lived at Carroll Lutheran Village, a CCRC in Westminster, Maryland, for the last five years. Hazel said she and her husband originally planned on moving to Carroll Lutheran Village "when we were ninety-four" but decided to make the move much earlier because the setting was ideal. There was a nearby college, shopping, and a small town. Due to a sudden illness, her husband lived there only seven weeks, so Hazel has lived there alone for five years. Hazel notes that "alone" is a strange word because her life includes, she says, "being a hospice volunteer and a Village Health Care Center volunteer, and singing with two groups, one in the Village and one in the community. I'm part of our Village book club, serve on various committees, and take water aerobics classes. And, with 650 residents in a mixture of independent living, assisted living, and nursing home care, we are like family. Loneliness is not part of the equation here."

The Commission on Accreditation of Rehabilitation Facilities (CARF) accredits CCRCs—lots of acronyms, but it's good to know.

To find accredited CCRCs, go to www.carf.org and click on "Find an Accredited Provider." Then, click on "Advanced Search" and put in your specifics: CCRC (under "program"), zip code, county, etc. Note that the average age in one of these communities tends to be around 80. For a good checklist of questions to ask when investigating this type of community, see the "Continuing Care Retirement Community Checklist" in Appendix 6A at the end of this chapter. Checklists from CARF are also available for independent living, assisted living, and nursing homes.

Green House Model

The green house model is a newer initiative for older adults that creates residences—single-family homes or apartments—within a community and incorporates the care and services that would be found in an ideal nursing home. Each home would generally have 6 to 10 residents. A private bedroom and bathroom is provided for each resident, and payment is through Medicaid, private pay, or, in some cases, Medicare or a charitable foundation. Around 230 of these homes are operating or developing in about 30 states. For more information, go to www.thegreenhouseproject .org. Examples of up-and-running green houses are The Green House at Calvary in Columbus, Georgia; St. Martin's in the Pines in Birmingham, Alabama; and Buckner Westminster Place in Longview, Texas.

Pocket Communities

Remember the toys called "pocket pets"? So little they could fit in a—duh—pocket? Well, that idea of compactness is now being applied to small homes, some under 1,000 square feet, that share a common outdoor area and emphasize community. Architect and author Ross Chapin (see his book in the "More 411" section) coined the term "pocket communities," and more than 40 have been built throughout the United States (www.rosschapin.com). Think cozy, close, charming, and caring. Examples: Inglewood in Carmel, Indiana; Riverwalk in West Concord, Massachusetts; Wyers End in White Salmon, Washington; and Salish Pond Cottages, Fairview, Oregon.

College Towns

If lifelong learning, generally stable housing prices, sports, a rich array of cultural activities, often cutting-edge medical care, restaurants, and perhaps bars are near the top of your list, consider a college town. For many of us, college was among the best years of our lives, so why not try to recapture the feeling? For example, after years of teaching ecology in a community college in northern New Jersey, Martha H. retired to Princeton, New Jersey, where she can take advantage of the famed Princeton University and all it has to offer. And, Martha loves how easy it is to take the "Dinky" train that connects to Philly or New York, enjoy the McCarter Theatre Center for the Performing Arts, or stroll to Palmer Square from her home with its shops and varied restaurants. But all those goodies don't come cheap. Princeton has a much higher than average price tag, more than one and a half times the U.S. average.

You could consider beautiful Bellingham, Washington, which has several institutions of higher learning, including Western Washington University and Whatcom Community College, and which weighs in at 10 percent more than the U.S. average cost of living. Or follow Dianne R.'s footsteps to Williamsburg, Virginia, which she chose because of her love of history, the proximity to the College of William and Mary, and the mild climate. Like Bellingham, Williamsburg also has a cost of living about 10 percent higher than the average. Keep in mind that if you're looking for a job, you could be competing with 30,000 college students! And you need to feel comfortable with the majority of people being about one-third of your age.

In addition to a home or apartment in a college town, you could consider a "university-linked" retirement community. About 60 of these exist, with an equal number on the drawing board. These types of communities are often continuing care retirement communities. Some require you to be an alumna of the institution. See "More 411" for examples of university-linked retirement communities.

Broads Abroad (Sorry, Couldn't Help It)

The idea of moving to another country has picked up steam. Looking to stretch those retirement dollars or to enjoy new experiences and challenges, relocating outside the United States has become an attractive option. Some women are taking their elderly parents with them; assisted-living arrangements are often 50 percent less expensive in a foreign country. The number of Americans living outside the United States is uncertain because the U.S. Census Bureau doesn't track this type of information, but the State Department estimates around 7 million.

A number of sites can help those of us considering this type of move (see "More 411" below). One well-known Web site is International Living (www.internationalliving.com). In business for 30 years, it sponsors trips to locations to consider for retirement and offers advice about purchasing property, moving, handling your money and mail, obtaining health care, and more. The site also includes a quiz about the best place to retire abroad. The quiz takes less than a minute and told me that, based on my answers, I should move to Mexico. International Living publishes all kinds of lists, such as the World's Healthiest Places, Quality of Life Index, Best Climate, and the World's Top Retirement Havens (for 2012, the top three are Ecuador, Panama, and Mexico). You can also sign up for free newsletters. Other Web sites include www.escapefrom america.com and www.liveandinvestoverseas.com.

I asked Kathleen Peddicord, founder and publisher of Live and Invest Overseas (www.liveandinvestoverseas.com), former editor and publisher of International Living, and author of *How to Retire Overseas: Everything You Need to Know to Live Well (for Less) Abroad*, for recommendations for single women considering relocating abroad. Kathleen's answer:

> To state the obvious, the most important issues for a single woman making an international move in retirement on her own would be safety and community. Where would she feel safe walking around and going out on her own? And where would she find an established and welcoming community, friendship, and companionship? In that context, here are three places that I'd recommend:
> - Ajijic, Mexico. Very safe, and home to a very established expat community. Living here, you wouldn't have to learn Spanish if you didn't want to. Immediately upon arrival, you'd be greeted by loads of like-minded people inviting you

to join book clubs and art groups and bridge clubs. You (a single woman) wouldn't ever want for something to do or for someone to do it with. Plus, speaking generally, this is an affordable, sun-filled option.

- Paris, France. Speaking personally, if I were going to make an international move in retirement on my own, this is where I'd go. Paris has anything . . . it has everything. Plus it's beautiful, romantic, and historic . . . as well as safe, easily navigable without owning a car, and, generally, very user-friendly for a woman on her own. This wouldn't be a budget choice, but Paris can be more affordable than you might imagine. As everywhere, it depends where and how you choose to live. Most all Paris is safe (even by the standards of a retired single woman), meaning you could settle in a non-central neighborhood (outside the 1st, the 7th, or the 8th arrondissement, for example), where rents are cheaper, and still not have to worry about coming and going, even at night. Endless opportunities for things to do and ways to spend your time. Big expat community to tap into.
- Ambergris Caye, Belize. This would be my top on-the-water pick for a single woman. This Caribbean island is home to an established and growing expat community that includes a number of 60-plus single women. Some have businesses. Some are active in the community. All feel safe and comfortable. The biggest complaint might be that there isn't a big selection of single men (as it's a small island!). On the other hand, this would be a great choice for a woman who wants to stay active. The main pastimes are walking, swimming, sailing, biking, fishing, etc. There's also a big fitness center (run by a friend of mine) that offers aerobics and yoga.

So that's a budget choice (Mexico) . . . a more "luxury" level and cosmopolitan choice (Paris) . . . and a Caribbean beach choice (Belize).

Is packing up and moving to a foreign land for you? Take a look at the questions from "International Living" in Appendix 6B at the end of this chapter to help you decide. And, read Louise O.'s in-depth and fascinating story about her international move to Boquete, Panama, in Appendix 6C.

Creative Living 101

In these difficult financial times, a little ingenuity goes a long way.

Barbara Traynor, author of *Second Career Volunteer: A Passionate, Pennywise Approach to Retirement* (www.secondcareervolunteer.com), has an inventive approach:

> As an administrative assistant for 45-plus years and a single parent to boot, I thought I would have to work forever. Not so! In 2004, I received a fortuitous email stating there were *"organizations that supplement their staff with volunteers, offering free room and board in exchange for workplace skills."* I only need to get there? Considering I would rely completely on Social Security income, I began to rethink retirement.
>
> I discovered that *free* room and board translates to clean, comfortable, and private. I might have driven there solo, but upon arrival was welcomed into a multigenerational, multi-cultural community of like-minded volunteers. For example, at Heifer in Arkansas (www.heifer.org) I shared a house with other married and single volunteers: an equipped kitchen, washer and dryer, a living room comfortable for games, visitors, TV/DVD. Had my own bedroom and bathroom. Meal: a *huge* ranch lunch plus supplemental stipend. I was a receptionist, delivered mail, and helped out with accounting. Oh . . . I do know how to make coffee, too, but most staff members (male and female) in volunteer organizations do not consider that a woman's job.
>
> This unique lifestyle keeps mind and body healthy and active. I've volunteered in Alaska, Florida, Arkansas, and New Mexico, and my next trip is to Russell Cave National Monument in Alabama. In between volunteer stints, I have an in-law arrangement with my son and daughter-in-law: a one-bedroom apartment, with a separate entrance, in their home. We do interact; however, they need to have their lives and

I have mine. When I leave for an assignment, I simply walk out and shut the door!

Retirement with travel—within my budget. It's a win-win!

No in-law arrangement? No problem. Extended-stay hotels might fit the bill while you're between volunteer assignments. The cost can be fairly reasonable, and it often includes breakfast and Internet access. And, someone else is replacing your towels and cleaning up for you. Or maybe you just want to move around, bum off relatives and friends, and have no fixed address.

A study by Lee Lindquist demonstrated that living on a regular cruise ship such as those of the Royal Caribbean or Princess lines ends up costing about the same as paying for assisted living, assuming you don't need help for daily living activities like bathing and getting dressed. Think about it: staterooms tidied; all the food in the world, and you don't have to buy it, make it, or clean it up; entertainment and lectures; social support; and even a doctor on board. If you're a whiz at planning inexpensive cruises, you can live on the seas for less than $100 a day. An assisted-living facility averages $111 a day, but of course price varies by region. See the world, and leave home insurance, mortgages, upkeep, property taxes, food, entertainment, landscaping, and perhaps car costs behind on a ship? All aboard.

Living with a Twist

These days, there's a place for everyone. Here are examples of locations and lifestyles that are unique or special in some respect, sites that you might seek out if you have a specific background or interest:

A Community of the Faithful. Ave Maria (www.avemaria.com) is a developing new urbanism/master-planned/highly walkable community 45 miles west of Naples, Florida, that has its own Catholic college built by Tom Monaghan of Domino's Pizza fame; an imposing church that is centered in the square; a variety of housing styles, including a Del Webb active community with homes starting in the mid-$100,000s;

and everything is brand-spanking new. Its Web site says all faiths are welcome—amen to that.

Serving Others. Pilgrim Place (www.pilgrimplace.org) is an intentional community of about 320 residents in Claremont, California. The mission of Pilgrim Place is to "provide quality housing and services for persons who have served in careers in religious, charitable, and non-profit humanitarian organizations." Residents include Christians, Jews, and Buddhists.

Homesharing. We mentioned *homeshoring* or working from home in a previous chapter, but more than a half-million single women are *homesharing*: finding roommates to save money, to have company, and to pool resources. About 40 percent of women in an AARP survey said they would consider having a nonromantic roommate. Kate and Allie, anyone? Can there be challenges in working things out? You bet your sweet bippy (remember that phrase from *Laugh-In?*), but it could be a viable choice if you find the right match, kind of like getting a great college roommate. Of course you can check Craigslist and ask friends and neighbors, or you can access the National Shared Housing Resource Center (www.nationalsharedhousing.org) or www.homeshareprogram.org (unique to Pinellas County, Florida). Or be like Shirley and her sister, Doreen. After both of their spouses died, they decided to be roommates and have lived contentedly for the last five years. Jill D. and Colleen F. are friends from high school; after Jill's spouse died and Colleen and her husband split, the two moved into a two-bedroom apartment to share expenses. Two can live more cheaply than one.

Lesbian/Gay Communities. An estimated 2 million to 6 million lesbian, gay, bisexual, and transgender men and women (LGBT) in the United States are between the ages of 50 and 64, and an additional 1 to 3 million are over the age of 65. The idea of communities where gays and lesbians feel welcome and have social support and services as they age are the driving forces behind these communities.

A new LGBT community for older adults, providing independent living and continuing care services, is Fountain Grove Lodge (www.fountaingrovelodge.com).

An all-women community that bills itself as "Southwest Florida's premier lesbian destination" and is thriving is the Resort on Carefree Boulevard (www.resortoncb.com) in Fort Myers, Florida. Manufactured homes are available for under $200,000, and residents range in age from the early 40s to the mid-80s on this community's 50 acres.

Kathy H. moved to Carefree in 2003, "lured by the idea of living in a community of women. We are a gated community, which provides privacy and some sense of security. Additionally, there are many activities open to all members at the Clubhouse; our weekly calendar is full of sports, games, arts and educational activities, and we offer special events and guest performers throughout the year. Golfers, kayakers, birders, photographers, etc. outside of Carefree welcome everyone to join in their activities, so singles need never be bored or lonely. At just 278 lots, we are small enough to be acquainted with everyone and help is always available if someone is in need."

Emily asked that her specific lesbian communities remain anonymous and her last initial be omitted:

Having lived in two different lesbian communities for the past 20 years, I am interested in sharing my experiences, especially my last eight years as a single woman. I grew up in the turbulent 1960s, graduated from high school in 1964, went off to college in Kentucky, and was very affected by the civil rights and antiwar movements. From early on I wanted to live in a community/commune. In 1969 I spent a year as a volunteer in Texas teaching a preschool class and running an after-school program. There were seven of us, and it was the beginnings of seeing what a community of individuals can do. After a short three-year marriage and having had lesbian feelings since high school, with much anxiety I struck out on my own and went back to nursing school in 1974, and finally faced the fact that my lesbian feelings were not going away.

It was during my first relationship with a woman that we discovered what we felt was a lesbian paradise. We went to a lesbian community in the southeast United States for a weekend getaway at the beach and discovered that it was a community that had the same values and radical approach to living that I had always wanted. I spent 12 years there, from my mid-30s to mid-40s, sometimes in a relationship, other times not, but always feeling included and part of a group that was trying to live a much kinder, simpler, egalitarian, and consciously-aware life. This community became a life-altering experience for me.

By the mid-1990s I was drawn into caring for my mother, who was diagnosed with Alzheimer's; she moved in with my partner and me. We had to move out of the community to have a house big enough, and for eight years I lived in town, with my total focus revolving around working at the hospital and my mother's needs.

At age 56, I was once again single after a 15-year relationship and very much wanted to get back to living in a community. Some of my friends from the previous community contacted me about joining them for a new adventure on 400 acres of forested land they had found, again in the southeast United States. The size of this land would allow us to do some of the things we always wanted to do. My dream to live more simply and sustainably was finally within reach. Worried about how this would work with my mother, who was now in an assisted-living facility, I went in to see her and said, "Mom, we're going on an adventure and moving to the mountains close to your relatives." Much to my relief, as her memory was failing, she responded with "Yippee," and what a trouper she was as I got her settled into an assisted-living facility close to the new community.

That was in 2002, after I built my small, 800-square-foot home on two acres of wooded land. Being single and living alone for the first time in the woods, I had to get over the fears of owl sounds and coyotes. The most wonderful thing was the safety I felt living in a space where only women were my neighbors behind a locked entrance gate. What a joy to walk at night, under the stars and not be afraid. It didn't take long for me to see that this was once again a situation that I felt comfortable with, especially as a single woman. My friends from before said, "You'll be bored to tears," and how wrong they were. I need at least eight more hours in every day to get all I want done. This community is really special in that the couples are very open to socializing with the singles.

For most activities all are invited, including things like game night, movie night, kayak trips, bicycling, and whatever else we decide to do. Then there are always the meetings and interest groups like our sustainability group, our community garden, and working to maintain our fire-wise status with the state. We also meet regularly to discuss aging in place, and other lifestyle issues. I have grown to love my single life and the pleasure of coming back to my sweet home after an activity and just relaxing. At this point I really don't have the desire to live with another person and I find that many of my needs are being met with all the wonderful friends that I have here. The support I received from this community when my mother was in her last days was beyond belief. Even though at times we struggle with getting along with each other, it is well worth it and amazing how we persist in getting through. There is rarely a dull moment for me in this very alternative life I have chosen, and I have no regrets.

If you're looking for a gay-friendly city and not a designated community, Clintonville, Ohio, is close to the capital city, Columbus, and has a strong lesbian presence. Clintonville's proximity to the 50,000 students of The Ohio State University, considered gay-friendly by Campus Pride, is a major reason for the almost 7 percent LGBT population of the Columbus area.

City-data.com (www.city-data.com) ranks cities with populations of at least 5,000 by the largest number of self-reported unmarried female-female households. The assumption is that this would indicate lots of lesbian couples. Its top five: Northampton, Massachusetts; Decatur, Georgia; Russian River–Coastal, California; Vashon Island, Washington; and Eldorado at Santa Fe, New Mexico. For all 101 of these rankings, go to www.city-data.com/top2/c15.html.

Letter Carriers. If you're in good standing with the National Association of Letter Carriers (NALC), you might want to head over to the community called Nalcrest, an acronym for the National Association of Letter Carriers Retirement, Education, Security and Training, in central Florida. Go to www.nalc.org and click on "Nalcrest." Guess what? No pets allowed! Call Nalcrest at 863-696-1121. Rent a one-bedroom apartment from about $400 a month.

The Sky's the Limit. Amateur astronomers are drawn to Arizona Sky Village (www.arizonaskyvillage.com) in Portal, Arizona. Dark heavens and a love of the natural world is the driving force behind this community. Fractional-share haciendas at $36,000 a month are available. You could say their prices are sky-high, but perhaps it's an option for some. Granite Gap (www.granitegap.com), with the same developer, has RV pads and cabins available. The closest cities are Animas and Lordsburg, New Mexico. The Web site also gives the location by coordinates—guess that's what you need to really be away from it all so you can see those glorious heavens.

Military Communities. For those who have served their country, it's now your turn to be served! Air Force Village (www.afvillages.org) in the wonderful city of San Antonio, Texas, is open to retired and honorably separated officers of all military branches and their spouses, widows, and widowers (62 and older). There are actually two villages, both CCRCs. Another community for retired military is Patriot's Landing (www.patriotslanding.com), located in the beautiful Pacific Northwest between Tacoma and Olympia, Washington.

Condo Ships. If "wanderlust" is your middle name, the World (www.aboardtheworld.com) might be the ticket. You could stop in Greenland, Brazil, and Antarctica as the ship leisurely circumnavigates the earth, and when onboard, play tennis and golf (biodegradable balls, of course), go to the spa, shop, or eat at one of the four restaurants. Life doesn't come cheap on the *World*, however. Studios start around $600,000 and suites can escalate to $14 million. Monthly fees are hefty, starting at around $20,000 a month. There are 165 residences. You do have the option to rent or to try out this lifestyle on a more limited basis. Although there has been talk of additional condo ships on the horizon (pun intended), the *World* is the only one that is a reality.

Multigenerational Communities. Almost 50 million Americans, or 16 percent of the U.S. population, live in homes with at least two generations of adults, according to the Pew Research Center. In many cases, this is an informal arrangement, but some forward-looking developers are getting into the act, building communities and homes that work for all ages. Del Webb is a leader in this area, with several developments designed for intergenerational living. In some cases, separate active-adult communities are incorporated into a larger all-ages master-planned community, such as the Falls at Eagle Crest inside the Ridge at Eagle Crest in Washington, or Windsor Lakes inside The Woodlands in Texas. See "More 411" below for several multigenerational communities.

Sure, you can convert a basement or garage into a living space. But what about creating a "granny flat" or a *casita*—a self-contained cottage in the back yard? You need to check out the zoning requirements. It's a way to generate income if the person living there is paying rent, live independently but with your family, or accommodate aging parents.

Manufactured-Home Communities. The term "mobile home" isn't used officially anymore. That moniker applies to homes built prior to June 15, 1976, before HUD instituted stricter building standards for factory-built homes. Big pluses of manufactured homes are cost, which is often 20 percent to 30 percent less than a site-built home, and the shorter time it takes to build since there are no pesky weather delays because they're built inside a facility. Many manufactured-home communities offer the same kinds of amenities—pools, tennis courts, golf, fitness centers— as do communities with site-built homes; they may also be age-restricted. In some cases, you purchase the lot; in other cases, you rent the lot. Manufactured homes frequently don't hold their value over time.

Live at the Racetrack. Do you feel the need for speed? If so, check out the 5-plus-acre lots at Competition Ridge (www .competitionridgeaz.com), located between Lake Havasu City and Kingman in western Arizona. It's a private car-racing community where all track time is free. Lots start at $150,000.

Martha Stewartville. If you're a fan of the domestic diva, you can live in a community influenced by Martha's own homes in the Northeast. KB Homes (www.kbhome.com/martha/) has teamed with Stewart to create communities in Florida and California. Homes start around $340,000 in Eastvale, California and around $270,000 in Orlando, Florida.

The Great Outdoors. Some women crave space and tranquility. Here is Jolene T.'s story about choosing her retirement location:

I recently retired from a 30-year career as an air traffic control specialist. I am originally from northeastern Ohio and moved to Texas as a result of marriage and my (ex) husband's job. Forced to retire by age 56 (federal law) and divorced 12 years ago, I'm ready to face new challenges and meet new people.

I have always loved the outdoors and activities such as hiking, camping, and gardening; missed the seasons; and wanted to move where I can have all of the above and enjoy a more relaxed, laid-back lifestyle with people who feel the same. Western North Carolina offers me all that I am looking for as far as outdoor activities, scenery, and culture without the harshness of long winters and traffic congestion. My goal is to have a timber-frame type of home on a couple of wooded acres outside any major city, but close enough to good medical care.

My friends wonder why I want to move where I have no family or friends, but all of my friends have boyfriends or husbands, kids or grandkids and now . . . jobs! So time with them is limited at best. Yes, it is nice to have someone around when

I need a ride somewhere or to be picked up after a surgical procedure, but I plan on finding a good church family, a new gym, and hopefully finding a fun, less stressful part-time job to meet new people and develop a new support group. I don't worry about living alone; I have been doing that for the last 12 years. What I am concerned about is finding good handymen, plumbers, electricians, a/c techs, etc.

Since I have no ties anywhere (we never had kids), it should be easy for me to be able to choose my ideal spot. What did I do? I looked at various places out West and, while I love the lore and feel of the West, every time I go back East I feel that that is where I belong. I am lucky that so far I have my health and the benefit of a good pension plus various other investments, so it is silly for me not to try to live my dream, although I worry about making the right decision and if I have thought of everything. I do not have a lot of close friends and I have a very, very small family so I personally have limited sources to contact for advice. I did lots and LOTS of driving around all of western North Carolina to try to experience the area firsthand. I attended city and county functions to get a feel for the communities. Basically it all came down to a gut feeling and I loved how I felt every time I went to Waynesville, North Carolina, and the surrounding areas. That feeling was really important to me.

I found myself going back to Sunset Falls at Bald Creek. The biggest drawback to that development, I thought, was that it was too far out of town. That's how it felt last year when I visited, but after spending three straight months in western North Carolina to try it out, it actually felt normal and a way of life that I decided I could embrace for the foreseeable future. I met some wonderful and helpful people and really started to feel a part of the community.

I purchased an almost-four-acre lot at Sunset Falls and will start building my home as soon as my house in Texas sells. I can't wait to get back to Waynesville!

Equestrian Communities. Cordillera Ranch (www.cordillera ranch.com), about 15 miles from San Antonio in the lovely

Hill Country of Texas, has an equestrian club on its 8,600 acres. This is one of seven clubs at the Ranch, including rod and gun, tennis and swim, river, social, and golf. Residences start under $200,000 and exceed $10 million; lots start around $100,000. The Golden Ocala Golf and Equestrian Club (www.goldenocala.com) in Ocala, Florida, has homes beginning around $400,000 and rocketing to the several millions.

Hangar-homes. If you'd like to literally fly home, landing your plane on an airstrip in your community and parking your plane in a hangar right next to your home, you'll find a number of airport communities, including Mountain Air (www.mountainaircc.com) in Burnside, North Carolina, and Fox Harb'r (www.foxharbr.com) in Wallace, Nova Scotia. At Spruce Creek Country Club in Port Orange, Florida (www.fly-in.com/country_club.html), homes (not including an individual hangar for your plane) begin around $150,000 and go up from there (like the planes). See www.livingwithyourplane.com for a detailed listing of these communities.

Golf. At my last golf outing, I was jokingly told that *golf* is an acronym for "gentlemen only; ladies forbidden." We haven't reached parity yet, but about 22 percent of golfers are female. If hitting that little ball is your passion, consider a community in or close to one of the best golf courses for women. About 15 percent of regular golfers live in a golf-course community. See "Lists, Lists, Lists" below for the top 10 women's golf courses. Or you could consider World Golf Village (www.worldgolfrealestate.com) in St. Augustine, Florida, which has courses designed by Palmer, Nicklaus, Snead, and Sarazen; the World Golf Hall of Fame; and even golf-themed restaurants. The community has condos, patio homes, single-family homes, and an active-adult community, with prices starting at $200,000.

Health and Wellness Communities. You can immerse yourself in all that the famous Canyon Ranch (www.canyonranch .com) has to offer. The Arizona-based company offers a very walkable Miami Beach, Florida, condo/hotel location with one-bedrooms units beginning around $325,000.

Calling All Oenophiles. For those into wine, the master-planned community of New Kent Vineyards (www.newkentvineyards .com) has a winery. The community is located about 20 miles from Richmond and 25 miles from Williamsburg, Virginia. Wooded lots begin at $150,000.

RV Home Yet? The Recreation Vehicle Industry Association (RVIA) estimates that between 400,000 and 800,000 people live on the road full time in their RV. Does this lifestyle intrigue you? Here is Laurel K.'s story:

After 15 years of marriage, I divorced and began again the single life. It was hectic caring for two boys, working, and attending law school, and I had owned a small RV for a short time while working. I retired at the age of 66, sold my home, and bought a 32-foot fifth-wheel travel trailer. On the day I retired, I put the two cats in the trailer and took off for the Southwest.

The first years I traveled and saw the sights; I went between California and Ohio, where grandchildren were located, and managed to see much of the West. I stayed in private RV parks and taught water aerobics, took line dancing, and enjoyed whatever fun events were being offered.

Then, I had the urge to do more. I did not need the money and did not want to have to file income taxes, so I decided to volunteer. I wanted to do something that was beneficial to the parks since I enjoyed visiting both state and local parks for many years. In my travels I learned that there were Web sites, such as www.nps.gov (click on "Get Involved"), where I could apply for volunteer positions.

I've worked as a volunteer interpretive ranger, in the visitor center, and on the trails of various parks. I like the lifestyle because it fits my personality. I enjoy meeting people, not only from the United States but also from around the world, and learning about new places. The hardest part is leaving new friends behind, knowing that you will probably never see them again, but I also know that in a short while I will meet new people who will become my friends. I will continue this lifestyle until I am unable to drive the trailer from park to park. I am sure even when I hang up the keys, I will continue to volunteer in the closest park.

Shakespeare Groupie. The Oregon Shakespeare Festival offers almost 800 performances annually in the just-about-perfect small town of Ashland. Ashland is tucked in a valley surrounded by mountains and boasts art, beauty, dining, shopping, rivers, and an educated population, with one in five residents having an advanced degree. The city is extremely pedestrian friendly with an average "walkscore" (see Chapter 5) of 70 and some areas with scores as high as 97. What's not to like in Ashland? Maybe the 10 inches of snow per year, but it usually melts by midday, sort of like in Camelot. Homes are on the pricey side, at a median of $375,000.

Start Your Own Community. An "intentional community" is one that is based on ideals or common interests, and you can find a blueprint for forming one at the Fellowship for Intentional Community (www.ic.org). Click on "Starting a Community" under "Useful Articles."

Lists, Lists, Lists

We all love lists. The Top 10 . . . , Best of . . . , Worst of . . . , 10 Most . . . National Public Radio even has a list about why we love lists. Not surprisingly, lists about where to retire are plentiful (you already read about them in the sections on city living and master-planned communities). Here are a few more lists that might appeal to you:

- **Top 10 Best Places to Live (and Retire) Affordably in the United States** (AARP): Gainesville, Georgia; Columbus, Indiana; Harrisburg, Pennsylvania; Portland, Maine; Ithaca, New York; Tulsa, Oklahoma; Midland, Texas; Winchester, Virginia; Wenatchee, Washington; Cheyenne, Wyoming.
- **Where to Retire If You Love the Outdoors, Live the Good Life, for Less,** and **10 Great Small Cities for Retirement** (Go to www.aarp.org and click on "Home and Family" then "Livable Communities.")

- **Best Places to Retire Abroad** (AARP): Buenos Aires, Argentina; Corozal, Belize; Central Valley, Atenas, Costa Rica; Languedoc-Roussillon, France; Le Marche, Italy; Puerto Vallarta Region, Mexico; Granada, Nicaragua; Boquete, Panama; Cascais, Portugal; Costa del Sol, Spain.
- **Best College Towns** (cnnmoney.com): Durham, North Carolina (Duke); Hanover, New Hampshire (Dartmouth); Lexington, Kentucky (University of Kentucky): Prescott, Arizona (Yavapai College); Bellingham, Washington (Western Washington University); Boise, Idaho (Boise State University); St. Petersburg, Florida (Eckerd College); Huntsville, Alabama (University of Alabama Huntsville); Austin, Texas (University of Texas at Austin); and Tucson, Arizona (University of Tucson).
- **10 Best Cities to Find a Job** (Ajilon Professional Staffing): Minneapolis–St. Paul, Minnesota; Austin, Texas; Salt Lake City, Utah; Boston, Massachusetts; Milwaukee, Wisconsin; Richmond, Virginia; Raleigh-Durham, North Carolina; Baltimore, Maryland; Pittsburgh, Pennsylvania; and Dallas, Texas.
- **10 Bargain Retirement Spots** (*U.S. News & World Report*): Portland, Oregon; Tallahassee, Florida; Tucson, Arizona; Wake Forest, North Carolina; Cathedral City, California; Wahiawa, Hawaii; Weatherford, Texas; Dover, Delaware; Sycamore, Illinois; and St. Charles, Maryland.
- **Most Singles 55 and Older** (*U.S. News & World Report*): Pittsfield, Massachusetts; Florence, South Carolina; Vineland-Millville-Bridgeton, New Jersey; Jackson, Mississippi; Springfield, Massachusetts; Miami–Fort Lauderdale–Pompano Beach, Florida; Eureka-Arcata-Fortuna, California; Memphis, Tennessee; and New Orleans, Louisiana. (Keep in mind that if you're looking for a future husband, the women often outnumber the men by a hefty margin—almost 2:1 in Pittsfield, for example.)
- **Top Places to Retire** (www.topretirements.com): Asheville, North Carolina; Sarasota, Florida; Austin, Texas; Venice, Florida; Prescott, Arizona; Fort Myers, Florida; Beaufort, South Carolina; Paris, Tennessee; San Diego, California; and

Green Valley, Arizona. (These are the top 10 of the site's "100 Best Places to Retire" based on page visits.)

- **10 Great Cities for Older Singles** (AARP): San Francisco, California; Boston, Massachusetts; Baltimore, Maryland; Minneapolis–St. Paul, Minnesota; St. Louis, Missouri; New York, New York; Cleveland, Ohio; Philadelphia, Pennsylvania; Pittsburgh, Pennsylvania; Milwaukee, Wisconsin.
- **Top Golf Courses for Women** (*Women's Golf* magazine): Pine Needles Lodge and Golf Club (Southern Pines, North Carolina); South Course at the Boulders Resort and Golden Door Spa (Carefree, Arizona); Old Macdonald at Bandon Dunes Golf Resort (Bandon, Oregon); Ocean Links at Amelia Island Plantation (Amelia Island, Florida); Running Y Ranch (Klamath Falls, Oregon); Seaside at Sea Islands Resorts (St. Simons Island, Georgia); Champions at LPGA International (Daytona Beach, Florida); China Creek at The Golf Club at Newcastle (Newcastle, Washington); Plantation at Kingsmill Resort & Spa (Williamsburg, Virginia); and East/North at Grand Cypress Golf Club (Orlando, Florida).

Whew! Lots of info and lots of choices. One community or lifestyle doesn't work for everyone, nor should it. The potential great locations for single women can't be all-inclusive, but perhaps you see yourself in one or more of these places, and thus have a good jumping-off point. Or maybe you'll feel more certain than ever that you should age in place. In the "Dollars and Sense" chapter, we'll address how taxes might affect your choice of retirement locations as well. But, first, let's take a look at a variety of "connections."

More 411

General Web sites for Finding a Place (many offer free newsletters):

www.aarp.org (click on "Home and Family" then "Livable Communities")

www.activeadultliving.com

www.bestretirementspots.com

www.golfcoursehome.net (you can search for other types of communities as well)

www.greatretirementspots.com

www.privatecommunities.com (search by state or by desired lifestyle)

www.retirementliving.com (good newsletter; part of site is restricted to paying members)

www.retirenet.com (also has a fun, easy quiz to help you locate your "spot")

www.topretirements.com (interactive and constantly updated)

Some Specific Active-Adult Communities to Consider (showing lowest-priced homes; prices can rise to $1 million or more):

Del Webb Orlando (find through www.delwebb.com): homes from $155,000; or contact Realtor Susan Melton (she also lives in this Del Webb community) at susan@thetropicalsun-team.com.

Pebble Creek (www.robson.com), in Goodyear, Arizona: homes from the low $200,000s.

Sun City Hilton Head (a Del Webb community in Bluffton, South Carolina): homes from $160,000.

The Villages (www.thevillages.com), in central Florida: all price points (manufactured pre-owned from $55,000 to estate homes for $850,000).

Victoria Gardens (www.sheaflorida.com) in DeLand, Florida, home to Stetson University (2,200 students): homes begin under $200,000. Contact connie.moore@sheahomes.com.

Active-Adult Communities (Developers):

Del Webb/Pulte (www.delwebb.com or 888-717-9777)

K. Hovnanian (www.khov.com or 732-737-7800)

Robson (www.robson.com or 800-732-9949)

Shea Homes (www.sheahomes.com or 800-685-6494) (active communities are under their Trilogy brand)

The Villages (www.thevillages.com or 800-245-1081)

Some Specific Traditional Neighborhood Developments (TNDs) or New-Urbanism Communities to Consider:

- Florida: Baldwin Park (www.baldwinparkfl.com) in Orlando. Rent a pet-friendly apartment for $1,200 a month or purchase a residence from the $270,000s to $1 million; Haile Plantation (www.haileguide.com) in Gainesville, five miles from the University of Florida, home of the revered Florida Gators. Residences under $200,000.
- Maryland: Kentlands (www.kentlandsusa.com) is in Gaithersburg, a suburb of Washington, DC.; Rockville Town Square (www.rockvilletownsquare.com) is in Rockville, north of DC, where you can walk to the Metro. Rent a one-bedroom from $1,600 a month and you can lease to own a condo. There are good employment opportunities since Rockville is the seat for affluent Montgomery County, many bio-techs are located in the vicinity along with the U.S. Food and Drug Administration and National Institutes of Health, and the Marriott headquarters is in nearby Bethesda. Not to mention adjacent Washington, with its more-resistant-to-the-downturn economy due to the federal government.
- North Carolina: Birkdale Village (www.birkdalevillage .net) north of Charlotte in Huntersville, where you can live above the shops and walk to the movies and retail stores. One-bedroom apartments rent for around $700 a month and three-bedroom townhomes rent for up to $2,200 a month.
- Oregon: NorthWest Crossing (www.northwestcrossing.com) in Bend is a perfect place if you love the great outdoors, beautiful mountains, and a charming downtown. Homesites start around $80,000, and homes start around $200,000.
- South Carolina: Daniel Island (www.danielisland.com). Airport, beaches, and historic Charleston are all within a

15-mile drive of this 4,000-acre community dripping with amenities, 23 miles of shoreline, and a wide variety of housing styles, with condos under $200,000 to homes over $5 million, and homesites beginning around $160,000. Rentals, including apartments, are also available from around $1,000 a month.

A Few Other Specific Master-Planned Communities Worth Considering:

- Ballantyne (www.ballantynenc.com) is a newer 2,000-acre planned "live, work, and play" community, considered a southern suburb of Charlotte, North Carolina. It has more than 12,000 residents and a variety of housing styles, including apartments with pricing from $800 a month, to condos/townhomes from $100,000 to estate homes from around $5 million.
- Hammock Beach (www.hammockbeach.com) is a 2,000-acre gated, oceanfront community south of St. Augustine, Florida, with golf, tennis, a marina, spa, pools, and other amenities (disclosure—I live here). Villas, condos, and single-family homes are available from $219,000 to over $2 million; homesites and rentals are available as well.

University-Linked Retirement Communities (from independent living to skilled care unless otherwise noted):

- Kendal Corporation (www.kendal.org) has partnered with such colleges as Dartmouth (New Hampshire), Oberlin and Denison (Ohio), Cornell University and Ithaca College (New York), and Washington and Lee/Virginia Military Academy (Virginia).
- Village at Penn State (www.villageatpennstate.com).
- University Commons at the University of Michigan (www.universitycommons.org). Independent living only.
- The Allegro at College Harbor (www.allegroliving.com), next to Eckerd College in St. Petersburg, Florida.

Living Aboard:

- www.cruisingworld.com (all things boats, including living aboard)
- www.liveaboardliving.com (all about living aboard; woman-created site)
- www.livingaboard.com (written by those living life aboard)

Living Abroad:

- Escape Artist (www.escapeartist.com). Living, working, and buying property overseas.
- Peddicord, Kathleen. *How to Retire Overseas: Everything You Need to Know to Live Well (for Less) Abroad.* New York: Plume, 2011.
- Sluder, Lan. *Easy Belize: How to Live, Retire, Work and Buy Property in Belize, the English Speaking Frost Free Paradise on the Caribbean Coast.* Create Space, 2010.
- www.belizefirst.com (includes retirement and relocation information).
- www.liveandinvestoverseas.com (Kathleen Peddicord's site).
- www.retiringsingles.com (if you're "a single baby boomer with a World view"—more than 200 members over the age of 45).

Multigenerational Living:

- Arroyo Grande at Anthem Parkside; Fireside at Desert Ridge; Fireside at Noreterra; Parkside at Anthem at Merrill Ranch. These are all in Arizona, with Parkside homes beginning in the low $100,000s. Find more details at www.delwebb.com.

RV Living:

- www.lonersonwheels.com
- www.rvingwomen.org
- www.womenrv.com

Pocket Communities:

- Chapin, Ross. *Pocket Neighborhoods: Creating Small-Scale Community in a Large-Scale World.* Newtown: Taunton Press, 2011.

Appendix 6A: Continuing Care Retirement Community Checklist*

First Impression

- Do you like the facility's location and outward appearance?
- Is the facility convenient for frequent visits by family and friends?
- Is the facility near a shopping and entertainment complex?
- Can the resident access a medical complex easily?
- Is public transportation available/accessible?
- Are you welcomed with a warm greeting from the staff?
- Does the staff address residents by their names and interact with them during your tour?
- Do you notice the residents socializing with one another and do they appear content?
- Can you talk with residents about how they like living there and about the staff?
- Is the staff appropriately dressed, friendly, and outgoing?
- Do the staff members treat each other in a professional manner?
- Are visits with the residents encouraged and welcome at any time?
- What percentage of the apartments has been rented and is occupied?
- Is there a waiting list? If so, how long do they estimate it will take to be admitted?

Living Area and Accommodations

- Is the floor plan well designed and easy to follow?
- Are doorways, hallways, and rooms accommodating to wheelchairs and walkers?
- Are elevators available for those unable to use stairways and handrails to aid in walking?

---

*Reprinted with permission from www.carepathways.com. (See additional checklists under the "Long-Term Care" tab on the site.)

- Are floors of a nonskid material and carpets conducive for safe walking?
- Does the residence have good lighting, sprinklers, and clearly marked exits?
- Is the residence clean, free of odors, and appropriately heated/cooled?
- What is the facility's means of security if a resident wanders?
- Are the common areas in general attractive, comfortable, and clean?
- Is there an outside courtyard or patio for residents and visitors, and can they garden?
- Does the residence provide ample security, and is there an emergency evacuation plan?
- Are there different sizes and types of units/housing available with optional floor plans?
- Are single units available and/or double occupancy units for sharing with another person?
- Does residence have furnished/unfurnished rooms? What is provided, or what can residents bring?
- May residents decorate their own rooms? Is there adequate storage space?
- Is a 24-hour emergency response system accessible from the unit with own lockable door?
- Are bathrooms private with handicapped accommodations for wheelchairs and walkers?
- Do all units have a telephone and cable TV, and how is billing handled?
- Does the kitchen unit have refrigerator/sink/cooking element and can food be kept in the units?
- May residents smoke in their units, or are there designated public areas?

Moving In/Contracts and Finances

- What's involved with the moving in/out process? How is the initial needs assessment done?
- Does the assessment process include the resident, family, and facility staff along with the physician?

- Is there a written plan for the care of each resident, is there an ongoing process for assessing a resident's need for services, and how often are those needs evaluated?
- What kinds of contracts are available to you? The CCRC contract is a legal agreement between you (the consumer) and a continuing care retirement community. This agreement generally secures living accommodations and services, including health care services, over the long term. Determine what fee structure and contract option best suits you.
- The three most common types of CCRC agreements are:
  - Extensive contract: This offers unlimited long-term nursing care for little or no substantial increase in your usual monthly payments.
  - Modified contract: This includes a specified amount of long-term nursing care beyond which you are responsible for payment.
  - Fee-for-service: You pay full daily rates for all long-term nursing care required.
- What is the payment schedule and can the residents own or rent their unit?
- What is the basic entrance charge, and what is included for that fee? What charges are extra?
- How much is the monthly fee? How often can it be increased and for what reasons? Is there a limit on the amount of increase per year? What is the history on monthly fee increases?
- Are refunds or rate reductions ever granted? Under what conditions?
- Are any portions of the charges covered under long-term-care insurance that the resident may already have or be eligible for? Are any charges duplicated?
- What happens if a couple moves into an apartment and then one of them must go to the nursing home or dies? Will the other one be allowed to stay in the same apartment, and how will this affect rates?
- What happens if someone wants to leave after just a few weeks or months, or if they die? Is any portion of the entrance fee refunded to their estate?

- What type of health and medical coverage is included in the entrance and monthly fees? Are dental work, vision exams, and routine wellness checkups included?
- What determines when a resident is moved to a nursing care facility and who decides?
- Will the facility guarantee that nursing home care will be available on the premises, or nearby, when needed? What rates will residents be charged for such care?
- Do billing, payment, and credit policies seem fair and reasonable? May a resident handle his or her own finances with staff assistance if able? Must a family member/outside party be designated?

Health/Personal Care/Services

- What type of health care and personal care services are available? Does the facility have both short- and long-term services, such as routine physical and dental examinations and pharmacy services, as well as skilled nursing and therapy services?
- Can the facility provide a list of available services and are residents and families involved in developing the service agreement? Who provides these services, and what are their qualifications?
- Is staff available to provide 24-hour assistance with activities of daily living (ADLs) if needed? ADLs include dressing, eating, mobility, hygiene, grooming (bathing, toileting, incontinence).
- Does the residence have programs for Alzheimer's, other dementias, and other specialized areas?
- How are medical emergencies handled? Does the residence have a clearly stated procedure for responding to medical emergencies? Is there an arrangement with a nearby hospital?
- Will the staff dispense medication to able residents? If so, what are the dispenser's qualifications? Will they monitor residents taking medications?
- Are housekeeping, linen service, and personal laundry included in the fees, or are they available at an additional charge? Are on-site laundry facilities available and convenient?

- Does the residence provide transportation to doctors' offices, the hairdresser, shopping, and other activities desired by residents, and can it be arranged on short notice?
- Are pharmacy, barber/beautician, and/or physical therapy services offered on-site?

Social and Recreational

- What kinds of group/individual recreational activities are offered, and who schedules them?
- Is there an organized activities program with a posted daily schedule of events?
- Does the facility schedule trips or other events off premises?
- Are the resident activity (social) areas appropriate and desirable to the prospective resident?
- Do residents participate in activities outside of the residence in the neighboring community?
- Are there supplies for social activities and hobbies (games, cards, crafts, computers, gardening)?
- Are religious services held on the premises? Does the residence arrange for transportation to nearby services?
- Do volunteers and family members come into the residence to participate in or conduct programs?
- Does the residence create a sense of community by allowing residents to participate in certain activities or perform simple chores for the group as a whole?
- Are there fitness facilities, as well as regularly scheduled exercise classes?
- Are residents' pets allowed in the residence? Does the facility have pets, and who cares for them?

Staff

- Do the staff members have professional backgrounds in continuing care and geriatrics fields?
- What are the hiring procedures and requirements for eligibility? Are criminal-background checks, references, and certifications required?
- Is there a staff-training program, and what does it entail?

- Is staff courteous to residents and to one another? Are responses for assistance timely?
- Is the administrator or appropriate staff person generally available to answer questions or discuss problems, and would you be comfortable dealing with them daily?
- Does the facility have a volunteer program, or is it affiliated with any student clinical program?

Food

- What are the meal programs? Does the residence provide three nutritionally balanced meals a day, seven days a week, and how does the menu vary from meal to meal?
- What about special diets; does a qualified dietitian plan or approve menus?
- Are residents involved in menu planning, and may they request special foods?
- Are common dining areas available, and when can residents eat meals in their units?
- Does the dining room environment encourage residents to relax, socialize, and enjoy their food?
- Are meals provided only at set times, or is there some flexibility? Are snacks available?
- How many meals are included in the fee? If a resident becomes ill, is tray service available?
- Can residents have guests dine with them for an additional fee? Is there a private dining room for special events and occasions?

Licensure and Certification

- Is the facility accredited by the Continuing Care Accreditation Commission? (Accreditation is not required, and not all CCRCs are evaluated.)
- Is the nursing center Medicare or Medicaid certified?
- What reputation does the facility have in the community? How long has it been in business? Is it in good financial health? Does the facility follow generally accepted accounting principles?

- If the facility is sponsored by a nonprofit organization and managed under contract with a commercial firm, what are the conditions of that contract?
- Is there a resident council or organization through which residents and families have a means of voicing their views about the management of the community?

Appendix 6B: Should You Retire Overseas?*

Here are some questions to consider if you're thinking of whether—or where—to retire overseas.

When It Comes to Climate:

- Do you enjoy a change of seasons?
- Would you be unhappy without regular sunshine?
- Do you mind rain?
- Can you handle heat? Humidity?
- Do you prefer a varying length of day?

When It Comes to Infrastructure:

- Do you lose your cool if you can't send an email the first time every time you try?
- Does your work require reliable Internet service 24 hours a day, seven days a week?
- Would you mind living on a dirt road?
- Would you mind your road access being temporarily cut off during the rainy season?
- Do you need U.S. television?
- Are you afraid of the dark? In much of the world, electricity isn't 100 percent reliable.
- Would you be comfortable owning a car and driving yourself around in a new country? If not, think about places where you could afford a full-time driver or where a car is unnecessary.

---

*Reprinted with permission from internationalliving.com.

- Would you want to travel outside the country often, either to visit family back home or generally? If so, consider how far it is to the nearest international airport.
- Would you be unhappy without your favorite comfort foods? If so, consider places with access to international-standard grocery stores.

When It Comes to Access "Back Home":

- Do you have children or grandchildren you want to see regularly?
- Are you going to be keeping a home in the country where you're moving from?
- Will you have some ongoing business concerns in other countries?

When It Comes to Language:

- Do you speak a second language?
- Are you terrified at the thought of learning a new one?

When It Comes to How You Like to Spend Your Time:

- What's your favorite thing to do on a Friday night?
- How would you rather spend a free Sunday afternoon—in a museum or taking a long walk in the woods?
- How regularly do you want to be able to dine out? To watch a first-run movie in English? To visit an art gallery or attend the theater?
- What would you like to see from your bedroom window? The ocean? A mountainside covered with wildflowers? A vineyard? A busy street scene?

When It Comes to Taxes:

- From where will you derive your income in retirement?
- Will you have earned, pension, dividend, interest, rental, or capital gains income to account for? The source of your income has a lot to do with your ultimate tax liability, especially if you're an American.

When It Comes to Safety:

- Are you moving with children?
- Do protests bother you? The French, for example, seem to assemble to make a point at the drop of a beret.
- Do you speak the local language? If you do, situations that might otherwise seem frightening won't bother you. If you don't, you may sometimes feel uncomfortable even if there's really no cause for worry.
- Have you traveled much internationally? If yes, again, you're probably better prepared for what otherwise might seem worrisome situations.

Appendix 6C: Going Solo in Panama by Louise O.

After a successful 23-year career in the fine-wine business, I decided to begin a new chapter in my life and moved to Panama at age 57, alone, in 2007. I had always been an adventurous person, and wished to live among like-minded individuals. Burned out on my job, tired of the mass consumerism in the United States, and facing the high costs of retiring early in the States, I set my sights on Panama. Many Internet sites had much to offer in my initial research. The name of Boquete kept popping up. I decided it was time to "put my boots on the ground" and go take a look!

By the time I returned home two weeks later, I knew I would move forward with my plan to retire in Boquete in this lovely, small, green country of Panama. I drew up a plus/minus sheet with all the good (location, price) and negative (that "hype" factor again, and price!). The result was a gated community 12 kilometers south of Boquete. Hacienda Los Molinos (www.losmolinos.com.pa), at 2,400 feet elevation, is a bit warmer and less damp than Boquete itself, at 3,400 feet. Elevation is everything near the equator.

Back in the United States, I started the due diligence required to obtain a *pensionado* visa. There are several types of permanent residency options offered by Panama's government. The value of the *pensionado* visa is the relative ease in obtaining it (one needs to prove a certain minimum monthly income from a pension or other source) and the discounts offered under this visa's umbrella (hotel, air transport, prescription meds, etc.). Eight months later

I returned to find construction on my home had begun; this second two-week visit was spent dealing with the immigration visa, checking out the Boquete area more fully and meeting some helpful people, including several of my neighbors-to-be at Los Molinos. This was the last time I would see Panama until my permanent move eight months later! This arrangement worked for me; I was secure in my decision, but readers might consider spending a longer time making this relocation decision; I would suggest renting for six months, part of that time during the rainy season.

After I arrived in late October 2007, I spent the next five months in a rental, got to know Boquete better, made some friends and gently pushed along the last phase of home construction. So, where is this place called Boquete where I have decided to hang my hat for perhaps the rest of my days? Located in the western highlands of Panama, it sits in a perpetually green valley of flowers, coffee *fincas* (farms), surrounded by mountains with the majestic Volcan Baru (at 11,400 feet the highest in Panama) dominating the landscape. The free-flowing (for now, depending on planned hydroelectric schemes) Caldera River rushes through the town, sometimes uncontrollably (as in the floods of November 2008).

A six-hour drive east along the Pan American Highway (or a 50-minute flight from David) is the capital of the republic, Panama City. A half-hour south is the provincial capital, David (pronounced "Daveed"), with the regional airport, hospitals, *tiendas* (stores) where we all visit at least once a month to stock up on necessities unavailable in little Boquete. . . . David is hot and humid at sea level, but what would we Boquetenian expats do without our Price Smart store (like Costco in the United States), the big Rey supermarket, the new Conway store (like a Target store), the car repair shops, the little Chinese store where one can buy rice wine vinegar, the movie theater, the furniture options (although limited), the big Arrocha pharmacy, and the hardware stores? It's not a particularly pretty place, David, but it is a godsend.

There are empty, wide Pacific beaches less than an hour from Boquete. Weather in Boquete is a constant spring-like 65 to 80 degrees. The seven-month rainy season lasts from May to December, with beautiful mornings, storms arriving in late afternoon (and they can be torrential), and calm nights. It takes about one or two full rainy seasons to realize (as many of us do) that the preferred season is that "green" one. Sure, in the dry season, you can confidently plan a late afternoon outdoor fiesta, but the wind can be fierce, and the sky is often smoky with slash-and-burn agricultural fires.

Boquete has a large and active expat community, mostly Americans, but also a sizable number of Canadians, Europeans, and a few South Americans. There are many and varied ways to become involved in the community, something I needed as I had no plan to just sit and soak up the sun (or rain) in my retirement. Soon I got involved in charity work, and currently I am chairwoman of a food program assisting nearby families. There is a chapter of Rotary International, a Spanish-language chapter of the Lions Club, a new hospice program, and several organizations that offer valuable volunteer opportunities.

On the social side, Boquete offers an endless round of activities. There is a nine-hole golf course, a bridge club, yoga and tai chi classes, two Spanish-language schools, two spas, a gardening club, a couple of good bakeries, a cooking school, a craft center/gallery, options for those interested in alternative health, two theater groups, dozens of restaurants ranging from *típico* Panamanian to first-rate dining, a single-women's group (the Boquete Chicas, of which I am a member), birding and hiking groups, and several active church groups. We have a unique support system in Boquete for the expats . . . every Tuesday morning there is a meeting with guest speakers covering all sorts of topics of interest to newcomers and established foreign residents alike, and some locals.

Most expats have a forwarding address in Miami, Florida, to which mail from the United States or elsewhere is sent, with ongoing transport to Boquete within five days or less. The company I use charges $39 per quarter for mail delivery to Boquete. There is no home delivery of mail. Speaking of communications, Panama is particularly advanced for its Internet connections; there are two or more competing companies; my TV/wireless Internet monthly charge is around $75, and it is 90 percent reliable (except during big storms that knock out the power). Keeping in touch with family and friends in the United States via telephone is generally available with the purchase of Skype minutes or a Magic Jack; both operate over the Internet.

An important expense to consider is health care. The nearest hospitals are in David, and they offer private insurance plans costing about $550 annually for a single individual. Care is excellent, although major surgery or cancer treatments are usually referred to Panama City. I broke my hand in a fall last year; the emergency room visit, x-rays, orthopedic doctor's visit, cast, and pain medications cost about $70 with my insurance plan. Compare that to similar treatment in a U.S. hospital!

Full and comprehensive automobile insurance is a must in a country with hazardous driving conditions . . . The roads are fine; it's the drivers on them that make for an adventure every time you get behind the wheel. My car insurance runs about $575 a year.

I built a modest home of about 2,000 square feet on an average-sized lot in this gated community of Los Molinos. With everything— the lot, construction and upgrades, landscaping, and furnishings—I spent about $205,000. This was in 2007. My monthly water bill is $10 for unlimited usage (Panama has lots of water, trust me!); my electric bill runs about $37 a month, and propane gas tanks (100-pound tanks last about four months) cost about $65 depending on the current oil prices worldwide. A haircut and color costs me $35, dental cleaning about $38, a weekly maid for housecleaning for four hours $15, and my twice-monthly gardener $17 for a half day.

If you decide to bring a vehicle, make sure it is a make that can be serviced here and that parts are available. Your cute Mazda Miata convertible is not practical here in the Land of Four-Wheel-Drive SUVs!

So, all of this sounds good so far, right? Here are the negatives: Nothing, even the simplest transaction like paying a bill, is ever simple. Nothing. Everything takes longer than it should: building a home; the opening of a business; the starting time for a concert; the road repairs . . . everything. Get used to it, and relax!

Living alone, I feel safer behind a gate, but that has not precluded break-ins in my community. Most crime is nonviolent and involves theft of portable items like laptops, jewelry, cameras, and such. In Boquete, we have a new anticrime organization, working closely with our police force, to address this growing issue.

As a single woman, it is difficult to meet eligible men in such a small town. Most expats have retired here with their spouses; the majority of my friends are married couples. The single men often seek much younger (and very attractive!) Panamanian women, so the competition is steep (and the pool is shallow!). There are a lot of single women like me, and we do provide great support and invaluable friendship to each other. But if you are single and female and looking for love . . . good luck!

For anyone to successfully relocate, it is important to always see the positive side of your new environment. For me, that is the wonderful climate, the affordable lifestyle, the chance to just take time and chat (who's in a rush?), the proximity to the United States, the dollar-based economy, the genuine friends I have made, the fulfilling opportunities to become involved and active, and the pleasure of discovering more and more of this beautiful place called Panama. Today, as I write this, I reflect on the decision I made in 2007 and have to admit it was the best decision I have made affecting my life.

—From my terrace, on a rainy July afternoon, in Panama and happy to be here!

CHAPTER 7

Divorce, Death, Dating, Dependency, and Deepening Connections

A woman is like a tea bag; you never know how strong she is until she gets in hot water.

—Eleanor Roosevelt

Sleeping Beauty . . . Snow White . . . Cinderella. Many of us listened to, read, or watched these stories from the Brothers Grimm. I loved these fairy tales as a kid, but when I became an adult, I always thought there was something ironic that two men with the name Grimm published stories about women rescued by princes and living "happily ever after," and I found it particularly annoying when the princes fell in love with women who were asleep or unconscious!

We know that there isn't always a storybook "happily ever after"—our princes die, they leave us, we kick them out, we never find one, we don't want one, they don't exist. Or, we make ourselves happy because we don't wait for Prince Charming to come along; we create our own joy, buy our own diamonds. Let's look at what to do if we are widowed or divorced, or if we decide we want to get back into the pool—the dating pool, that is. We may be responsible for caring for aging parents or welcoming a not-so-wee one back into the nest. And for many single women, retirement is also a time for deepening, developing, or renewing connections with family, old friends, and new friends. Those are the topics this chapter will address.

Divorce

You may be reading this book because you're divorced, or you're *thinking* about divorce (by the way, January is the most popular month for divorce filings). Either way, you have plenty of company. About 37 percent of marriages end in divorce or annulment, according to the 2010 U. S. Census. With the difficult economy, the divorce rate has dipped a little, since some people can't afford to get unhitched. About a quarter of a million women over 50 get divorced each year, and two-thirds of divorces are initiated by women; if you're college educated, that percentage is even higher. It's a scary time, even if you are the one who put the wheels in motion.

In addition to the emotional aspects of divorce, the financial aspects can be daunting. If you're considering divorce or have reason to think you are going to find yourself "suddenly single," prepare ahead of time. Get a credit card and open a bank account in your own name; formulate a budget and put aside some extra money; if your spouse controls the money, start learning about your mortgage, taxes, investments, bank and retirement accounts, and insurance. And change your passwords to ones your soon-to-be-ex won't figure out. Cynthia C. learned the hard way—her estranged husband read all her e-mails from his computer since he knew her password.

If you're the one who wants the divorce, don't let guilt get in the way. Start getting savvy now and request what is fairly due to you, even if you want it to be over as quickly as possible.

For More Information

Here are more tips about what to do if you're in the divorce process or potentially headed there. Janice Green is a lawyer and the author of *Divorce After 50: Your Guide to the Unique Legal & Financial Challenges.* The following tips may help your transition to single status:

Financial Planning Advice. Especially if you are over age 50, with less time to recover economically after a divorce, financial planning is a relevant and crucial part of divorce. Financial planning tools include designing a mixed portfolio, assessing your tolerance for risk, and coordinating the timing of retirement income. The best way to use such services is for you and your attorney to consult with an independent advisor while analyzing options and making decisions before the divorce is final.

Women often want to end up with the marital residence no matter what. This may be an emotional decision, so give yourself time to consider other options. The downside of not opting for a mixed portfolio is obvious in the following scenario: Wife wants to end up with the family home (and substantial $250,000 equity). She is thrilled when Husband agrees to take his 401(k) Plan (valued at $100,000) and a $25,000 note, payable by her in five years and secured with a second lien on the home. Of course, his note is accruing interest. Five years later when her former Husband's note is due, a serious real estate market downturn occurs. Wife is "upside down"—she owes more to the mortgage company and former Husband than what the house is then worth. She sells the home, pays off the primary mortgage, but still owes her ex-spouse $25,000. While we cannot always predict the course of market risks, this is a good example of asking yourself if you really want to put all your eggs in one basket or take a share of multiple assets (mixing your portfolio).

Social Security Benefits. If your marriage lasted 10 years or more, you are unmarried now, and you and your former husband are at least 62, you may qualify for Social Security retirement benefits based on your former husband's income credits. (His check is not reduced, either!) This is a good thing for women who have accumulated no, or only nominal, Social Security income credits.

Should your former spouse predecease you and your marriage lasted 10-plus years, you may be eligible to receive survivor benefits of up to 100 percent of your former spouse's benefit, as long as your own Social Security retirement benefit is not equal to or greater than his at the time of his death. You can compare the potential benefits by requesting a copy of your earnings records (www.ssa .gov/online/ssa-7050.pdf) and estimating your benefits at www.socialsecurity.gov/estimator.

Your ex-spouse can't take these benefits away—even in a divorce settlement. Remarriage, age, and other factors may affect your eligibility. These details, and more, are explained on the Social Security Web site (www.ssa. gov) or in AARP's *Social Security for Dummies* by Jonathan Peterson.

Collateralize Buyouts and Alimony. If your spouse buys out your interest in one or more assets or if he is paying you alimony, try not to settle for an unsecured promise to pay you. Whenever possible, secure these obligations with collateral (assets) and with life/disability insurance.

Length of Marriage. Sometimes how long you are married affects your eligibility for a number of benefits—Social Security benefits, as discussed above, is an example. A 10-year marriage is also required before some states will award alimony and, if you are the spouse of a military man, before the federal government will pay you your share of his military retirement. There is a 20-year marriage requirement before former military spouses are eligible for commissary and military exchange privileges, called the 20-20-20 Rule: 20 years of qualifying military service, 20 years of marriage, and 20 years of overlap between the two. If you are just a few months shy of meeting a marriage-duration requirement, consider delaying the finality of your divorce.

COLAs. Cost of living adjustments may be a feature of pension plans, such as state, local, or federal government or military retirement plans. The former spouses may share COLAs proportionately to the amount of retirement they receive. The divorce orders must specifically spell out that you are entitled to the COLA or else you will not share in it, and usually the retirement benefit awarded is described as a percentage rather than a fixed dollar amount.

Under-the-Radar Assets and Liabilities. Here are examples of assets some people overlook (or do not reveal) in divorce.

- Bonuses to be paid in the future, yet the amount is based on employment during the marriage.
- Employer contributions to retirement plans or other deferred compensation plans made after the date the divorce is final, but earned on employment during the marriage.
- Club memberships, season tickets, and frequent-flier miles and rewards.
- Tax refunds based on returns filed during the marriage.
- Overpaid estimated taxes.
- Refunds on credit cards.

Credit Reports. Request a copy of your own and your spouse's credit report. You may discover credit cards and other debts that otherwise you would never know about.

Brokerage Accounts. Consider dividing brokerage accounts that contain a variety of investments by percentages rather than by dollar amounts. Doing so spreads the tax advantages and risks between the spouses. If you reach an agreement for a specific dollar amount, what happens if there is a substantial increase or decrease in the account between the time the agreement is reached and the time the divorce is final (or account divided)? This possibility should be addressed in the agreement and court orders.

Estate Plan Revisions. Most states have laws that automatically delete former spouses designated as beneficiaries or named as administrators under wills executed before the divorce. If your divorce agreement involves a spouse continuing as a beneficiary under a life insurance policy, will, or trust, be sure that the paperwork is executed immediately after the divorce.

Alimony. Be sure you ask your attorney whether your spouse can later reduce the amount of court-ordered alimony, and if so, the rules in your state for modifying alimony.

Be Creative. Here are two examples of creative settlements:

- Wife needed to return to college to retool for the workforce after the divorce. Husband agreed to create a 529 Plan for her education and gained some tax breaks in doing so. The couple also agreed that if she decided not to return to school, the funds would be used for the benefit of a grandchild's education.
- Wife wanted the house, but it was a strain for her to afford it. After the divorce, she rented the house to her daughter and son-in-law, and she turned her former husband's workshop/garage into a small apartment that met her vision for downsizing.

Gray Divorce

The term *gray divorce* describes the dissolution of marriages that lasted 20 or more years. These represent about a quarter of all divorces, according to the U.S. Census Bureau. Susan L., Barbara J., and Lisa B. share their stories about their gray divorces:

Susan L. explains why it was the "right time":

It seems like the right time. I guess I am one of a growing number of people who have realized the possibilities of living out the second half of life as a "me" rather than as a "we."

At nearly 24, it seemed like the right time for me to get married. R and I had been dating for over two years and we were in love. Some women my age already had children. He was 27 and an only child and was waiting for the right time to tell his parents that they would no longer be number one in his world. He was smart with a great sense of humor and would probably be a good provider. He knew so much about so many things, like science, how to ski and golf, boating, and how to build and fix things. I admired these talents and still do. So what changed over 30 years of marriage? We never had that much in common, although I enjoyed many of the things he introduced me to. He would go to my "character study" movies and hike in the woods and lie on the beach for a period of time. But then he would get antsy when time slowed too much and all that was left was either conversation or self-reflection.

After eight years of marriage, it seemed like the right time to have children. We had a son and then, three years later, a daughter. Perfect. But because we were a two-career couple, children introduced a whole new level of stress to our already busy lives. My career and workaholism, combined with R's excellent time management skills despite the demands of his job, meant R was always home first, always the one to be greeted by the needy children, always fixing dinner while I toiled away at the office. R's resentment built.

When our son was six and daughter three, I was burned out at work and it seemed like the right time to take a leave of absence from the frantic pace of life. I took up a new career as mother, health nut, and enjoyer of some free time. A year later, R decided it seemed like the right time to start a business with a colleague, and so they struck out on their own. R and I temporarily became a no-income couple, but lived nicely on our savings. After a couple more years, I returned to work and R's business was doing pretty well. It seemed like the right time to design and build a dream home on a big lot with a pond and lots of trees. This venture, in addition to the two careers, intensified the stress on our marriage.

Shortly after the four of us moved into our lovely new home, mysterious symptoms that our son had suffered for a few years became more pronounced, so we took him to another professional for another battery of tests. It turns out that the stress of the change in homes plus puberty exacerbated the three neurological disorders that had been simmering inside our son since kindergarten. These disorders affected him cognitively, so as to undermine his abilities as a student; socially, so as to destroy many of his friendships; emotionally, so as to lead him to doubt his own sanity; and behaviorally, so as to cause incredible conflict and frustration at home among the family members. The constant calls to my office from the school regarding problems with our son and the clear need for a more hands-on approach to assist him in his many struggles prompted me to take another leave of absence from my career.

It is said that marriages of parents of children with special needs often end in divorce. Well, R and I emotionally supported each other for over eight years of dealing with the challenges of medications, meltdowns, and near mayhem. I ended up on antidepressants. We tried marriage counseling a couple of times. But it was all about the kids, not about us, and we slowly drifted even further apart without realizing it.

It eventually dawned on me that R and I were living separate lives whenever we had free time beyond the process of managing our children. And I liked it. He did his manly pursuits like fishing and shooting, which I did not care for at all, and I returned to school to pursue a whole new career (it seemed like the right time). In addition, our daughter had gone from being the perfect, hassle-free kid to an angst-ridden teen with wildly swinging moods. With this new stressor, R's moodiness greatly increased and I was in danger of becoming stuck in the fretting over our daughter, whose mental health diagnosis came with a whole new set of psychiatrists, medications, counselors, and school problems.

Over time, it was clear to me that I was happier when I was not around R. There were never any hostile exchanges, cheating, or outward signs of deep unhappiness. Just a weariness of unsatisfying routine, lack of intimacy, and, with the children older, no more common goals. I had fallen out of love and preferred to be by myself instead of with him. He preferred to stay married but was not interested in going back to marriage counseling. Some women, factoring in their age, the financial insecurity, length of the marriage, and the effects on the children and extended families, would come to the conclusion that separation or divorce didn't make sense or was too risky or too big of a change. But for me, living apart from R represented positive change, a feeling of optimism, and hope for continued personal growth.

And so it seemed like the right time to go our separate ways. I bought my own condo, we sold our dream house, and he bought his own place. Our son is on his own (doing very well), and my daughter lives with me. After several years of separation, R and I both found it to our liking and obtained an amicable divorce.

Although neither of us will have as financially comfortable a retirement as if we had stayed together, sometimes one of the spouses needs the courage to declare the marriage dead and move on. Although we were raised with "till death do us part," that phrase came about when our life expectancy was half of what it is today. So instead of waiting for that individual death, for some of us, we see the marriage has died and therefore it is the right time to part.

Barbara J. has kept her sense of humor intact:

July 4, 1976 . . . The Bicentennial, celebrations, fireworks . . . and an engagement ring, the promise of love everlasting? Okay let's be realistic . . . it was an opportunity to get out of my parents' house. Ah, the blindness of youth. Why can't we be born older, wiser, and then work our way backward? Or at least be given a chance for a do-over!

Twenty years and four children later, the end of a marriage. I often wonder how I survived that period of my life without a breakdown. Taking one day, or week, at a time seemed to help. Going back to the corporate world after 20 years of staying home was quite the challenge. I knew I had developed a strong work ethic and time management and organizational skills. I just had to be convincing to employers that these skills that worked so well in the home would be as valuable in the corporate world. My house was always clean, the kids fed, laundry done, homework done, yard work done, trips to the doctor, piano lessons, dance lessons, the orthodontist, soccer practice, football practice, hockey practice, birthday parties . . . whew . . . no wonder I was tired. Unfortunately, this was not exactly resume material.

I did get a job at a big insurance company; the next big hurdle was developing computer skills. When I left the workforce as an accountant to be a stay-at-home-mom, we punched our computer cards and took them to the computer room. The next day we picked up our computer printout and lugged it back to our desk. Now, everyone had their own PC and monitor. I took several evening computer classes at the community college so I would at least be able to find the "on" button. I was overwhelmed. I felt like Wilma Flintstone among the younger generation sitting next to me. Luckily I shared a work cube with a sympathetic young girl who never seemed to tire of my questions. Maybe she was just a good actress? She actually left the company about two years later. It wasn't my fault, really! She reported to a miserable woman that no one could stand. My young friend left and the miserable woman was promoted. I was beginning to understand the corporate dance.

More than a dozen years later, I'm still employed with the same company. I've survived the cutbacks and work sent offshore. I tried to take advantage of any opportunity that would increase my value to the company. Sadly, I've realized you can be replaced in an instant. I just hope my "instant" won't arrive before I'm ready. My youngest is now a senior in college. I remember when my oldest was just starting. How was I going to afford the tuition bills? My divorce agreement reflected the fact that my ex's attorney was more effective than mine. Thank goodness for child support.

To be honest, I don't know what I'd do with myself all day if I didn't have a job. I currently have the option to work from home a few days a week, and I do enjoy being home. I can get caught up on the laundry, watch the snow fall rather than trying to drive in it, get a head start on mowing the lawn . . . and even enjoy quality time with the cat. But there are other days when it feels good to wear something nice, put on a pretty piece of jewelry, and interact with other adults. It's also a good thing to have some face time with your manager so when it comes time for that annual review, she remembers who you are. What would I do if I were home all the time and the only responsibility I'd have was to clean? I think I'd go crazy. And although I've developed some handyman skills (I've almost become the man I wanted to marry!), I certainly couldn't keep myself busy with home improvement projects.

So much for the mental impact. What about the financial impact? One word comes to mind . . . HELP!! My goal is to be as thrilled saving every penny as I am receiving goodies in the mail from the home shopping channels. I admit it. I'm a QVC/HSN junkie. The show hosts are all my friends. I enjoy hearing the sound of their voices as I move from room to room in the house. How can you feel lonely when someone is showing you an item that is just perfect for you and in so many sizes or colors? Too bad I didn't find my ex on QVC. I could have used the return label and shipped him back for a full refund. I would have even spent the extra money for delivery confirmation.

Lisa B. is in the process of a divorce:

As a poster child of the 1970s, I went to college and majored in anthropology because it was interesting. Not great for a career, but then I planned on getting married so what did it matter? And right after I graduated from The Ohio State University, I did marry, at age 21. (Wow, does that sound young now.)

I worked for five years until our first child was born, and then I became a stay-at-home mom. I didn't miss the corporate games but did miss adult conversation. I threw myself into leadership positions in volunteer organizations while working for my husband in his dental practice whenever and however needed. Our children grew up and are now successful, productive members of society. Time to relax, travel, and enjoy the fruits of our labor, right? Wrong.

The day my husband told me that he had rented an apartment and was moving out will forever be frozen in my memory. Never in a million years did I imagine that my marriage of 38 years would end in divorce. Shock, denial, unfathomable hurt for many months, then a little voice that said, "Get up off your ass and figure out how to live the rest of your life!"

As we go through the actual divorce process, I have enlisted the help of a financial advisor who only works with individuals getting a divorce. She looks at the various scenarios presented by the attorneys and helps me determine what my best options will be. She helps create a budget that can be projected years into the future so I will have a clue about how much money I will need for future taxes, insurance, expenses, etc.

Once the divorce is final, she will recommend several fee-based advisors from whom to choose to assist with getting my investments in order. This process will include some buying and selling of stocks in order to rebalance my portfolio because during my marriage, we never did that. We bought and held individual company stock and never sold, so I feel like there is way more there than I care to handle. Our multiple IRAs and investments are spread out over six brokerage companies as well as several banks, so I am quite concerned about how to get this into a manageable form.

Don't even get me started on my search for health insurance (which used to be through my soon-to-be ex), long-term-care insurance, a new home, how to take care of my 90-year-old father, and how to define myself since I will no longer be Mrs. So many questions to which the only answer so far is to take it one day at a time.

It has been a slow, painful process, but I really am trying to look forward to each new day with hope. Some days are more successful than others. And . . . remember to breathe!

Death of a Loved One

I hope I don't remind you of Debbie Downer from *Saturday Night Live* with this subtitle of "Death," but we need to be realistic.

If we're married, our husbands may die. There are over a million boomer widows in the United States, and 70 percent of married boomer women will outlive their spouses.

You may recall the five stages of grief that Elisabeth Kübler-Ross described, based on talking with more than 500 people in the process of dying and their families: denial, anger, bargaining, depression, and acceptance. These stages are not necessarily complete, and some people may get "stuck" in one stage. As Kübler-Ross said, "The stages are not linear. People do not necessarily go through all of them or some of them." According to Kübler-Ross, women are more likely to experience all stages. As she so eloquently states, "Our grief is as individual as our lives."

George Bonanno, professor of clinical psychology at Teachers College, Columbia University, has studied bereavement for 30 years and has found three common patterns in response to a death. Bonanno's studies show that about 10 percent of people experience "prolonged grief," which lasts for years and years, doesn't relent, and may become worse as time goes on. Another approximately 20 percent exhibit what he calls the "recovery" pattern. This describes those who suffer tremendously for as long as a year and continue to feel pain from their loss but operate in many respects as they did before the death of the loved one. The third and most common pattern (one-third to two-thirds of people) is the "resilience" pattern. People grieve tremendously for up to several weeks, but the intense grief fades and the bereaved adapts to the new reality and moves on with life, although still feeling sad about the loss. Bonanno's studies are comforting because they demonstrate that many people can recover from the death of a loved one and that humans are hard-wired to bounce back from adversity.

In Chapters 5 and 6, we discussed how a number of women choose to move after their spouse dies, perhaps downsizing and finding a location with strong social support and new opportunities. Here are some additional specific strategies from real women who lost their spouses. Their thoughts mirror the advice that experts provide about coping with grief, but include their personal touch:

- I rescued a dog. I needed to come home to someone who loves me and is happy to see me. I needed to hear life in my house. I knew there was a dog out there I needed and who needs me—and I found Rosie. (Ann N.)

- Plan for "triggers" such as anniversaries, holidays, and birthdays. Are you better off distracting yourself, focusing on the good memories, or allowing yourself to grieve? All are options, and what is right is what is right for you. My husband loved St. Patrick's Day, so every March 17, I pour a cold one on his grave! It's a tradition that makes me smile and brings me comfort. (Leanne N.)
- Don't make any big decisions for the first three months. If you're not financially savvy, get help; don't automatically turn everything over to your adult kids to handle. Try to remain in control. You're not stupid, just financially uneducated, but that can be remedied. I did it; you can, too. (Marcia O.)
- I knew that I would have to take care of myself so I could be there for my children—they were my first priority. I started working out, watching my weight, and went to counseling. I have since remarried. (Martha W.)
- I looked for the "silver lining." My husband was a workaholic. When he became ill, he stopped working and spent more time with our family than he would have if he were healthy and lived to be 100! (Kim O.)
- I am very independent and always had my own interests. The main issue was the loss of my best friend. I speak to him every night and tell him how much I miss him, talk about how he would react to the goings-on in today's world, and most of all, I cherish the memories we had. (Gayle C.)
- I learned to ask for help, which was not typical for me, but in learning to ask for help, I learned that people really want to help. My life was so much easier once I let go of having to do it all. (JoAnne F.)
- I decided to fulfill one of my husband's goals. We have a son with autism; I started an autism foundation. I did not want his plan to die with him. (Claudreen J.)
- Hospice grief groups. They're free, open to anyone, available in nearly every county, and miraculously, through helping others bear their own grief, provide stability and reassurance

at a time when everything in one's life can otherwise feel like pure free fall. (Sam J.)

- Besides the sorrow and grief, there were overwhelming practical considerations—my husband had handled all the finances, and I was totally unprepared to deal with money issues. I met with a certified financial planner to figure out what to do—bills had to be paid, I had to figure out where our accounts were, and then there was the whole investment arena. It was very hard, but now, after 18 months, a lot of help, and forcing myself to become financially literate, I'm much more confident. Word to the wise—don't be like me; get involved in the finances when your spouse is alive. (Kathleen K.)

- Be prepared for good days and bad days. Waking up with no desire to get out of bed doesn't mean you aren't moving on; it just means that for today, this is part of your grieving process. Having a support system to lean on is so important. Use them. Call up a friend and say, "I don't need to be alone right now. Can you come over?" (Laura C.)

- Years ago, when giving birth to my son, the midwife said: "You never have to do more than one contraction at a time. Anyone can handle one contraction. Just do that one. When it is over, forget about it. Then do the next one; this one is the only one in the world. Don't think about how much longer this might go on, how many more there might be. Just this one." I used that advice after my husband died, and it has gotten me through the last 14 years without him. This is how it works: Immediately after the loss, don't think about how long you have to live with this kind of pain. Just bargain for five minutes. Can you live with this pain for five minutes? Chances are you can do five minutes. Then, re-up for another five minutes. After a while, you will be able to imagine living for another half hour. Then an hour. Then just this morning, I can get through the morning. Then, just the afternoon. Just this one night of staring at the ceiling. Just one. As you recover, you can negotiate for longer amounts of time. If you backslide, go down to the increment of time you think you can imagine dealing with. We can generally cope with truly awful pain if we stay in the present. It is when we start imagining how long our situation will continue that we become overwhelmed. A journalist once asked the Dalai Lama how he had managed to escape, on foot, from Tibet in the middle of winter, which should have been impossible. He replied: "One foot in front of the other." (Cerridwen F.)

- The death of a loved one can be a beginning or an end. I became very close to God and His purpose for my life and found great fulfillment. (Ann C.)
- I said "yes" to every request made of me for six months. This sounds very hard to do and it was, but by forcing myself to just say "yes," I met wonderful new friends and opened my world beyond my dark house and learned to cope with the new challenges of being alone. I was very happy to say "no" again when the six months were over, yet that time made a huge difference and forced me to live through grief rather than just endure it. (Susan B.)
- Take one day at a time and don't feel pressured by people expecting you to pull yourself together; allow the feelings to surface . . . there is no such thing as a normal grieving process. (Judy S.)
- Consider writing in a diary/journal. (Sharon O.)
- I promised Dick I would laugh every day, and I do. I was working part-time as a travel agent and decided to continue and make "lemonade out of lemons." There are so many divorced and widowed people who like to travel and have no one to go with. I began to plan cruises and tours for solo travelers and would often match them up with roommates. We are older now and most of us like our own rooms, but I am still planning the trips. (Marilyn A.)
- Visit "neutral" places and family. I spent a few weeks at a Florida vacation home of friends. I also visit my daughter, son-in-law, and new granddaughter regularly. (Susanne A.)

For a more financially oriented checklist developed by Kathleen Rehl, a certified financial planner (and widow), see "What to Do When Your Husband Dies" in Appendix 7C at the end of this chapter.

For More Information

You can find an online grief support group through Otrib (www.otrib.com) or Groww (www.groww.org).

Dating

Ready to get back into the dating scene? About a third of boomers are or have been divorced. After the death of a spouse, divorce, or the end of a relationship, you may be considering dipping your toes into the sometimes anxiety-filled waters (cue the *Jaws* theme music) of dating.

Before looking at the online dating scene, let's go low-tech. I asked a lot of singles, both women and men, where they had success meeting someone. The most original answer had to be from Ann W. She met her now-husband in a funeral home; they were at separate wakes (in both cases, a friend of their families had died). They started chatting in the foyer that connected the two visitation rooms, and the rest, as they say, is history . . . or herstory.

In general, get involved in activities that are of interest to you, and be open to new relationships. But, here are some specific places to meet someone: dog parks; classes at Home Depot/Lowe's; classes at your local college or through your county such as conversational foreign language, cooking, computer, finance, dance, or rock climbing; singles groups at houses of worship; community events such as wine/scotch tastings (men are more likely to attend a scotch tasting than a wine tasting), concerts, book signings, or lectures at book stores or libraries; sports (this is a big one—think of joining a co-ed softball team or running, skiing, bowling, archery, or a gun club). If you're not a participant, be a spectator at sporting events. Of course, it's nice if you actually enjoy the sport. Dawn A. met her boyfriend through the American Singles Golf Association (www.singlesgolf.com). Most members are 45–60, and as its site says, you don't have to be a good golfer, "just a good person."

Significant Statistic

The over-50 crowd has increasing rates of sexually transmitted diseases (STDs) due to longer lifespans, no need for birth control (so no condoms), more sex due to the "little blue pill" and other treatments for erectile dysfunction, more fragile vaginal tissue that can allow the entry of microbes, a less effective immune system, and frankly, because STDs are something mature people often don't think can happen to them so they don't protect themselves. No matter your age, you still need to practice safe sex.

Of course, friends, family, and colleagues can be potential matchmakers. And you can meet people through volunteering, such as through Habitat for Humanity, a political or environmental group, a historical society, or a hospital—maybe you'll meet your own McDreamy. Farmers' markets, flea markets, and coffee shops (how many people are there for hours working on their computers?) are other possibilities. Charity auctions, art galleries, museums, airports, trains (Frances A. met her now-spouse in Europe while traveling from Prague to Budapest on a train), single travel (discussed in Chapter 2), bars, the health club, a park bench, grocery stores, and restaurants (where one of my sisters met her husband) are worth a try. Belinda V. met her current boyfriend through a coed divorce support group, and Amanda Z. met the man she is dating when she went to listen and dance to a band that used to perform at her high school dances. Realize that you might be the one initiating the conversation in any of these scenarios. You don't have to wait for the guy to approach you.

Rekindled Romances

Have a first love or an old boyfriend you've lost touch with—maybe for 20 or 30 or 40 or more years? Research about reuniting with lost loves offers some pretty compelling data. Dr. Nancy Kalish, an expert in this field and professor of psychology at California State University, Sacramento, found that those who reconnected with past flames (and it didn't matter if they had sex or not when they had dated) had a very high success rate, even if both the man and woman had happy marriages (to others) before reconnecting. The stat for widows was particularly amazing; 87 percent of reconnected loves remained together. But Kalish also reported that all was not rosy. Often adult children saw the new old love as an "interloper" or in it for the money, or were doubtful of their parent's mental health, and were concerned with the speed at which these rekindled relationships progressed. Reunited couples often married within days, weeks, or months.

When I lived in New Jersey, I had a hairdresser named Kristine. At one appointment, Kristine told me she was getting divorced. Six months later, she told me she was going to her 40th high school reunion. I asked her if she had an old boyfriend from that time and if he would be there. Kristine said not only would he be there, but also a friend had told her he was recently single. I told Kristine about the research by Kalish and that a wedding would be in her future. Guess what? They are now married.

Kalish found that when old loves reconnected but one of the partners was still married, it often led to affairs, so you do need to tread carefully if you look up an old flame. The Internet has made tracking down that lost love so much easier.

The Internet

It's an understatement to say that the Internet and social media have changed the way we interact with others. About 90 percent of adults between 50–64 use the Internet; about a half of adults in this age group participate in social networking (such as Facebook, LinkedIn, and MySpace), according to a 2011 Pew Research Center survey.

Two sites before we move to the "traditional" online dating sites:

- Meetup.com (www.meetup.com). This is an easy way to meet up with people in your area with similar interests, and you can start your own Meetup group if you can't find one that fits your needs. There is also a specific site (www.seniors .meetup.com) for those 50 and older.

- Eight at Eight (www.8at8.com). Dinners are arranged for four single men and four single women. Targeted ages are 21–55. Right now, Eight at Eight is "open to single professionals looking for dating opportunities in New York, Chicago, Atlanta, and Washington, DC." Chances are there is a singles dinner group in your area. Type "dinner groups" along with your location into your search bar, and you'll probably find one. Add in "mature" or "seniors" if you're looking for dinner groups that cater exclusively to an older age group. These are easy ways to meet people who could become friends—or more. And at least you'll have a good meal.

Dating sites are springing up like mushrooms after a summer thunderstorm, and singles 50-plus are logging on. The research firm comScore reports that the number of online dating site users overall who are 50 and older has grown twice as rapidly as all other age groups.

First, the usual warnings about using dating sites: Don't share specific, personal information upfront, such as your real name, e-mail, or home or work address or phone numbers; look for consistencies and plausibility when exchanging information to avoid scams and to be sure the guy is really single; research the prospective person online and see what comes up; keep the first meeting short—if things click, you can always meet again; meet in a public place and let a friend know where you are; and follow your gut and don't do anything that feels creepy.

Read the disclaimers and warnings on each site that explain how to minimize your chances of being a victim of fraud, charges associated with joining, how to opt out of the site, what to include in your profile, and so on.

When you're setting up your dating profile, as shallow and unfair as it sounds, your picture is the most important thing. We're visual beings, and most people scan pictures before reading profiles. So use a picture that is flattering and recent, not 30 pounds and 30 years ago, as well as the image you want to project (do you really want to attract potential dates by showing your cleavage?).

As an example of an online dating experience gone bad, here is Andrea C.'s story:

I had been divorced for almost three years. After dating unsuccessfully for a while, I decided to join one of the biggest online dating sites. My story is in no way blaming the Web site; it is totally my fault for a bad decision.

My profile was viewed 167 times and not one of the men actually contacted me. That chipped away at my very fragile ego. I have been told I'm attractive and have a great personality. So I was a little miffed as to why so many views and no contacts.

One night, I received an e-mail from this man who saw my profile and picture and was so over the top interested in me that it was just a smidge strange, but extremely flattering. I checked his profile and pictures and he seemed too good to be true. He was very handsome and a successful businessman. He sent at least three e-mails every day and after I gave him my phone number, he proceeded to call me several times a day.

His name was Thomas, and he was attentive, flattering, and romantic. His e-mails were in the form of love letters. He was a good writer and I really looked forward to reading his e-mails as soon as they arrived (me being just a little needy and lonely). He told me that his wife was killed in a car accident six years ago by a drunk driver; this would be his first date since that tragedy. He also had a 13-year-old son, James, who was home schooled by a tutor.

After a few weeks of all this attention, I suggested we meet for coffee and for him to bring James if he'd like. I certainly did not want to exclude his son, who was so important to him. Coincidentally, the very next day he called and told me he had been awarded a contract to build a road in Malaysia and would be gone for six weeks. Thomas e-mailed me a copy of the contract; it was for $10.5 million. He asked me to wait for him, because when he returned he would retire and have all of the time in the world for me. Well, I was very excited that this man seemed to be madly in love with me, sight unseen, and he had a ton of money, too. So, naturally I said I would wait for him to come back to meet him. He left for Malaysia and called me 24 hours later but on a different cell phone number since he was out of the country. Just for fun I tried to call him back on this new number but "the call could not be completed as dialed." Well, after all, he was in another country.

Two days into his trip, Thomas frantically called and told me that James fell and injured himself riding a bicycle, was in the hospital, and needed surgery. The next phone call, a few hours later and more frenetic than the last call, Thomas proceeded to tell me he used all of his money to pay the surgeon for his son's operation that would take place on Friday. He needed me to send him $3,000, but just for two weeks and then he would pay me back. I felt sick to my stomach because I knew then that this was a scam.

I didn't feel so bad about Thomas himself because I never met him, but the humiliation of believing him for even a split second is why I had a hard time. How lonely and pathetic was I? After calling the police and contacting the Web site to report him, I felt a little better. No crime had been committed, according to the police, and they get at least 1,000 calls per month about this exact same scam, different stories but same outcome.

I have picked myself up, brushed myself off, and will get back on the horse again, but I think I'll try the bar scene for a while instead.

Of course, there are many success stories as well. I recently attended a wedding in Rhode Island between two divorced people, both in their 60s, who met, fell in love, and got married after meeting through eHarmony (www.eharmony.com), which matches based on "29 dimensions of compatibility." The eHarmony site claims that an average of more than 540 weddings a day result from its scientific matches. Other popular sites include Match.com (www.match.com), Chemistry.com (www.chemistry.com), and Zoosk (www.zoosk.com), which matches based on personality. A newer site is Find Your FaceMate (www.findyourfacemate.com), based on the premise that "findings prove that passion is subconsciously ignited when we spot someone whose facial features are similar to our own."

Using a site that is targeted to older adults may also be helpful; you've already narrowed the age range. Examples of age-specific sites (I wish they would dump the "senior" in these names):

- www.eons.com (go to groups, then put "40+ singles" into the search bar)
- www.ourtime.com
- www.seniorsmeet.com
- www.silversingles.com

There are also several specialty online sites:

- www.bbpeoplemeet.com (for big and beautiful singles)
- www.blacksingles.com
- www.catholicmatch.com
- www.christianmingle.com
- www.jdate.com (Jewish singles)
- www.singleparentmeet.com

Pet Peeves

Women's pet peeves on a first date? According to Zoosk, it's (in order): men who smell, are on their cell phone too much, arrive late, talk about themselves too much, and ask too many questions. If you want to know what annoys men, it's pretty similar: a date too obsessed with her cell phone, smells, arrives late, asks questions like it's a job interview, and wears too much makeup.

Dependency (Grandkids, Boomerangs, and Parental Care)

Single women, in addition to caring for themselves, may care for three other generations: parents, children, and grandchildren. No wonder phrases like "sandwich generation" (caring for parents as well as children) and "club sandwich generation" (caring for three other generations) are frequently heard. Let's take a more detailed look at caregiving.

Our Kids' Kids

The term "grandmother" might conjure up images of "Grammy" dandling a baby on her knee, watching the grandkids in an emergency or on a regular basis, taking them on a trip, or providing relief so the parents can have a child-free date night. There's another reality, though. About 7 percent of kids younger than 18 live in households headed by grandparents, and more than 60 percent of those grandparents are women. We're talking 1.7 million single women responsible for the feeding, sheltering, and clothing of their grandchildren, according to the U.S. Census Bureau. This growing lifestyle is fed by the challenging economy; military deployments; death, incarceration, or mental illness of the parents; and the mandate to place children with relatives rather than in foster care. Most of these grandparents are under 60, and most are still working.

A broader term, grandfamilies, describes grandparents who are sharing their homes with some combination of their children, grandchildren, nieces, nephews, and perhaps other relatives. This may be a win-win situation, such as a single grandmother with adult children living in her home, while she happily cares for her grandchildren while the parents are working. But in a third of these grandfamilies, the parents are not present.

So while in some cases the arrangement can be economically and emotionally rewarding, in many instances the unexpected and unplanned costs of providing and caring for other family members can put a huge dent in retirement savings or alter the lifestyle you envisioned.

Possibilities for help, depending on your situation:

- Your local Department of Social Services is a good place to start. Find out about financial help, food stamps, Medicaid, daycare assistance, and other programs, such as Temporary Assistance for Needy Families.
- Contact the Social Security Administration if the parents of your grandchildren are deceased. Your grandkids may be eligible for survivor benefits or benefits based on the earnings records of a grandparent who is supporting them. Your local Social Security office can also tell you if you're eligible for Supplemental Security Income (SSI).
- Places of worship often provide help.
- Other organizations such as United Way, Catholic Charities, and the local Health Department may be of assistance.
- The AARP Foundation offers assistance through this link: www.giclocalsupport.org.

Tip

If you're looking for grandma-like opportunities that pay, check out www.rentagrandma.com. There is a $25 fee for a background check and processing.

Our Kids

Perhaps "they're baaaacck" or they never left. There are 10 million single mothers living with kids under the age of 18, and 40 percent of these single moms are 40 years of age or older, according to the U.S. Census Bureau.

Looking at older children, more than four out of five 2011 college graduates returned to the parental nest, often with the double whammy of student loans (averaging $25,250 in 2010, according to the Project on Student Debt) and bleak job prospects. Whatever the reason, they are back.

The good news: In homes with just one parent, it's not always a one-way street with moms providing fresh laundry, hot meals, stocked pantries, and rent-free lodging to boomerang kids. In fact, when living with a single parent, adult children were shown to contribute more money and help than those who moved back to a married-couple home, according to researchers at Bowling Green State University. If this is the case for you, sweet, since the extra money spent on children can undermine your own retirement savings. If that's not how it is in your house, remember that young adults have a much longer horizon than you do for getting out of debt and saving for their own retirement. If you spend an additional $400 a month by having your adult kids live at home (with you providing food, health/car insurance, etc.)—say for five years—that amounts to $24,000 less for you—and that's assuming no return on your investment.

This transition period for kids, roughly five years beyond college graduation (and I recognize that not everyone goes to college) has been termed "adultolescence" by social scientists. The dynamic between adult children and parents has changed over the years, with adult children often viewed as friends and intellectual equals.

"Not that there's anything wrong with that," as Jerry Seinfeld might say. Many single mothers enjoy having their children with them, as long as they are still plodding along the road to adulthood and self-sufficiency. But will they ever get there? When we look at older "kids," those 25–34, 19 percent of guys and 10 percent of women are living with a parent or parents, says the 2011 March Current Population Survey. If you hear the pitter-patter of big feet, at least you know you're not alone.

Here's an example: Rebecca V. became a widow in her mid-50s. When her husband died, she had a daughter in high school and a son and a daughter in college. Rebecca has a revolving door of adult kids moving in and out of her home. The older daughter landed a job when she graduated, moved out, and then the place she was renting ended up being sold by the owner, so she moved back home, stayed there for six months, and recently moved out to new digs. The son graduated with a degree in history, dabbling in low-paying jobs unrelated to his major (although he was sending out resumes), living at home all the while. Just recently he found a full-time position working at a museum and is still living at home. When the younger daughter graduated from college, she got a job teaching, moved in with some girlfriends, but recently became engaged and moved back home to save money. Rebecca feels that there are definite benefits to having the kids at home. They help fix things around the house, walk the dog, cut the grass, and she loves them and enjoys their company, but she decided she will need to work longer as a result. Rebecca feels she needs to keep the house, which is too big if it were only for her, because she needs the space for the kids, and her retirement savings aren't what they should be with the extra expense of two adult children living at home.

Rebecca is like the 7 percent of respondents to a National Endowment for Financial Education Survey who said they would postpone retirement to help their kids. She is also like the 30 percent who said they have less privacy with live-in adult children, and the 59 percent who said they help their out-of-school children financially by providing housing, subsidizing transportation and medical costs, paying for insurance, and giving them spending money.

Having a live-in adult child (or children) can be the best of times, the worst of times, or a mixture of the two. Don't redirect retirement savings to your adult kids' support. Let your children know you don't want to be a burden to them when you're too old to care for yourself, so your first priority is to support yourself, and that means putting money into retirement savings. Discussing your finances to the extent you feel comfortable can help drive the message home. Establish ground rules for meals, chores, money matters, visitors, and applying and networking for jobs, and set out a timetable for departure (six months seems pretty reasonable).

Remember that the door can swing both ways. Harriet P. lost her job, couldn't pay her rent, and had to move in with her 26-year-old son!

Perhaps the United States will become more like other countries, such as South Korea and Italy, where children routinely live at home until they are married. Or perhaps some will follow the model of my Aunt Kay, who never left home, remained single, worked as a pianist, retired, cared for my grandparents until they passed away, and then lived in the family home until she passed away.

Caring for Parents

Women are much more likely than men to care for aging parents, and about 18 percent of caregivers are single parents as well, according to AARP and the National Alliance for Caregiving. In Chapter 1, we addressed the general challenges and rewards of being a caregiver. As a single woman responsible for funding your own retirement, being a caregiver is an additional financial and emotional burden. Women who are caretakers are more likely to retire, quit, work part-time, and take a leave of absence, and they suffer six times as much from depression or anxiety, according to the Family Caregiver Alliance.

Looking for some help? AARP has a terrific comprehensive site at www.aarp.org/caregivers. Caregivers can access an online community where they can seek advice and help others. Sometimes just being able to vent is therapeutic, and who better to help one another and offer support than other caregivers? There is also a ton of information on all aspects of caregiving, including in-home and community care options, caregiving from afar, addressing sibling disagreements, meal programs, senior centers, choosing the best housing option, managing your loved one's finances, and end-of-life care. Another source is the National Association of

Geriatric Care Managers (www.caremanager.org), which specializes in helping those caring for older relatives.

Dr. Marion Somers, an expert in elder care, provides these tips:

- Talk to your company's human resources department and find out if there are any policies about telecommuting and flexible hours. Also, the same flex spending accounts that allow workers to set aside pretax dollars for child care can often be used for elder care needs.

- Figure out whether the services/assistance your elder needs can be coordinated in the home environment first. If not, look into all the options: assisted living facilities to CCRCs or nursing homes (described in Chapter 6); www.retirementhomes.com is a great place to start. www.3in4needmore.com has a calculator that breaks down living costs by location and type of care.

- Gather your elder's legal papers and put them in a safe spot, such as a lock box, safety deposit box, or fireproof safe. This includes birth certificate, marriage certificates, divorce decrees, Social Security card, military records (including discharge papers), and tax records.

- Determine your elder's income and expenses and set a budget. For income, factor in things like pension, current salary (if any), bonds, dividends, CDs, annuities, rental properties, Social Security, disability, and unemployment. Expenses can include everything from mortgage and rent, property taxes, equity loans, home maintenance fees, utilities, and more.

- Determine assets including checking and savings accounts, stocks, bonds, homeowner property, IRAs, 401(k)s, vehicles, items stored in safety deposit boxes, furs, and jewelry.

- Contact any Area Agency on Aging, which can help you find reputable professionals in your area—financial, health care, and more.

- Try the Eldercare Locator, www.eldercare.gov, a tool to help any family looking to find more information or resources about caregiving. It offers everything from financial resources to health and nutrition information, and resources are narrowed down by location.

- Find time (no matter how little) every day to go on a walk, ride a bike, meditate, practice yoga, read, go to the gym, and meet up with friends.
- Consider respite care, since it's a great option for someone who needs care for only a short time. Ask a local nursing home what its options are, or go through the nursing aide registry at www.ncdhhs.gov/dhsr/hcpr/links.html.
- Keep track of doctors' appointments and financial outlays, as well as short- and long-term goals. Caregiving can be stressful and overwhelming. It's easy to lose track of your own goals as well as the goals for your elder's care. By tracking your short-term goals (your daily/weekly tasks), you'll stay organized and more easily reach your long-term goals (for the month or year).
- Keep all receipts and track all conversations.

Dr. Marion (Marion Somers, Ph.D.) is the author of *Elder Care Made Easier* and an expert in elder care. Check out www.drmarion.com for more information.

For More Information

As a caregiver, you will find it extremely helpful to have ready access to your loved one's important papers. AARP provides an excellent checklist: http://assets.aarp.org/external_sites/caregiving/resources/pdfs/organize_documents.pdf.

Lynn T.'s story provides one snapshot of caregiving. Lynn's dad died while she was living in another city, and when a job promotion provided the opportunity to move back home, she did, moving in with her mom. As Lynn explained, "Fearing my mother would not be around long and knowing I was an only child with no one to help care for her, I moved in with her."

We lived together for 13 years. In many ways, she took care of me more than I did of her. We had our conflicts, but enjoyed

Tip

One of my single sisters moved from New York to care for my mom, who had Alzheimer's disease, into my mom's home in Maryland for several years (my dad had passed away). My sister wrote up a contract for her services (she consulted her five siblings before doing so) and was paid $10 an hour for her help. Something to consider if a parent has the means to pay.

trips and many other experiences together. Some may think it's weird to live with your mother as a single woman in your 40s, but she was my only immediate family and it was fine. Crimped my love life, but that wasn't much, anyway!

What I wasn't prepared for was the sense of loss when she finally died. I was 51. I thought I was prepared, but I had no idea. It incapacitated me for months. If I could advise someone else facing the same situation, I'd say to have a good support system in place. You'll need it.

For Your Information

For a handy form on which to record your parents' (and your) medical info, see the Medical Form in Appendix 7D at the end of this chapter, courtesy of MedIDs.com.

It's a good thing to have a will, an advanced health care directive, a power of attorney for finances, and perhaps some guidelines for making funeral arrangements ahead of time. If your parents haven't made any decisions regarding these important issues, perhaps you can discuss them together—for their benefit and for yours; check out Appendix 7A, "Taking Care of Business," at the end of this chapter. And, although nobody likes to think about it, if your parents and you want some control over how the end will play out, see the Preneed Funeral Planning Checklist from www.funeral plan.com in Appendix 7B.

Did You Know?

Do you worry about your elderly parents on the road? "Yellow dot" is a simple, free, and elegant way to assist accident victims. A yellow dot on the left rear window notifies first responders to look for a yellow folder in the glove compartment; it contains emergency contacts, medication, allergies, medical conditions, and a picture. It's an easy way to have a little more peace of mind. Type "yellow dot" and your state into your search bar and see if your state offers this growing program.

Deepening Connections

Parents, siblings, children, grandchildren, other relatives, friends. As mentioned at the beginning of this chapter, retirement is an opportunity to deepen existing connections, reconnect, and forge new relationships. For many, it's also a time to become more religious or spiritual. And, as we age and our testosterone levels increase relative to our estrogen levels, many women have a newly awakened or heightened desire to start or continue to make their mark in the working world. (Men often become more family-oriented and nurturing as their estrogen levels increase relative to their testosterone; this is sometimes called "andropause.")

Susanne B.'s story sums up many of the issues discussed so far—divorce, working, children at home, finances, spirituality, and health issues—all with an emphasis on connecting, reconnecting, and deepening her family and community connections:

I was lucky when I became a single mom at the age of 40. My girls were 12, 13, and 16, so old enough to sort of understand. I had a career that allowed me flexibility and many job opportunities that would better match my daughters' schedules and interests, and I had a decent income. Not that the divorce was expected or wanted; I thought I had married for life when I married my childhood sweetheart. I was aware that we had some problems but did not think they were insurmountable. I thought we had worked out a nice compromise—he did not like social activities and I did, so he managed the home and I took care of all of the kids' activities. I guess that wasn't the case.

The first year after the divorce I worked on automatic pilot. I resented that he had left. I didn't discourage the girls from going with him but I also didn't encourage them. I felt I was in the parenting game alone. I had to explain why this happened without making him the bad guy. I had to monitor grades, make sure the girls had their homework done, arrange rides to and from activities, shop for food, and be the parent to cheer them on. Although I loved all the time I spent with them, I had no time to myself except late at night. I stayed so busy I didn't have time to think about where my life was going. Although I thought about when I would date again, it was not worth the effort of dealing with teenage drama should I bring someone else into my life. I had one daughter who was pretty adamant that no man could grace my door. I wasn't up to that battle so dating never happened after the divorce or to this present day.

Although I had a good career, money was always a worry. As the girls approached their college years, their expenses became my responsibility because their dad did not think he should help with college. That meant college loans, second jobs, and most recently up to four jobs to cover expenses. Plus, I was not very responsible with my money. I did not want to disrupt the girls' lifestyles that they had become used to when we were a two-income family. So Christmas and birthdays remained lavish, credit cards were used to cover school expenses and treat friends to meals. We ate out often; I hated housework and cooking so it was easier to have someone else prepare the meals. I never learned to say "I can't afford that." Needless to say, the resentment against their dad continued. I often had to bite my tongue to prevent negative comments about him. I knew in the end that I would be held responsible for that negativity. It took me several years to realize they needed him in their lives, so I had to encourage them to deal with their anger, stay in contact, and maintain a relationship with him. Again, more resentment that I was the one responsible enough to acknowledge this need of theirs. I really was filled with such self-importance and self-righteousness—I needed a knock in the head.

The scariest part of being a single parent is dealing with my most recent health issues. Although the girls have been phenomenal in their presence and support, they still have their own lives to live, and at the end of the day, I'm still alone to wonder who will take care of me if and when death is closer. They ask me to share my fears, concerns, and tears with them but, ultimately, I'm still Mom. I have to find the balance of truth and positive energy when I talk to them so they do not feel the need to have to always be present to "take care of me." I save my tears for nighttime, alone in my bed or at church during Mass. Commercials and movies sometimes cause tears that are not equal to the sentiment expressed on the screen.

Along with the fears have come many blessings in my illness. My silent child now initiates conversation, my social child has found the strength in herself to manage her life and finances, and my responsible child has found the courage to step outside of her comfort zone and live away from family and friends. My extended family—siblings, nieces, and nephews—have learned to say "I love you" when talking to one another (we wouldn't do that before). I have discovered a support system that is so awesome that whatever the outcome of this illness my daughters will have many "aunts" to turn to in time of need.

My illness has provided some insight and relief from the resentment that lingered over the past 14 years of single life. I have accepted that I was equally culpable in the breakup (I don't compromise well, and I did not ask for his help because I wanted to be the super parent). If I have learned nothing else, it is no matter the plans for yourself, life and God often have different ideas. I believe God's will works in my life, but I struggle with prayer. I focus on living one day at a time now because thinking of the future is too scary. I try to live each day to its fullest despite the fatigue. I make time for friends and family. I have reconnected with in-laws and old friends. I explore the city where I live and grew up with new eyes. I take mini trips around town. I attend Bible studies. I read. I continue to fight. And I rely on my friends and family to keep praying because I can't right now.

"I plan to enjoy life now and I'm not worried about retirement/tomorrow." More than half of respondents to a Wells Fargo survey agreed with that statement, and those who did were making less than $25,000 a year. Only a fourth of those who made more than $100,000 a year agreed there's nothing to worry about. Do people have their heads in the sand, or is it "carpe diem" time? Let's change directions and talk about money. Interesting topic for some, boring to others, scary for many, but important to all. That's the focus of the next chapter.

More 411

Divorce and Dating

Green, Janice. *Divorce After 50: Your Guide to the Unique Legal & Financial Challenges.* Berkeley: Nolo, 2010.

Kalish, Nancy. *The Lost Love Chronicles: Reunions & Memories of First Love.* Amazon Kindle, 2009.

Manfred, Erica. *He's History, You're Not: Surviving Divorce After 40.* Guilford, Connecticut: GPP Life, 2009.

Death of a Loved One

Bonanno, George. *The Other Side of Sadness: What the New Science of Bereavement Tells Us About Life After Loss.* New York: Basic Books, 2009.

Ginsburg, Genevieve. *Widow to Widow: Thoughtful, Practical Ideas for Rebuilding Your Life.* Cambridge, Massachusetts: Da Capo Press, 2004.

Kübler-Ross, Elisabeth. *On Grief and Grieving: Finding the Meaning of Grief Through the Five Stages of Loss.* New York: Scribner, 2007.

Rehl, Kathleen. *Moving Forward on Your Own: A Financial Guidebook for Widows.* Land O' Lakes, Florida: Rehl Financial Advisors, 2010.

Caregiving

Gross, Jane. *A Bittersweet Season: Caring for Our Aging Parents— and Ourselves.* New York: Knopf, 2011.

Kardasis, Arline. *Mom Always Liked You Best: A Guide for Resolving Family Feuds, Inheritance Battles, and Eldercare Crises.* Norwood, Massachusetts: Agreement Resources, 2011.

Sheehy, Gail. *Passages in Caregiving: Turning Chaos into Confidence.* New York: Harper, 2011. (Sheehy cared for her spouse; lots of good info)

Somers, Marion. *Elder Care Made Easier.* Kensington, Maryland: Atticus Books, 2006.

Deepening Connections

www.allthesinglegirlfriends.com (a social site for single women over 40)

www.nabbw.com (National Association of Baby Boomer Women)

www.vibrantnation.com (boomer women community)

Appendix 7A: Taking Care of Business

Caring for your parents, caring for your children, caring for your grandchildren—what about *you?* Although you may feel overwhelmed plowing through the demands of everyday life, there are several things to address before the need arises. Be sure to consult your attorney.

- **A Will.** Hmmm . . . would you rather get a root canal or craft a will? According to a Harris Interactive Survey commissioned by Rocket Lawyer, a third of those asked would prefer the former. Fewer than half of boomers have a will, and 22 percent of those over 65 lack one. About a fourth of women cite cost as the reason for not creating a will. And most of us don't want to think about dying.

  If your state decides who gets what, and you are okay with its rules, maybe you don't need a will. Or, if your situation is simple and you don't own a business, perhaps you can do a will yourself (see Chapter 8 for more information on this). Or, you can pay for an estate attorney to create a will.

- **Advance Health Care Directive.** If you want to be in control of your health decisions, an advance health care directive lets others know what you would like or not like and under what circumstances. Only 30 percent of people have an advance health care directive. Become part of this elite group.

  There are often several parts to the advance health care directive: choosing what you want or don't want medically (sometimes called a living will); choosing who will speak for you if you become incapacitated (a health care agent); and specifying your wishes regarding organ donation or an autopsy. You may address any or all of these areas through forms specific to your state. AARP has free downloadable forms by state at www.aarp.org/advancedirectives. Each state has its own requirements for witnesses and notaries.

  It's vital to share your advance health care directive (and where you keep your copy) with doctors, family, friends, religious advisors, or any others who would or should need to know your wishes. And, it's important to do this before there is a health crisis, so your desires are known. You can revoke your advance health care directive (or portions of it) at any time, but if you do, you need to notify those who have a copy so there's no confusion.

- **Power of Attorney for Finances.** It's important to name someone you trust who will represent you in money matters if you should become unable to do so. This person will have limitations—such as the inability to modify your will or give away your money as gifts to others or to herself or himself. She or he will be able to handle your general financial affairs. You can use the same person to be both your health care agent and hold your power of attorney for finances, but the documents are usually signed separately. You can find an example of a form here: www .expertlaw.com/library/estate_planning/durable_power _of_attorney.html.

  Some experts recommend the same person handle both your finances and health care decisions; other experts recommend the opposite.

216

Appendix 7B: Preneed Funeral Planning Checklist*

This preneed checklist shows you how many decisions must be made by a family member at the time of a death. This does not include choosing a casket or urn and outer burial container, notifying relatives, preparing a family history for the obituary, arranging for floral displays, and more. By taking time now to consider the items below, you (or your loved ones) can make your wishes known.

- ☐ Name of house of worship (if service to be held)
- ☐ Clergy to preside over service (name)
- ☐ Music? Vocal? Instrumental?
- ☐ Special musical selections?
- ☐ Would you like to have a visitation?
- ☐ Open casket? Closed casket?
- ☐ Funeral home preference
- ☐ Obituary
- ☐ Names of pallbearers
- ☐ Memorial contributions
- ☐ If veteran, flag on casket? Folded?
- ☐ Clothing
- ☐ Glasses
- ☐ Jewelry
- ☐ Location of cemetery property and deed
- ☐ Type of property: burial space/lawn crypt/mausoleum/niche
- ☐ Other instructions

Appendix 7C: What to Do When Your Husband Dies**

Disclaimer: These suggested steps are generic and certainly not all-inclusive for each widow's situation. Consult your attorney, accountant, and financial planner.

---

*Reprinted with permission: www.funeralplan.com

**Adapted with permission from *Moving Forward on Your Own: A Financial Guidebook for Widows* by Kathleen M. Rehl, Ph.D., CFP®

When your husband dies, you may be faced with a dark shadow of grief, fear, and uncertainty. Just when you feel least able to cope with life, when you are low on mental and physical energy, there are many decisions to be made that can permanently affect you—your finances, your family, your livelihood, and so much more.

It might seem no one really understands what you are going through. But there are immediate concerns to take care of after your spouse's death, including the funeral or memorial service. Then you'll deal with critical issues, including settling his estate and collecting death benefits. You used to make choices with your partner, but now you feel alone.

Review these items with members of your support network in the days, weeks, and months during the first year after your husband's passing. Only time will help to heal the grief you experience. Organizing your finances and taking the right steps will help you regain a sense of control, well-being, and reduced financial worry during your time of healing.

Funeral/Memorial Period:

☐ Follow directives if body or organ donation was planned.

☐ Select a funeral home, if not already arranged.

☐ Discuss costs with funeral director with the assistance of a family member or friend. Select what is within your budget.

☐ Order preprinted "thank you" cards.

☐ Decide on cremation or burial, if not already determined.

☐ Make arrangements for the service, in consultation with your place of worship if appropriate.

☐ Write an obituary and send this to local newspapers. Include information about memorial gifts if appropriate. A family member or friend can help you follow guidelines supplied by your newspapers. The funeral home will also assist if requested.

☐ Notify friends, relatives, and others.

☐ Order at least 15 copies of the death certificate from the funeral director or health department.

☐ Allow family and close friends to assist with food preparation and housekeeping tasks.

☐ Arrange care for children, if needed.

☐ Make a list of contacts you can reach in an emergency.

☐ Set up a system to record and later acknowledge cards, letters, phone calls, food, and other gifts.

Begin to Organize Information:

☐ Start a filing system for quick and easy retrieval. For example, use colored manila folders. Here are some possible file headings: bank correspondence, bills, business-related, credit card statements, employer correspondence, estate documents, household, income-tax related, investments, life insurance, other assets, and personal documents.

☐ Create a calendar with important due dates.

☐ Keep a log of actions taken, including the date and contact person if someone else was involved and pertinent notes. (If you don't create a list, you're likely to forget the dozens of contacts you'll make and things done.)

Work with an Attorney and Tax Preparer:

☐ Gather significant documents, including your husband's will and trust if applicable.

☐ If you have not previously worked with a tax preparation professional, inquire about which documents to keep and your pertinent tax issues for the current year.

☐ Ask friends or a professional advisor for names of a lawyer who does estate work, if you don't already have an attorney. This person will guide you during the probate process.

☐ If you're the executor, process and manage the estate settlement process with the guidance of your professional advisors. (Also see section on estate settlement.)

Review Cash Flow and Liquidity Needs:

☐ Be certain you have sufficient cash flow during this transition period. Prepare a statement listing where money will come from and where it needs to go in the coming months. Include a list of regular bills.

☐ Tap certain investments that may be available at face value without penalty, as they carry an "estate feature." (For example, certificates of deposit with a "death put" or a variable annuity with a death benefit greater than its current market value.)

Collect Benefits:

☐ Locate birth certificate, Social Security number, marriage license, military discharge papers, W-2 earnings statements, financial account statements, and company benefits brochure you may need to collect certain benefits. Keep these papers readily available in your organizational folders.

☐ File a benefits claim form through the nearest Social Security Administration office or go online at www.ssa.gov if you qualify for benefits. Call 1-800-772-1213 and ask for Publication No. 05-10084: "Survivor Benefits." If your spouse paid into the Social Security system for at least 40 quarters (10 years) and was eligible to receive Social Security, you will receive a lump-sum death benefit of $255. Unmarried children under age 18 (or older if attending high school or if disabled) are eligible for benefits, and if you are caring for these children you may qualify for survivor benefits. You can apply for Social Security survivor benefits as early as age 60 if you are a widow with limited employment income (or in some cases, even earlier).

☐ Contact your life insurance agent to start collecting benefits. You may have various payment options. Be certain you understand your choices before selecting the payout method. Check the following sources for other life insurance: your spouse's employer or former employers; insurance through your mortgage company, credit cards, or certain other loans; and professional association or unions.

☐ Collect veterans benefits if you qualify. Contact the Department of Veterans Affairs if your husband served in the military. You and children of active-duty or retired military may be eligible for certain benefits, such as medical care, commissary exchange, and veterans' mortgage life insurance. For more information on benefits and procedures, go to www.va.gov or visit a local VA office.

☐ Roll over your spouse's individual retirement accounts (IRAs) into your own. Or, if you are less than 59½ years old and need extra income, consider making his account a beneficiary IRA. This will minimize income tax you'll pay on early distributions. (Other exceptions may exist. Consult your tax professional or financial planner before making choices.)

☐ Contact the human resources department of your late spouse's employer if he was employed at the time of death. Staff can assist you with unpaid salary, vacation pay, sick pay, medical-care flex or reimbursement account, bonuses and commissions, life insurance, pension benefits, access to qualified retirement accounts, stock options, and any other benefits due. If the death was because of an accident on the job, there may be accidental death benefits.

☐ Take a pension from your spouse's qualified retirement plan or roll over money into your IRA, depending on your options. Review the employer's retirement plan document.

☐ Contact the financial aid office if you have a child in college. Your son or daughter may be eligible for special assistance or increased financial aid.

Adjust Health and Other Insurance Coverage:

☐ Make sure you have your own medical insurance coverage. If you and your family were covered under your deceased spouse's policy at work, inquire about continuing under the group plan through COBRA (Consolidated Omnibus Budget Reconciliation Act) coverage. (You are eligible to enroll for up to 36 months after your spouse's death—more than the standard 18-month period.) You will have to pay the premium. Another option may be to convert from existing group coverage to an individual plan. If you previously had your own policy, notify the agent of your spouse's death so premiums may be reduced. Notify Medicare if covered.

☐ Inform insurance agents for your auto, homeowner's, liability, long-term care, and other policies. Premiums may be reduced for one fewer driver. If your husband had long-term-care insurance, you may be eligible for the return of part of his most recent premium payment.

Review Assets and Liabilities:

☐ Create a financial net worth statement, a list of all you own and what you owe.

Complete the Estate Settlement:

☐ Change the title and beneficiaries, at the appropriate time, on investments, vehicles, and your safe deposit box. It may not be necessary to change the title on your residence, depending on how it's titled now. You may want to hold off temporarily on changing names on credit cards so you will continue to have use of the existing cards. (When you are ready to change ownership of a credit card, write a letter to this effect and send this to the company, along with a copy of the death certificate.)

☐ Don't change your joint checking account name for a year or so, as checks may still come payable to your spouse for some time. You'll be able to deposit these into your joint account.

☐ File an estate tax return if federal or state estate tax is owed (due nine months after death).

Take Care of Yourself:

☐ Remember self-care, which may include exercise, yoga, meditation, facials, manicures, bubble baths, enjoying a beautiful sunset, spiritual practices, and chocolate! Do not let this slide!

☐ Read a good book about widowhood to give you guidance and inspiration. Here's one to start with: *For Widows Only!* by Annie Estlund (iUniverse, 2003).

☐ Consider joining a support group for widows or talking with a counselor.

☐ Keep in touch with your women friends.

In the Future, Move Forward with New Goals and Your New Life:

☐ Create an updated financial plan. Focus on short-term goals first, especially during the first year or so. Keep your plan simple and manageable.

☐ Update your will and estate plan. You may want to include charitable bequests for those organizations that you and your spouse supported previously.

☐ Think about writing a legacy letter (also known as an ethical will) that passes on your values, beliefs, hopes for the next generation, insights, special stories, history, and so much more.

☐ Expand your social circles. Meet new people who know you as yourself and not as half of the couple you were before your spouse died.

☐ Be careful about "coupling" too quickly if you are interested in a new relationship. Give yourself some time. Be careful about new partners looking for a "purse." Keep your finances to yourself.

☐ Try to keep in mind that there is life after grief. You will be able to reframe parts of your life positively as you continue your journey as a widow. Postpone major decisions during the first year when possible! You don't need to rush. Especially take time with your big decisions. You are going through a grieving process, and your life may feel like it's been turned upside down. Your mental, emotional, and physical condition may be very different than before your husband's death. Well-meaning acquaintances, extended family, or salespeople who don't really know your entire situation might bombard you with suggestions. It can be helpful to have a friend help you think through some decisions you'll face. For example, right now may not be the time to pay off your home mortgage. It might also not be wise to move in with your adult daughter and her family, either. If you don't want to make some decisions alone, consider asking a trusted professional to assist you. Be careful about whom you select, because widows are sometimes viewed as easy targets by those who sell financial products. You are at a very vulnerable time following your husband's death. Go slowly. Be gentle. Give yourself time to heal.

Ask yourself this question: Does this decision have to be made right now, or can it wait for a future date, which might be a better time for me to make the right choice or take action then? Just don't rush!

Appendix 7D: Medical Form

This form is provided as a courtesy of www.MedIDs.com.

Name:			
Address:			
City and State:			
Home Phone Number:			
Cell Phone Number:			
E-mail Address:			
Primary Medical Insurance:			
Secondary Medical Insurance:			
Other Medical Insurance Info.:			
Date of Birth:			
Medical Directives: (Select)	Organ Donor:	DNR:	Other:
Physician:	Phone:		
Physician:	Phone:		
Physician:	Phone:		
Physician:	Phone:		
Physician:	Phone:		
Physician:	Phone:		
Wear Contact Lens:	Blood Type:	Weight:	Height:
Primary Medical Condition:			
Other Medical Conditions:			
Other Medical Conditions:			
Other Medical Conditions:			
Other Medical Conditions:			
Other Medical Conditions:			

Drug Allergies:	
Drug Allergies:	
Drug Allergies:	
Food/Insect Allergies:	
Other Allergies:	
Implants, (Hip Replacement, etc.):	
Hospital Name/ Phone No.:	
Pharmacy Name/ Phone No.:	
Previous Surgeries:	
Previous Surgeries:	
Previous Surgeries:	
Hospitalizations:	
Hospitalizations:	
Hospitalizations:	
Lab Test:	
Lab Test:	
Other:	
Other:	
Other:	

Enter in form below people to contact in the event of an emergency.

Name	Relationship	Home Phone	Work or Cell

Enter the medications and supplements that you are taking at the present time.

Drug/Supplement Name	Dosage	Frequency	Pharmacy Rx No.

Dollars and Sense

The amount of money in your bank account is a fact. The amount you spend today is your choice.

—Sarah Ban Breathnach

We noted previously that 80 percent to 90 percent of women will be responsible for *all* financial decisions at some point, and that many single women are concerned about running out of money in retirement or becoming a bag lady. If this is an area that you're worried about, know that an awful lot of our sisters—and our brothers, too—feel the same. In an Allianz survey, 61 percent of respondents said they were more afraid of outliving their assets than they were of dying.

We also discussed what you might want to do with those 168 hours a week when we retire. Determining how much money you need in retirement is really planning for the kind of lifestyle you want in retirement. If you want to travel to every continent, live in a resort-type community, and fund your grandchildren's education, you'll obviously need more than if you're a homebody and plan to grow your own food, continue to work until you die, and live in a modest residence with a roommate. Planning for your finances can be daunting, but it's not as complicated as it initially appears. It's important to decide what you hope your lifestyle will be, and then be willing to change your plans if your retirement income can't support it. You may need to dial down your retirement expectations, or distinguish your true needs from your wants.

One consoling statistic: Three out of four pre-retired women are enthusiastic about retirement, according to Ameriprise Financial.

If you're looking for the quick and dirty CliffsNotes approach to not running out of money in retirement, take a look at "Retirement by the Numbers: Basic Cheat Sheet for Being Prepared," below. The rest of the chapter looks in more detail at expenses in retirement, funding your retirement, advisors, tax issues, and some money-saving ideas.

Retirement by the Numbers: Basic Cheat Sheet for Being Prepared

No matter your age, there are certain things you need to do to prepare financially for retirement, and of course, the earlier you start, the better. Specifically:

1. *Save, save, save.* How much of your salary should you put aside? Experts recommend at least 10 percent to 15 percent of your annual income, and more if you're closer to retirement and haven't put much aside. If you've hit your 40s or 50s and haven't started saving, you may need to save two or three times as much from each paycheck. One simple calculator that tells you what you need to put aside can be found at www.morningstar.com (click on "Real Life Finance" and the calculator is in the middle of the page—"Are you saving enough for retirement?"). Several assumptions are built into this calculator: You'll need 80 percent of your present income (net of savings) for retirement, you'll retire at 65, inflation will be 2.5 percent a year and your income will increase by the same 2.5 percent a year, you'll receive Social Security, and you'll invest your money in a "life-cycle" or "target-date" mutual fund, which rebalances your investments (stock, bonds, and cash) based on your age and retirement date. For example, if you're 55, make $40,000 a year, and have saved $10,000, you'll need to save 26.2 percent of your income each year until retirement. No guarantee, of course, but this calculator is one easy way to come up with an actual percent of

what you need to save to have a 90 percent chance of outliving your money. If this seems daunting, remember that saving something is better than saving nothing.

2. *Establish an emergency fund of three to six months.* Remember, it's for an emergency ... and the newest designer shoes don't qualify as an emergency.

3. *Pay down debt.* If you're struggling with debt, personal finance guru Dave Ramsey suggests a technique called the "debt snowball." List your debts from lowest to highest. Pay the minimum balances on all debts except the smallest, and pay down that smallest debt fast. Once you've rid yourself of the lowest debt, pay off the next lowest one. Continue until all debt is gone. Some experts suggest you tackle the debt with the highest interest rate first, but Ramsey's idea is that you'll feel better getting rid of the smallest debt first, and you'll be motivated to continue and pay down the rest of your debts. Paying off the smallest debt is the beginning of your "snowball," and once it gets rolling, there's no stopping you! Once your debt is paid down, pay all of your credit cards in full each month.

4. *Pay yourself first for retirement.* Put your retirement savings before your kids or grandkids' college education. They have more time than you do to save for their own future, and can work, take out loans, or attend a community college for the first two years. Of course, if you have the excess money to pay for their education, it is a great investment in their future.

5. *Contribute the max to your retirement savings program at work.* At a minimum, contribute enough to get the maximum employer match available.

6. *Consider where and how you'll live.* If you're living alone, consider a roommate, or downsize to something less expensive. Or move to an area that costs less. This can go a long way toward making your money stretch, both when saving for retirement and when you retire.

7. *Be flexible about work.* You may need to work in retirement, even if it's part-time. Match your retirement lifestyle to your retirement income.

8. *Stay healthy.* Many health care costs are related to lifestyle, and we have control over them.

9. *Postpone taking Social Security, if you can.* Don't take Social Security until you reach your full retirement age or even later, if possible.

10. *Rinse and repeat.* Review your financial status on a regular basis, getting professional help if necessary.

Significant Statistic

The current definition of poverty for a single woman under 65 living alone: income under $11,702, according to the U.S. Census Bureau.

Expenses in Retirement

Although financial planners suggest a number of ballpark formulas for estimating your costs in retirement—70 percent to 80 percent of your pre-retirement expenses is commonly cited—the only real way to properly estimate is by categorizing your major spending areas and then estimating each one separately. The best place to start figuring out what you need in retirement is to summarize your current spending and then project your retirement costs category by category. Begin with the biggest expenses: housing, food, transportation, travel, medical, insurance, personal care, entertainment, and so on. Some expenses, such as work-related expenses, including your contributions to your 401(k) plans, business wardrobe, and lunches out, will go down, while other expenses, like travel, entertainment, and medical, will likely go up. Some experts say we'll spend up to a fifth of our after-tax retirement income on health care. After you finish estimating your monthly ongoing expenses, add in large one-time costs, such as buying a new car, replacing your washer and dryer, or putting a new roof on your home.

Many worksheets available online can help you work through the estimate of your retirement expenses; one you might try is from Vanguard (https://personal.vanguard.com/us/insights/retirement/tool/retirement-expense-worksheet).

Complete this worksheet assuming your ideal retirement. You may find great comfort in the results, or you might find you need to make some small or large modifications to your expected retirement lifestyle. It'll be a start. For example, do you have a "bucket list"? You might have to move some of these items to the "chuck-it" list.

How Much Money Do You Really Need, How Much Can You Spend, and What If You Have Less Than You Need?

Let's consider needs versus wants. Shelter, clothing, and food . . . this is what we used to think were our basic needs. That changes, though, the more comfortable we are. In a recent survey by MainStay Investments of consumers 45 to 65 with $100,000 or more of investable liquid assets, more than half of respondents declared that an Internet connection, shopping for birthdays and special occasions, an annual vacation, and pet care were needs, not wants or luxuries. Almost half said weekend getaways and professional hair coloring/cut were basic needs, while about a third said dining out, ordering take-out, and going to the movies were considered non-negotiables in everyday life. So, when answering the question "How much money do I need for retirement?" a reality check might be in order.

Your assets at retirement will need to fund your expected lifestyle. If they aren't enough, you may need to work longer at least part time during retirement and perhaps also reduce your expenses. There are many ways to significantly reduce your expenses, and lots of suggestions are included a bit later in this chapter, but the single biggest way may be to move to less expensive housing, possibly in a lower-cost area. And yes, you won't get as much for your home as you want in today's depressed real estate market, but you'll buy another one for less.

The cost of living in different areas varies significantly. In a previous chapter, we mentioned the Cost of Living Index. And it's not just that housing, food, and transportation (factors the index takes into account) are cheaper in many areas of the country, but state taxes can also be important. The impact of state taxes on your overall retirement expenses are addressed later in this chapter. Another option, of course, is to move to a less expensive location abroad; go back to Chapter 6 for that discussion.

Essentially, the best way to determine how much money you need for retirement is to estimate your retirement expenses (have you completed the worksheet referenced above?) and then

For More Information

A new Web site from Wider Opportunities for Women (WOW) allows you to search the basic cost of living (food, housing, transportation, and health care) in the United States by state and county. It's designed for those 65 years of age and older, and it's bare bones; it doesn't factor in extras such as taking vacations, buying gifts, going to the theater, or eating out. What's nice is that you can specify whether you're single and own your home with or without a mortgage, or whether you're a single renter. Check it out at www.wowonline.org (click on "Economic Security Database" then "Elder Index"). You do have to register to use this free site.

reduce them by the total of your retirement income that comes from sources other than your IRA, 401(k), and other investment accounts, such as Social Security, employer pensions, and employment. The balance represents the expenses you need to cover from your investment accounts. It would be great if you could just guess at how many years you will live in retirement and multiply your annual expenses by your remaining years and compare it to your investment accounts. But, as you probably suspect, it is not that easy. Investment accounts produce income each year, and expenses increase with inflation. Plus, who really knows how many years we have left to live? Surely we don't want a financial plan that is based on an early death.

So how do you know how much of your investment portfolio you can safely spend each year without running out of money before you die? A commonly cited rule of thumb has been the 4 percent rule. This rule says that you will likely not run out of money if you only withdraw 4 percent of your portfolio, starting with the year you retire and only increasing the withdrawal rate by inflation. Variations of this rule suggest the annual withdrawal rate should be between 3 percent and 5 percent. For example, Carla L.'s assets at retirement are $600,000. Using a 4 percent withdrawal rate and a 3 percent inflation rate, Carla would take $24,000 in the first year, $24,720 in the second year, $25,462 in the third year, and so on. Although using a constant withdrawal rate of about

4 percent could work out fine, there is always a risk of a significant market decline, depleting your portfolio and risking that you will run out of money. This can be particularly disastrous if the decline takes place in your early retirement years. Planners generally recommend that you reduce the withdrawal rate in years of significant market declines to help preserve the principal balance of your investments.

Tip

Many advisors are now recommending a safe withdrawal of 3 percent, instead of 4 percent, as in the past. The combination of low interest rates on investments and relatively poor stock market performance throughout the first decade and into the second of the 21st century suggests this is a good time to err on the conservative side.

Another way to look at the 4 percent rule is that your investment assets at retirement need to be about 25 times your estimate of your initial annual retirement expenses reduced by your retirement income from sources other than your investment assets. This is the amount that needs to be funded from your investment assets each year. If, for example, this amounts to $25,000 in the initial year, you should have a portfolio of at least $625,000 ($25,000 × 25).

Inflation Can Be a Nasty Surprise and Expense

Your expenses will rise each year with inflation, and you must factor this into your calculations. Although inflation has been averaging around 2 percent the last several years, the average rate for the first decade of the 21st century has been a bit under 3 percent and from January 1990 through December 2011, it averaged close to 3.5 percent. If inflation were 3 percent each year, an item that cost $200 in 2012 would cost $361 in 2032 and $485 in 2042. If you ignore inflation, you will be seriously overestimating your ability to fund your retirement expenses. On my personal retirement projections,

I inflate all my estimated expenses by 3.5 percent per year. This has turned out to be a bit high over the past few years, but my preference is to be conservative. Keep in mind that a 65-year-old woman has a life expectancy of about 85, while a 75-year-old woman can expect to live to 88, and many of us will live longer (look at the growing number of centenarians and supercentenarians). I base my projections of retirement income and expenses on a life expectancy of 90, and I hope to live even longer.

Did You Know?

Although many retirees expect their monthly expenses to drop in retirement, 50 percent found their expenses were the same or more, according to an Employee Benefit Research Institute study.

Don't Forget the Expense of Health Care

Remember heath care costs when you're thinking about expenses. At the magic age of 65, you're eligible for premium-free Medicare Part A if *"you or your spouse worked for at least 10 years in Medicare-covered employment and you are 65 years or older and a citizen or permanent resident of the United States,"* according to www.medicare.gov. If you haven't worked a total of 10 years, or if your ex-spouse or deceased spouse worked in Medicare-covered employment for 10 years, you may still be able to acquire Medicare on your own. Medicare is a federal health insurance program for people who are 65 and older and for some younger people with disabilities. There are two options for how you can receive Medicare:

1. Original Medicare is a fee-for-service plan where you choose any doctor or health care facility that accepts Medicare.
2. Medicare Advantage is an alternative to Original Medicare and is offered through private insurance companies such as HMOs and PPOs.

Original Medicare includes Part A (hospital insurance) and Part B (medical or doctor's insurance) and covers many of your costs.

Many people with Original Medicare also enroll in Medicare Part D, which provides coverage for some of your prescription drugs, and Medicare Supplemental Insurance (Medigap), which helps pay some of the costs that Medicare doesn't, such as your deductibles and copayments.

Medicare Advantage plans typically combine Parts A, B, and D, and they might offer a few additional services. Most Advantage plans require you to use doctors and hospitals on the plan list. Your rights under Advantage plans may be different than under Original Medicare.

Medicare does not cover all of your health care costs. Depending on which plan you choose, you'll probably be paying deductibles, copayments, premiums, and coinsurance. How much will this cost? For a single woman retiring in 2012, it can be $300 a month for the extra Medicare coverage (Parts B and D and Medigap insurance), with the cost gradually increasing. Go to the Medicare site for more information. If you have questions about Medicare or need assistance paying for Medicare, you can call the Medicare Hotline at 1-800-633-4227. If your income and resources—such as bank accounts, stocks, and bonds—are limited, you may be able to get help with paying some of these costs. Contact your state or local office of the State Health Insurance Assistance Program at www.shiptalk.org.

Tip

You can switch from Original Medicare to a Medicare Advantage plan and vice versa during Medicare's annual open-enrollment period. If you switch back to Original Medicare after being on an Advantage plan, you may not be able to get Medicare supplemental insurance (based on pre-existing conditions) or your premiums may have increased.

You have the right to enroll in a Medicare supplemental (Medigap) policy without taking into account pre-existing conditions only once during the six months following your initial enrollment in Medicare Part B at age 65 or over.

If you're age 65 or older and still covered by a group health plan from your employer, you might not need Medicare right away. Check with Medicare to find out how it works with other insurance.

What if you retire before the age of 65 and your health care costs aren't covered by your employer or you don't have an employer? For Diane R., who worked outside the home only during her first few years of marriage (she married right out of college and left her job to care for her children), part of her divorce settlement included her ex paying for her insurance until she reached the age of 65 and could start receiving Medicare (she had been married for 33 years). Tamara L. was downsized from her position at the age of 59. She checked with her employer to see if she could be covered for 18 months by COBRA (Consolidated Omnibus Budget Reconciliation Act), and she could. If you're 55 or older, a few states let you continue COBRA coverage until you're eligible for Medicare. You may not be eligible for COBRA—for example, employers with fewer than 20 employees don't have to offer COBRA—so check with your state insurance department for insurance options. Although COBRA is more expensive since you have to pay your employer's portion too, and there's a 2 percent administration charge, COBRA is often a better deal than purchasing insurance on the open market. When COBRA runs out, you may have the right to buy an individual policy from the former group insurer without being subject to pre-existing conditions. Check with your state Health Insurance Department if you lose your group health insurance.

About 13 percent of women in the United States between the ages of 45 and 64 are uninsured, according to the National Center for Health Statistics. If you have to seek health insurance coverage on your own, see what the rules are for your state. Your state determines the rules that govern insurance companies, and some states are better than others in regulating fees, coverage, and how easy it is to drop you from their rolls. Go to www.healthcare.gov to read more about health care options. A comparison site such as www.ehealthinsurance.com or www.coverageforall.org provides thorough and easy-to-understand information.

The 2010 Affordable Care Act was designed to help individuals get health care coverage; check out www.healthcare.gov for descriptions and updates. For example, under the act, starting in 2014, women wouldn't be charged higher premiums than men would be charged or be denied coverage for pre-existing conditions.

Remember that some companies offer health care coverage even if you work only 20 hours a week (examples of these are listed in Chapter 3). You can also often get free or low-cost dental care at dental and dental hygiene schools; or go to a site such as www .freedentalcare.us and look by state; or contact a federally funded health care center through www.hrsa.gov (U.S. Department of Health and Human Services)—click on "Get Health Care." And, of course, exercising and eating right might help lower medical costs, too. Many health issues, such as diabetes, some cancers, and cardiovascular disease, can be related to lifestyle.

Another Possible Expense: Long-Term Care Insurance

As a single woman, you need to think about how you will be taken care of should you eventually be unable to live on your own. Perhaps if you have kids you'll move in with them or they will move in with you. Perhaps you'll find a roommate and you'll help one another. Perhaps you can manage by hiring a home health aide or nurse aide. Perhaps you'll move to a cohousing community, naturally occurring retirement community, continuing care retirement community, or green home care model, which we discussed in Chapter 6.

While family and friends generally provide the majority of care people receive in the United States, you'll find out quickly that long-term care can be expensive if you need to purchase it. The cost varies widely depending on location, but in 2011 the average cost for a private room was $239 a day, or $87,235 a year. The average price of an aide coming to your home to help with bathing, eating, and dressing was $21 an hour, according to the 2011 MetLife Market Survey.

You might want to consider long-term care insurance. It's not for everyone, so you should consider whether you can afford the premiums both now and well into the future. In addition to the cost, many people see purchasing long-term care insurance as a gamble. According to Nolo, as a woman 65 or older there is a two-in-three chance you will need a long-term-care facility, and if you do, only one-fourth of women will stay more than a year, and only 10 percent longer than three years.

Did You Know?

Medicaid pays for nursing homes and home care aides for those who have limited incomes or have exhausted their resources. Medicare does not cover those costs, unless you need skilled nursing care or rehabilitation such as physical therapy. Even then, care is limited. Most long-term care is not skilled care but rather help with daily activities such as bathing, dressing, or eating.

The cost of long-term care coverage varies by the age of the insured as well as by the term of the policy, particularly with respect to the waiting period before benefits start, the number of months the policy will pay benefits, and how much the total benefits will be, both per day and for lifetime maximums. Newer policies, unlike older policies, often include home health care, assisted living care, and inflation riders.

Long-term coverage is expensive, and many will find that they can't afford it, or if they can afford it, they don't need it because they have enough assets to pay for their long-term care. What are "enough assets"? Experts advise that $1.5 million in savings should allow you to self-insure for long-term health care and still afford your retirement. Rule of thumb: If you are having difficulty paying basic expenses, this insurance may not be for you. If you purchase long-term care insurance, limit premiums to around 5 percent of your income, according to the National Association of Insurance Commissioners.

Did You Know?

To be eligible for Medicaid coverage, the largest payer of long-term care, you need to have no more than $2,000 in "countable" assets. In some states, you may need to sell your home and use the proceeds to pay for your long-term care. When your money is (virtually) gone, Medicaid will kick in. Your Social Security checks will also go toward your care, minus a small amount (about $60 a month) for your personal use. Medicaid is a joint federal-state program, so rules vary by state. If you think you can transfer your assets to your loved ones and qualify for Medicaid, you're in for a surprise. There are severe penalties affecting your eligibility for Medicaid based on an inappropriate transfer of assets. For a good discussion of this topic, check out www.elderlawanswers.com/elder_info/medicaid-rules.asp.

For an estimate of the cost of long-term care insurance, go to AARP's calculator, www.aarp.org/longtermcarecosts, or try the calculator at the Federal Long Term Care Insurance Program Web site, www.ltcfeds.com, and click on "Calculate FLTCIP Premiums." Note that not everyone can purchase a policy with this company, but you'll get an idea of cost without having to divulge any personal information except a birthday. As an example, this site shows that a 55-year-old woman purchasing long-term-care insurance would have a monthly cost of $92.39 for coverage of $150 per day, for a maximum of two years, a 90-day waiting period, a 4 percent inflation protection feature and a lifetime maximum benefit of $109,500. Going to a three-year maximum with the lifetime benefit capped at $219,000 raises the monthly premium to $155.34. Examples of companies that offer long-term-care insurance are John Hancock and Transamerica Life Insurance Company. Although you probably won't be able to get a guarantee that rates won't increase over the life of the policy, you should at least ask for a history of rate increases by the insurance companies you are considering. Recent stories in the press have reported increases as much as 90 percent charged to existing policy holders.

Compare at least three policies using the checklist developed by the National Association of Insurance Commissioners, in its Shopper's Guide to Long-term Care Insurance (www.ltcfeds.com /documents/files/NAIC_Shoppers_Guide.pdf).

Some General Savings Guidelines

Before we look at managing your investments for retirement, a few words about *saving* for retirement:

Tip

Consider how to frame questions you ask yourself. For example, when a researcher asked participants if they could save 20 percent of their income, half said no, but when the researcher asked if they could live on 80 percent of their current income if they had to, 80 percent said yes. Same question, different answer. It's all about how the question was framed.

As an alternative to the Morningstar calculator referenced earlier, both AARP (www.aarp.org/retirementcalculator) and Yahoo! (www.finance.yahoo.com/calculator/retirement/ret02) have good calculators. Filling in the numbers could be a big wake-up call. For example, I looked at a scary but not atypical scenario: a 50-year-old woman (we'll call her Sally), making $60,000 a year, who has $2,000 in retirement savings. I assumed Sally needs to replace 75 percent of her current income to live for 20 retirement years, is retiring at age 65, is collecting Social Security, and will earn an 8 percent return on investments (an optimistic return these days). I assumed an inflation rate of 3 percent. What did it show? Sally will need to save about 24 to 26 percent of her annual income each year, including any employer match she receives, until her retirement at age 65. Of course, the lesson is to start saving early; it's very hard to catch up.

Tip

One trick to save more effectively is to establish one savings goal (such as retirement) rather than multiple goals. Research has shown that when you have competing goals, people are often overcome by choice and do nothing, but saving for one goal seems manageable and often results in more specific action.

Should You Pay an Advisor or Do it Yourself?

For many of us, the thought of handling our own retirement planning is scary, boring, or too overwhelming, and something for which we need the services of a professional advisor. Others may find the world of finance fascinating, and a challenge they are ready to tackle (see "More 411" at the end of this chapter for resources). If you were once married, your spouse was in charge of the financial portion of the marriage pie, and you used an advisor, your husband may have been responsible for choosing the advisor. Interestingly, about 70 percent of women drop their current financial advisor within one year of their husband's departure.

You may be deluged with mail from investment professionals seeking your business. There are stockbrokers, accountants, financial planners, insurance salespeople, purveyors of annuities, and the list goes on and on. Although the expertise of these individuals is more important than their credentials, it is probably better to stick with advisors who have received the appropriate training and passed the requisite tests to receive relevant professional certifications.

There are two kinds of financial advisors, who have different standards of advice. Investment advisers have a fiduciary duty and are supposed to serve the best interests of their clients. (Note that the term *financial advisor* is a generic term, but *investment adviser*—with an "e"—is a term of art and the adviser's responsibilities are defined within federal and state law.) Financial advisors, including brokers and their representatives, only have to give investment advice based on suitability, a lower standard. The terms may be different, but the point is that you should know whether your financial advisor is subject to the higher standards and is required to operate in your best interest. I would recommend that you also consider a certified financial planner (CFP) or possibly a certified public accountant (CPA) who also has a personal financial specialist (PFS) designation. These professionals should be able to help you plan out your likely financial needs in retirement as well as set up a plan for how you can get from here to there, including assistance with your investments and planning for a lifestyle that fits your situation.

Keep in mind that such advisors are compensated by fees, either hourly or as an annual percentage of your investment portfolio (in the area of 0.75 percent to 1.5 percent, with the lower percentages used for the larger portfolios), by commissions from your purchase of investment products, or through a combination of both. Although the method of compensation should not be the most important determining factor in your selection of an advisor, many feel that receiving a commission from a client's purchase of investment products presents a conflict of interest to the professional. Other investors prefer commission-based compensation because they think it is more transparent.

Did You Know?

About 47 percent of households preferred to pay commissions, compared to only 27 percent who preferred paying a fee based on assets, according to a survey by Cerulli Associates. Even fewer preferred paying a retainer or hourly fee for investment advice.

Those holding themselves out as financial advisors (the generic term) may be licensed as brokers, investment advisers, insurance agents, lawyers, accountants, or even financial planners. In some cases, like financial planners, there is no state or federally issued license. "Certified financial planner" is a title conferred by the Certified Financial Planner Board of Standards. Many financial advisors also use various titles or designations showing their specialization in planning for retirement or investing by older adults. These designations vary in how much is required to get and maintain them and can be misleading. For more information about the use of designations, go to www.aarp.org/money/scams-fraud/info-06-2008/senior_specialists.html.

One way to locate financial professionals in your area is by talking to your friends and acquaintances, as well as to your attorney and accountant. Another way is to contact the National Association of Personal Financial Advisors (NAPFA), which will locate planners for you by zip code, at www.napfa.org/consumer/index.asp or call them at 847-483-5400. To locate a certified financial planner (CFP), contact the Certified Financial Planner Board of Standards at www.cfp.net. For a certified public accountant, contact the American Institute of Certified Public Accountants (AICPA) at www.aicpa.org (go to "For the Public" then "Find a CPA") or call 888-777-7077. Once you identify a few possible candidates (many women prefer to work with women), you should visit with them to see if they meet your needs and are individuals you can work with and charge fees that you can afford. Finding an advisor you click with who is both a CFP and a CPA would be a real coup.

Tip

Always be alert to possible fraud when dealing with your finances. About 20 percent of Americans older than age 65 have been victimized by a financial scam, according to a survey by Investor Protection Trust. Remember how Bernie Madoff's financial management business turned out to be a house of cards, with investors losing around $20 billion? Consider spreading your investments around among managers and putting your investments in custodial accounts rather than accounts held in the name of your financial advisor. If you don't understand the investment being recommended, don't invest in it, and if the promised returns seem too good to be true, they probably are. One other bit of bad news—we become about 2 percent less financially savvy each year after we hit 60, according to a study by Texas Tech University, while at the same time we become more confident in our financial abilities! For more information about financial scams and fraud, go to www.aarp.org/fraud.

Sources of Money in Retirement

For many single women, the primary source of retirement income will be Social Security, hopefully supplemented by earnings from investments in 401(k) plans, IRAs, and savings. Although our parents may have retired with a pension from their employers, these traditional pension plans are disappearing and today only about 15 percent of private-sector (non-governmental) employers still have such plans. This means that most of us are now responsible for ensuring that we don't outlive our assets. So, here are the sources:

Working in Retirement

I know, working in retirement sounds like an oxymoron. Go back to Chapter 3 for a discussion of hot careers, part-time jobs with health benefits, working from home (yes, sometimes it is legit), and tips for networking, resume writing, and interviewing.

Social Security

In 2011, 66 percent of singles 65 and older relied on Social Security for at least half of their income; 41 percent of singles 65 and older relied on the program for 90 percent or more. No wonder it's called the "third rail" of American politics. The average retirement benefit? In 2012, it was $1,229 a month. Let's examine a few scenarios. First, assume you worked for at least 10 years and never married. In that case, your payments from Social Security will be based on your earnings history during your working years, using your 35 highest years of earnings, but the calculated benefit is reduced, or increased, if you retire before or after what is considered your full retirement age. Full retirement age used to be 65, but it is gradually increasing to age 67 (for those retirees born in 1960 or later) by a change to the rules enacted years ago.

Did You Know?

You're eligible for Social Security retirement benefits if you have 10 years of work (40 credits) subject to Social Security taxes. You can earn up to four credits per year, based on your earnings. For 2012 you earned one credit for each $1,130 of earnings. This amount goes up a little each year as average earnings increase.

If you haven't worked for the full 35 years, you will have some years with no qualifying earnings, which will reduce your benefit. The amount of the reduction may be mitigated somewhat because the calculation is based on your average monthly earnings and gives more weight to lower average earnings than to higher average earnings. Your actual benefit is based on 90 percent of the first $767 of your average monthly earnings, 32 percent of the next $3,857, and 15 percent of your average monthly wages over $4,624.

Fun Fact

Social Security benefits are calculated using inflation-adjusted earnings, so today's retirees are not hurt by the lower wage levels of past years. For example, $5,000 of earnings in 1972 currently counts as $29,200 of earnings in the formula.

If you were married for at least 10 years, you can claim Social Security benefits based on your ex-husband's earnings record, as long as you have not remarried. In fact, multiple former spouses can collect Social Security benefits based on the same ex-husband's earnings record, as long as they otherwise qualify. If your former spouse is deceased and you were married for at least 10 years and did not remarry before age 60, you can claim benefits based on his earnings as early as age 60.

Today, full retirement age is 66 for those born before 1955, and it gradually increases to age 67 for those born in 1960 or later. Should you elect to begin receiving Social Security benefits early at age 62, or delay receiving them as long as up to age 70, your actual benefits will be actuarially adjusted to be as much as 30 percent less or 32 percent more than the benefit payable at your full retirement age, with the actual adjustment based on how many months early or late you start collecting Social Security.

As an example, a woman born in 1947 who retires with a very high earnings history and starts collecting Social Security at age 66 might get a benefit of as much as $30,000 a year. But should she retire and start taking benefits at age 62, the payments would be reduced by 25 percent to $22,500. Likewise, should she delay the start of benefits to age 70, the annual total would be increased to $39,600. All this raises the question of whether you should start collecting Social Security as early as possible, which is age 62, or delay it as late as age 70, to increase your benefit.

In general, if you are going to continue working after age 62 and will earn more than a specified amount, your earnings could reduce your benefits, at least temporarily. On the other hand, high earnings may increase your Social Security benefit when you eventually collect it—depending on your earnings history. But in an interesting twist of the rules, earnings from working after you reach your full retirement age do not reduce your Social Security benefit.

If you start collecting your Social Security benefits before your full retirement age (your full retirement age is somewhere between age 66 and 67, depending on your year of birth) but continue working, your benefits will be reduced temporarily if you earn over a specified amount, which is adjusted each year for inflation. For 2012 this specified amount is $14,640 for any year before the year you reach your full retirement age, with any earnings over that amount reducing your Social Security benefits in a 1-to-2 ratio. This benefit reduction rule changes in the year you reach full retirement age by using a specified amount of $38,880 with earnings in excess of that amount reducing your benefit in a 1-to-3 ratio, and does not apply at all once you reach full retirement age.

As an example of how this rule works, assume Carla L. started collecting Social Security in 2012 when she was 64 years old and she earned $24,640, or $10,000 more than the limit in 2012; her Social Security benefit would have been reduced by $5,000. It is important to know that the reduction in your benefits will result in an increase in your benefit once you reach full retirement age, to reflect the effect of losing benefits during the years you worked while collecting benefits. Over a lifetime, all of the reduced benefit payments could be repaid to you.

The question that is often hotly debated is whether or not to start collecting Social Security early, at the full retirement age, at age 70, or somewhere in between. The major considerations are whether you plan to continue working, your life expectancy, and whether you need the money before full retirement age or are better off delaying the start of benefits to increase your monthly checks for the rest of your life.

In the example above, a woman born in 1947 must decide between an annual benefit of $22,500 at age 62, $30,000 at age 66 (full retirement age), and $39,600 at age 70. If she has an average life expectancy as shown in the mortality tables, waiting until full retirement age, or, if possible, to age 70 to start collecting Social

Security could be preferable. In fact, waiting as long as possible to receive benefits is the advice given by most financial experts and AARP. Yet data compiled by the Office of the Chief Actuary showed that from 1997 through 2005, over 43 percent started their Social Security benefits within one month of their 62nd birthday and over 72 percent started their benefits before age 65. Only about 14 percent waited for the full retirement age, and less than 3 percent delayed beyond age 66.

The decision to start benefits early or delay them as long as you can largely depends on an assessment of how long you expect to live, and if and when you need the money to live. If you are 65 now, your average life expectancy is another 20 years on average. You may not live that long, or you may live longer.

Many women want to load the first years of retirement with travel and new experiences and need or want more money toward the beginning; they may also be assisting elderly parents or have adult children who need some financial help. If you can tap into other resources rather than claiming Social Security benefits, do so. Social Security might be the only inflation-adjusted life annuity that you will have. By delaying, you'll be buying an inflation-adjusted annuity, likely at the cheapest price available.

For More Information

If you haven't started receiving Social Security and you qualify for benefits, you can get your online statement (www.ssa.gov/mystatement) showing what your benefits would be at age 62, at your full retirement age, and at age 70, as well as other useful information. At www.socialsecurity .gov/estimator, you can create scenarios such as changing your annual income and the age at which you stop working. The site also has a longevity calculator (It said I have 27 years left). You can also get information from the Social Security Administration by calling 800-772-1213. Another site that can help you decide when to start receiving benefits is at www.aarp.org /socialsecuritybenefits.

Fun Fact

Women pay 40 percent of Social Security payroll taxes (we make less and are out of the workforce for longer stints), but receive 49 percent of Social Security benefits (we live longer), according to the Social Security Administration.

Pensions

Although pension plans, a term which generally refers to employer-sponsored retirement plans under which the retirees get a fixed monthly benefit for life, have almost disappeared in the corporate United States, they remain dominant in state and local governments and can be found in some nonprofit schools, hospitals, colleges, and other entities. Under these plans, the monthly benefit, which may or may not adjust in future years for cost of living increases, is generally based on a formula that looks to the number of years the retiree worked for the entity and the average compensation over the last three or five years of employment. The retiree does not have to worry about how to invest the retirement funds, as the employer takes care of all that. There is always some risk that the employer would go out of business and the plan would be terminated without sufficient assets to continue paying the pensions. Under these circumstances, however, the Pension Benefit Guaranty Corporation (PBGC) guarantees up to an annual benefit of $55,840 at age 65. If you retire earlier than age 65, your guaranteed benefit would be actuarially reduced.

If you have the opportunity to take a lump-sum distribution from your employer in lieu of getting a pension, you should at least find out the amount of the distribution and compare it to the annuity payments you could get by rolling the distribution over tax-free into an IRA and buying an annuity from an insurance company (see discussion of annuities below) to replace the pension. Although the current low interest rates have the effect of reducing the amount of annuity payments you can obtain, they also have the effect of increasing the amount of the lump-sum distribution itself. This strategy might be particularly useful if your pension is larger than the PBGC guarantees and your employer's future is at all uncertain.

"Lost" Retirement Accounts

You may have "lost" retirement funds. We live in a very mobile society; many of us have changed jobs a number of times and moved from location to location. It is possible that you have one or more pensions due to you, but your former employers don't know where you are. Over the years, the tax rules for vesting of retirement programs have changed a number of times, and you may have a vested benefit that is yours for the asking. Wouldn't an extra few hundred dollars a month for the rest of your life help in your retirement planning? Although your former employers should have reported your pension to the Social Security Administration and you should find out about it when you apply for Social Security benefits, relying on this reporting system is not your best bet. One place you can search for lost retirement plan funds is at www.unclaimedretire mentbenefits.com. A better course of action would be to call your former employers and ask if you have a vested pension benefit or 401(k) account from your years on the job. Most larger employers have an employee benefits group, or at least a human resources department, and that is where you should direct your call. Kate C., who recently did just that with a major corporation, discovered a vested benefit earned by her now-deceased husband, who worked there in the 1960s and 1970s.

Individual Retirement Accounts and 401(k) Plans

The tax law provides tax-friendly rules to help you save for your retirement. The two principal saving vehicles are the individual retirement account (IRA) and the 401(k) plans. Originally, each of these provided you with the ability to contribute tax-deductible or tax-deferred amounts into an investment account, which could then grow tax-free over your remaining working years and be taxed only when withdrawn. The benefits were obvious: a tax deduction now, with taxability potentially many years later, when your tax rate might be lower. Eventually, these rules were enhanced by allowing a variation: With a Roth IRA or Roth 401(k), the money you contribute to your account is not tax deductible or tax deferred, but qualified withdrawals upon retirement or after reaching age 59 ½ are tax-free.

Which type of IRA or 401(k) you should choose to contribute to depends on your expected tax rate today, at the time of contribution; your expected tax rate in retirement; and the number of years before you plan to start withdrawing from your retirement accounts.

If your tax rate in retirement will be equal to or higher than your tax rate while working, you would generally want to forego the current tax deduction and go with a Roth. If the converse is true, and you expect your tax rate in retirement to be lower, you would tend to pick a regular IRA or 401(k). But if there are many years to go before you plan to start making withdrawals, you may still want to consider using a Roth even if your tax rate in retirement will be lower, because the benefit of many years of compounding tax-deferred income in a Roth account could more than offset the effect of the higher tax rate.

Many rules control how much you can contribute each year to your IRA and 401(k) plan. In 2012 a single woman could contribute up to $17,000 to her 401(k), or $22,500 if she is age 50 or older. For IRA accounts, the maximum that could be contributed in 2012 was $5,000, with up to an additional $1,000 for people age 50 or older. If you have a 401(k) or other retirement account (including a pension) at work, your ability to make a tax-deductible contribution to a traditional IRA starts to phase out when your modified adjusted gross income (essentially your total income with certain adjustments) reaches $58,000 and is eliminated at $68,000.

Tip

If your adjusted gross income meets certain restrictions (in 2012, under $28,750 if you file as a single, $43,125 if you file as head of household), you can get a saver's credit of up to $1,000 on your federal income tax return by making a contribution to a qualified retirement account such as a traditional or Roth IRA or a 401(k) plan.

Investments

Most of us will need to rely on investments in addition to Social Security to provide an income that is adequate to cover our expenses. This is true whether our retirement funds are held in a tax-deferred or tax-saving regular or Roth IRA or 401(k) retirement account or in other taxable investment accounts we have accumulated over the years. A major issue is where to invest our savings so that they not only produce an appropriate amount of earnings, but also last for the rest of our lives. For most, depending on your age and circumstances, a combination of stocks, bonds, and savings accounts works best, but for some, annuities and reverse mortgages may also fit well into their retirement planning.

Banks are paying interest rates so low on savings that the accounts are little more than a place to keep funds safe, while their values are eroded by inflation. Depending on your age, assets, and risk tolerance, to fund a retirement far into the future you will probably need to have a portion of your assets invested in stocks and bonds. If some of your investments are in an employer 401(k) account, your choices of investments will be limited to those offered. When you either retire or leave your employer, you should give some consideration to taking a lump-sum distribution of your 401(k) account, and roll the proceeds into an IRA to have more options available for investing your funds.

Investment of Short-Term Cash   Savings and other similar type accounts and cash-equivalent investments need to be a part of your investments, if for no other reason than to have a ready source of funds to meet current expenses. Right now, interest rates are so low that it is counterproductive to have too much of your portfolio invested this way. Bank accounts generally pay less than ½ of 1 percent interest per year—not enough to pay for your morning coffee. And now that recent legislation has restricted the fees banks can charge for many of their services—such as merchant-paid debit card fees and overdraft fees—institutions seem to be planning on new charges, such as monthly fees for your checking accounts. One good way to avoid these fees and to get a higher interest rate on your bank funds is to use an Internet-based bank. I have accounts at

Bank of Internet (www.bankofinternet.com), Emigrant Bank (www .emigrantdirect.com), and ING (www.ingdirect.com), but there are a number of others as well. Many Internet-based banks pay interest rates that are currently double or more the rates paid by the brick-and-mortar banks, and they can also be used for checking and electronic bill paying. Currently they do not impose monthly fees for their checking and saving accounts. Whatever bank you choose, make sure it is insured by the Federal Deposit Insurance Corporation (FDIC).

One way to have cash funds available on a regular basis, while getting higher interest rates than would be available on bank accounts, is to purchase FDIC-insured bank certificates of deposit and ladder their maturity dates. This allows you to have CDs with longer maturities, and therefore higher interest rates, while still giving you regular penalty-free access to your money. As an example of this, rather than putting $10,000 in a bank savings account paying almost no interest, you would invest the $10,000 in five CDs as follows (using rates available in 2012):

$2,000 in a five-year CD @ 2.00 percent

$2,000 in a four-year CD @ 1.55 percent

$2,000 in a three-year CD @ 1.40 percent

$2,000 in a two-year CD @ 1.15 percent

$2,000 in a one-year CD @ 1.05 percent

After one year, the first CD matures and you can use the funds either to pay for expenses or to purchase a new five-year CD. After four years of reinvesting, all your CDs will have five-year terms, with one maturing every year and paying you more interest than having your funds in either a bank savings account or in one-year CDs, and throughout the initial four years while you are building up to all five-year CDs, you are earning good interest rates—or at least good for the current environment. As interest rates rise you will also be purchasing five-year CDs at the higher interest rates.

Diversifying with Stocks, Bonds, and Other Investments
Every study I've seen makes the point that an investment portfolio

that does not include stocks as well as bonds is unlikely to keep pace with inflation. Although historically stocks generate larger returns (gains and dividends) than bonds, it is also true that stocks carry more risk of market fluctuations than bonds. Because single women are often more cautious with investments, stocks are something that they often shy away from. (Only 27 percent of women, compared to 40 percent of men, express confidence in the stock market—though this is justifiable, considering its recent volatility.) Yet depending on your age, it'll be tough to make your investments last as long as you do without stocks, unless you can work forever or find a money tree. We also have to be aware of psychological issues such as loss aversion; most of us are much more sensitive to loss than to gain. So, a downturn in the stock market can scare us away more than an uptick encourages us to invest.

A portfolio balanced between both stocks and bonds tends to achieve returns almost as good as one invested solely in stocks over a long period, and with less risk. As an example, a recent analysis by Morgan Stanley compared the average annual returns, for all of the 10-year periods starting in 1926, of portfolios composed of 90 percent stocks and 10 percent cash; 60 percent stocks, 30 percent bonds, and 10 percent cash; and 0 percent stocks, 90 percent bonds, and 10 percent cash. Results:

Stocks	Bonds	Cash	Average Return
90%	0%	10%	10%
60%	30%	10%	8.5%
0%	90%	10%	5.4%

It is clear that the portfolios with stocks outperformed the portfolios without stocks. Since any portfolio will likely have many ups and downs over your lifetime, one that is diversified will soften the swings and could prevent you from cashing out in the down markets and missing the inevitable upswing. The balance changes depending on your age and circumstances, such as how close you are to retirement.

Bonds generate more or less fixed returns by virtue of the interest they pay, while a stock investment will generate returns from dividends and from increases in the stock price. Although the market price of bonds fluctuates based not only on the perceived creditworthiness of the company that issued the bond but also on the current market rates of interest, holding the bond to its maturity makes such fluctuations somewhat irrelevant. Stocks are generally considered riskier investments than bonds because of their market fluctuations, but over an extended period will usually produce higher returns than an investment in bonds. As noted, a portfolio balanced between both stocks and bonds tends to have only slightly lower returns but with less risk than a portfolio that is invested only in stocks, and a higher return over time than a portfolio that is invested solely in bonds.

A significant consideration in diversifying a portfolio is how much of your assets should be invested in stocks, bonds, and relatively short-term cash accounts. Since stocks generally have higher returns but more risk than bonds or short-term cash accounts, a younger investor would be well advised to heavily concentrate her portfolio in stocks, and very little in bonds or short-term cash. She has a long time horizon before retirement and, therefore, her stock portfolio has time to recover from a large market decline. An older investor who suffers a large market decline in her portfolio as her retirement date nears could put her retirement in jeopardy, particularly if she plans to start withdrawing from her portfolio early in her retirement years. As she ages, more and more of the portfolio should be shifted out of stocks and into the other two categories to reduce the risk of declines in market value as the retirement date gets closer.

Some mutual funds are designed to rebalance their investments between stocks and bonds as the fund holders' retirement date approaches, thus relieving the investor from having to do this herself. These funds, known as target-date or life-cycle funds, are discussed under "Mutual Funds" and have had mixed reception and success.

In addition to having a portfolio that is diversified among stocks, bonds, relatively short-term cash accounts, and perhaps commodities, it is also important that you diversify within these broad categories. Your stock investments should include large capitalization stocks (think Apple and Exxon), midsize capitalization stocks, and small capitalization stocks, as well as both U.S. and foreign stocks. In fact, many financial specialists now recommend that the portion of your portfolio invested in stocks include as much as 25 percent foreign stocks, and should have a part of this invested in emerging market stocks (countries like Vietnam, India, and China). When considering foreign stocks, keep in mind that your overall gains or losses in these stocks is derived from the performance of the stock itself as well as from the fluctuations in the value of the U.S. dollar to the currency in which the foreign stock is denominated.

Think of a diversified portfolio as a well-landscaped yard, using trees, grass, large bushes, and small bushes, with a few flowers sprinkled in between. A number of different plants are used, and together they produce a beautiful picture.

Fun Fact

Studies show that we tend to buy high when the market is going up and sell when it goes down, earning much less than the average returns in the market. For example, a study by DALBAR of returns for the 20-year period ending in December 2010 concluded that the average investor in stock funds earned a market return of only 3.8 percent a year while the S&P 500 Index averaged 9.1 percent a year. The moral: Don't overreact to market fluctuations.

Commodities

Another asset class you might include in your investment accounts is commodities. These are things like gold, oil, and copper. Investments in commodities are readily available from stock brokerage companies such as Merrill Lynch, Quick & Reilly, TD Ameritrade, and Vanguard.

Reverse Mortgages

Single women make up half of those who obtain reverse mortgages, but reverse mortgages aren't suitable for everyone and should be used only after careful consideration of all possible options. Homeowners age 62 or older who have equity in their homes can draw on this equity to cover living and other expenses without having to sell their homes. The most popular reverse mortgage is the home equity conversion mortgage (HECM), which is insured by the Federal Housing Administration (FHA) and administered by the U.S. Department of Housing and Urban Development. Unlike a home equity line of credit, no payments are required on reverse mortgages, although the initial proceeds of the loan must be used to pay off any existing mortgage debt and you must continue to maintain your home and pay property taxes and homeowner's insurance premiums.

Currently, these mortgages are available regardless of your income, but that may change. The actual amount you can borrow depends on your age, current interest rates, and the value of your home. There are also limits on the total amount that can be borrowed. You can get an estimate of the amount you can borrow using the reverse mortgage calculator at www.reversemortgage.org. With a reverse mortgage, you can access loan proceeds in one of several ways or as a combination: a lump sum, monthly payments for a set period, monthly payments for as long as you live in the home, or a line of credit.

The loan becomes due when you cease to live in the home permanently; that is, when you sell, move out, or die. The loan also becomes due if you fail to pay property taxes or homeowner's insurance premiums. If the value of the home at the time the loan is due

Did You Know?

The senior staff attorney for Consumer's Union (publisher of *Consumer Reports*) has stated, "Reverse mortgages should only be a last resort for seniors who want to stay in their homes and have no other alternatives to supplement their income." On the other hand, a survey by the National Reverse Mortgage Lenders Association found that 74 percent of borrowers of reverse mortgages felt using their reverse mortgage was a positive experience.

exceeds the loan balance, the excess proceeds will belong to you or your estate. If the loan amount exceeds the home value, you or your estate will not be liable for the difference, and the FHA insurance will cover the lender for the loss.

Although this brief description of a reverse mortgage may sound great, these are complicated transactions and can include high upfront costs and fees. The FHA recommends that you do not use any service that charges to refer you to a reverse mortgage lender, nor should you use any lender that wants you to invest in its financial products with the proceeds of the loan. You can download a free booklet on reverse mortgages from AARP at http://assets .aarp.org/www.aarp.org_/articles/money/financial_pdfs/hmm _hires_nocrops.pdf. The National Council on Aging also publishes a booklet for consumers. Type "Use Your Home to Stay at Home NCOA" into your search engine or call 800-510-0301.

For More Information

Check out more than 170 free, 10-minute courses on various aspects of investing at www.morningstar.com/cover/Classroom.html. You will need to register to sign up for the courses.

Mutual Funds

One way to invest in a variety of stocks and bonds without having to select each one individually is to invest in mutual funds. That said, there are more than 10,000 mutual funds, according to recent estimates, so even investing in mutual funds requires that you do your due diligence. Mutual funds invest in stocks, bonds, and commodities and generally have professional managers who charge a fee to the fund for their services. In addition, the funds have their own expenses. Many funds are so-called load funds, for which an investor pays the commission that goes to the broker who sells the fund, while others are no-load funds, where no commissions are paid.

A short primer on mutual funds: Mutual funds can be separated into broad categories including money market funds, equity mutual funds, bond mutual funds, and balanced funds. How do you pick a good one? Morningstar mutual fund ratings use one to five stars to rate most funds, and this is one way to compare funds with similar investment profiles. These ratings are readily available on a variety of Internet sites, including Morningstar (www .morningstar.com) and Yahoo! Finance (www.finance.yahoo.com). Morningstar lists its fund ratings, categorized by fund type, and provides the fund's rating, expense ratio (lower is better), and lots of additional information about each fund. Although you need to register on Morningstar's Web site, you do not need to purchase a subscription to access this information. Go to www.morningstar .com, click on "Funds," and then go to "Star Ratings," which are shown by type of fund. Select a fund type and you will be taken to an alphabetical list of rated funds within that fund class.

Although Morningstar ratings are a useful source for evaluating potential fund investments, the effect of fund expenses has been shown in studies to be equally if not more important. The impact of an extra 1 percent or more in expenses each and every year over an extended investment horizon is huge. In addition, other studies have shown that managed funds (as contrasted with index funds to be discussed momentarily) as a group do not beat the market most of the time. In fact, according to Vanguard, 72 percent of actively managed U.S. equity mutual funds underperformed the market over the 20-year period ending in 2010. And when you think about it, why should managed funds as a group be able to beat the market averages when they have to generate gains in excess of the market just to cover their expenses? For example, a major benchmark for funds to measure themselves against is the Standard & Poor's 500 index—derived from the values of 500 large corporation stocks, chosen based on their market size, industry groupings, and other factors. The S&P is a more significant indication of the overall stock market performance than the Dow Jones Index, which is based on just 30 companies. If the S&P index increases by 8 percent in a given year, a mutual fund that is measuring its performance against this index would need to have pre-expense gains of 9 percent or maybe even 10 percent to end up with the same 8 percent after its expenses.

In 1975 John Bogle created the first index fund, a fund designed to track the S&P 500 index. The idea behind this fund was essentially that most mutual funds do not beat the market indexes, partly because of their inherent expenses incurred for research and management, so why not just invest in the index itself by buying all the stocks comprising the index, without the costs of the research. Although the concept was derided at the time, index funds have become very commonplace today and can be a great way to invest in the market, providing the opportunity for a well-balanced portfolio with funds that often have very low expense ratios. After all, these funds can be largely managed by a computer program since there is no need to evaluate and select specific investments to include in the fund.

There are numerous index funds, including funds investing in the S&P 500, the NASDAQ 100, the Russell 2000, bond indexes, and foreign indexes. It is important not only to select a diversified mix of index funds for your portfolio, but also to carefully look at the expense charges (generally referred to as the expense ratios) of each fund you select. Currently, for example, annual expense ratios of mutual funds can be as low as 0.05 percent per year (that is, $50 per year on a $100,000 investment) to as high as 2.00 percent per year ($2,000 per year on a $100,000 investment), with the average being about 1.3 to 1.5 percent. The effect of paying just a half-percent less in expenses each year over an extended investment horizon can add up, so it's important to pay close attention to the expense ratio. The less you pay in expenses each year on your investment portfolio, the more you will have to spend for travel, health care, and other expenses. Index funds are available from a number of fund families, including low-cost providers such as Fidelity Investments (www.fidelity.com), T. Rowe Price (www.troweprice .com), and the Vanguard Group (www.vanguard.com).

Tip

Investing $100,000 for 20 years in an index fund with an 8 percent annual return and an expense ratio of 0.20 percent will be worth over $75,000 more than a similar fund with the same annual return but an expense ratio of 1.12 percent.

Target-date funds are mutual funds designed to match the mix of investments within the fund to the investor's expected retirement date, seeking to simplify things for the investor. Thus, a 40-year-old woman planning to retire at age 65–67 would pick a target fund aimed for retirement around 2040. As the retirement date approaches, the fund would take care of shifting its investments from largely stocks to a heavier concentration in bonds. Lots of these funds are available, each with its own approach to what the investment mix should be at any particular point. For example, Vanguard's Target Retirement 2060 Fund is invested 81 percent in stocks, 9 percent in bonds and 10 percent in cash, while its Target Retirement 2010 Fund has a mix of 45-54-1. Fidelity's Freedom 2055 Fund has a mix of 90 percent stocks and 10 percent bonds, while the Fidelity Freedom 2010 Fund has a mix of 50-45-5. The mix of these funds changes over time to reduce the mix of investment in stocks and increase the investment in bonds and cash. Clearly, there are major shifts to bonds as the retirement date approaches, and this shift will continue into the retirement years.

What About Annuities?

If you long for the good old days when many retirees received a monthly pension check from their former employer and had few worries about how to invest their retirement portfolios, maybe an annuity is the answer for you. Women purchase 6 out of 10 annuities, and although sales of annuities increased more than 10 percent last year, according to the Insured Retirement Institute, they still aren't that hot of a commodity. Be careful about buying immediate fixed annuities when interest rates are low, because low rates mean smaller monthly checks from your annuity. If an annuity is attractive to you, consider waiting for interest rates to rise before purchasing one. While it is impossible to predict what interest rates may rise to in the future, it is pretty easy to conclude that the current 2.0 percent interest rate on a five-year certificate of deposit is a clear indication that interest rates are presently too low for this to be a good time to purchase a fixed annuity. In fact, as a point of comparison, the February 2012 interest rate on 10-year Treasury Bonds of 1.97 percent was far less than the 7.34 percent interest rate in February 1992 and the 14.43 percent interest rate in February 1982. All market pundits expect interest rates to rise from their current levels.

Tip

Social Security is one of the best annuities available to you, and it includes a cost-of-living adjustment feature. If you are considering the purchase of an annuity, you should also be thinking about delaying the start of your Social Security benefits to maximize the total monthly payments you receive.

In simple terms, an annuity is an insurance product. You make a payment to the insurance company in return for its promise to make a periodic payment to you, generally for the rest of your life. Unfortunately, annuities are not all that simple; there are many types of annuities, with many features that can be included or excluded from your contract. Examples are annuities that start paying you right away, called immediate annuities, and those that don't start paying until some date in the future, known as deferred annuities. Some include cost-of-living adjustments. Annuity payments can be fixed under the contract (see the discussion above about fixed annuities and the current low interest rates) or can be variable, based on investments in the stock market, using either actively managed accounts or even indexes.

If you change your mind after purchasing an annuity, you'll probably pay surrender charges, with the amount of the charge generally decreasing each year that you hold the annuity contract. If an annuity sounds right for you, get assistance from a financial planner or other expert to help you select the right annuity. Keep

Fun Fact

A recent survey by the Society of Actuaries found that 20 percent of Americans age 45 to 70 plan to buy an annuity or similar financial instrument.

in mind that an annuity locks up your funds; keep enough of your portfolio outside of an annuity so you are prepared for any emergency that may require immediate access to cash. Also remember that even though the annuity payment to you may be "guaranteed," the promise is only as good as the solvency of the insurance company. Annuities are issued by insurance companies and are marketed by mutual fund companies and brokerages as well as by insurance sales representatives. As with any insurance product, it is important that the insurance company issuing your annuity is financially strong. You can find financial strength ratings from sources like AM Best (www.ambest.com). Some experts recommend buying annuities from several insurers to minimize the risk.

Tip

A major concern of single women is that they will run out of money before they run out of time. Annuities seek to solve this dilemma, but they tie up your money and, in the past, typically disappeared when you died, leaving nothing for your heirs. (Some annuities sold today include riders that allow annuitants to pass money on to their heirs.) A new product called longevity insurance may be the solution for those of us who worry about outliving our money. This insurance is essentially an annuity that starts paying only when, and if, we reach a pretty advanced age, at which time we might run out of money. A typical policy might cost $25,000 at age 65 and pay out $3,000 per month beginning at age 85. If you die before reaching 85, no payments will be made and premiums are not recoverable. Among the insurance companies selling longevity insurance are Hartford Financial Services Group and MetLife.

Eugenia L. discovered many money lessons after her divorce:

After my divorce—we were married 17 years—I struggled to balance living within my available means. With a nod to Scarlett O'Hara's famous quote, I'd frequently chant to myself, "As God is my witness, we'll never be hungry again." After several years of juggling, I improved my employment situation, renegotiated child custody (the divorce included five children ranging in age from 3 to 17), and renegotiated my financial life. By 1996, I had only two children under my roof (the oldest had moved out and the two middle children moved to California to live with their father and stepmother), was working full-time, and was willing to make more changes.

I pored over every penny and devised a tracking sheet of annual, quarterly, monthly, and weekly expenses. (I should mention that arithmetic and math were my academic phobias throughout grade school, high school, and into college.) By this time, the child support I was receiving was being garnished so the income flow was still small but steady. I talked to a friend who also was a real estate agent, and he suggested I downsize and move into a smaller, less-expensive home. I did.

Major lessons:

I learned not to give cars to children who need them but rather to children who will maintain them and the paperwork that goes with them.

I learned that every divorce that involves child support should have wage garnishment as the means of collection of the support. That provides third-party verification of the support payments, and one less potentially nasty conversation to have about finances.

I learned that helping to pay for a child's college education is nice but not a requirement to be a loving or a supportive parent. If you cannot afford to give someone money, do not loan them any, either! This goes double, triple for kids! Let them enjoy (it's a relative term) the satisfaction and the strength that comes from growing their own financial muscles and the discipline to be self-supporting.

I learned that if you can be flexible and responsible with your automobile "requirements" and learn to make the most of public transportation, you can save an *enormous* amount of money and reduce the stress in your life.

I learned to create "escrows" for each major area of spending. For example, you can pay auto insurance monthly and pay a processing fee or you can set aside from each paycheck an amount that will allow you to make fewer, larger payments and pay fewer processing fees. This can be applied to auto maintenance (why do we act as if repairs are a surprise?) and also to saving money to replace the current car when its useful life is over (a well-maintained car should run safely for at least 8–10 years, right?).

I learned to *save something from each and every paycheck or income stream! Five hundred or fifty or five dollars, or fifty cents!* The amount is of less overall importance than the consistency of the savings.

I learned that there is life after divorce. It's more frugal and still good.

Taxes, Taxes, and More Taxes

Did you ever notice that when you put the words "The" and "IRS" together, it spells "THEIRS"

—Author unknown

First the good news—the percentage of Americans' income spent on taxes dropped to its lowest rate in many years in the first quarter of 2011, according to an analysis by *USA Today* based on Bureau of Economic Analysis data. The total burden for taxes, including all federal and state income, sales, and other taxes, was 23.6 percent, compared to a rate of about 27 percent in the late 20th century. And of course your taxes pay for valuable protections and services—everything from public schools to libraries to Social Security and Medicare.

The bad news is that any taxes paid take away from the amount we have available to spend in retirement. Clearly, we cannot ignore the impact of taxes on how we save, how we spend, and even where we live. On the other hand, it would be a mistake to let tax consequences dictate your life. Certain tax issues of particular interest to retirees are discussed below.

Where You Live Affects Your Total Tax Cost

As a general rule, the amount of federal income taxes you pay will be the same no matter where you live. The only significant exception to this rule is for employment earnings of certain individuals living in foreign countries, which is likely not an important issue for most retirees.

Each of our 50 states and the District of Columbia has its own tax system that determines your state and local income taxes, sales taxes, property taxes, gas taxes, inheritance taxes, and more. Few of us would move to a new state just to reduce our tax bite, but if a decision is made to move for any or all of the other personal reasons (climate, proximity to relatives, overall cost of living, infrastructure, etc.), you might also consider the tax consequences of the move. In addition, even though your federal tax bite doesn't depend on your state of residence, the move itself has several significant federal tax issues, the most important of which is the potential tax on a gain on the sale of your residence, should you be lucky enough to have a gain. Still, on your principal residence you only have to pay tax on gains above $250,000. And you may be able to claim a tax deduction for your moving costs.

Let's consider the variation in the tax systems of the 50 states, starting with income tax. Forty-one states have a broad-based income tax, seven states have no income tax, and two states, New Hampshire and Tennessee, tax only interest and dividends. The seven states with no income tax are Alaska, Florida, Nevada, South Dakota, Texas, Washington, and Wyoming.

But before you start packing your bags for one of these states, you might also want to look at your sources of income and find out whether other states have beneficial rules with respect to taxing that income. Only 14 states tax Social Security benefits, an important source of retirement income, and then only if your income is above a certain level. Ten states exclude from taxable income all pensions from the federal, state, or local governments, and a few of these 10 states also provide for a full or partial exclusion of income from nongovernmental retirement plans.

The amount of taxes you pay on your income is important, but so is the sales tax you pay on your spending. The sales tax rates vary from state to state, and there are often significant local sales taxes, too. Only Delaware, Montana, New Hampshire, and Oregon have no state or local sales taxes. Alaska has no state sales tax but allows for local sales taxes. For the others, the combined state and maximum local sales tax rates range from 4.5 percent in Hawaii to 12.7 percent in Arizona.

Another important determinant of your total state tax cost is the amount of property taxes you will pay, either on a home you buy or on rent that factors in property tax. Property tax rates vary significantly, as does the percentage of market value upon which homes are assessed. A tax rate of 1.8 percent on a property's full market value is the same thing as a rate of 3.6 percent on a property assessed at only 50 percent of its market value. In addition, the total tax rate often varies from county to county and from city to city. Calling the county tax assessor's office to ask about both the tax rate and the percentage of fair market value at which homes are assessed will help you get a better handle on this. Another way to get a general idea of the impact of property taxes is the summary of "Property Taxes on Owner-Occupied Housing as a Percentage of Median Home Value, by State," published by the Tax Foundation. This summary, which you can find at www.taxfoundation.org /publications/show/2181.html (go to Table 29) shows that New Jersey has the highest real estate taxes, with an effective tax rate of 2.01 percent, and Hawaii has the lowest, at 0.27 percent. Although you might expect that the nine states without a broad-based income tax would have the highest property tax rates, this is not always true. By way of example and considering only states with no income tax, the effective property tax rate for New Hampshire is 1.92 percent and Texas is 1.90 percent (ranking the second and third highest on the summary), but other no-income-tax states such as Wyoming, Washington, and Florida have reasonably low effective property tax rates of 0.62 percent, 0.98 percent, and 1.09 percent, respectively. But also factor in that low property taxes can sometimes mean high property prices or substandard public services.

How about the tax bite after you are gone? Estate taxes are imposed on the value of the decedent's estate. Currently 17 states and the District of Columbia impose an estate tax with exemptions from the taxable estates in 2012 ranging from $338,333 in Ohio to $5,000,000 in Delaware and North Carolina. The top tax rates in these 17 states range from 12 percent in Connecticut to 19 percent in Washington. Ohio has repealed its estate tax effective on January 1, 2013. Inheritance taxes are imposed on the transfer of property by the estate to its beneficiaries in 7 states, often with unlimited exemptions and/or lower tax rates for bequests to lineal heirs (typically children, parents, and grandparents) and often spouses and other family members, and limited exemptions and higher tax rates for bequests to other heirs. For example, in Indiana the exemption for bequests to lineal heirs is only $100,000 and the top tax rate is 10 percent, while Iowa, Kentucky, Maryland, and New Jersey allow an unlimited exemption for bequests to lineal heirs. The top tax rate on bequests to nonfamily members ranges from a high of 20 percent in Indiana to a low of 6 percent in Kentucky. Only two states, Maryland and New Jersey, impose both an estate tax and an inheritance tax.

How do you make sense of all of this? One summary that might be of interest is Kiplinger.com's 2011 analysis of the 10 most tax-friendly and tax-unfriendly states for retirees. It lists the "tax heavens" as Alabama, Delaware, Georgia, Kentucky, Louisiana, Mississippi, Oklahoma, Pennsylvania, South Carolina, and Wyoming. Kiplinger.com's top "tax hells" are California, Connecticut, Iowa, Maine, Minnesota, Nebraska, New Jersey, Oregon, Vermont, and Wisconsin. It's an interesting list to keep in mind as you go through your own analysis.

Each state needs to raise adequate revenue to provide the goods and services necessary for its residents, but they don't all accomplish it in the same fashion. So you can't just focus on the states that don't have an income tax. In fact, of the nine states without a broad-based income tax, only one (Wyoming) is included in the tax-friendly list above. On the other hand, of the 14 states that tax Social Security benefits, only six are included in the tax-unfriendly list.

"How the States Tax Singles" is a chart in Appendix 8, at the end of this chapter, showing the range of individual income tax rates, state and local sales tax rates, and information on whether the state taxes Social Security benefits and whether it has an estate and/or inheritance tax. This chart will be a good starting place, but you need to consider the impact of your own circumstances in coming to any useful conclusions. You might also want to consult a tax accountant to help you understand the impact of the various state tax laws on your particular set of facts.

Your Social Security Benefits May Be Taxable by the Federal Government

The general concept is that Social Security received by lower income retirees is tax-free, while up to 85 percent of your Social Security could be taxed if your income is above certain minimum thresholds. IRS Publication 915 (go to www.irs.gov and type "Publication 915" into the search bar) provides an overview of the tax rules related to Social Security income and provides examples and worksheets to help you with the calculations. Happily, the various income tax preparation programs available, such as TurboTax (www.turbotax.com) and H&R Block At Home (www.hrblock.com), make these calculations for you.

Selling Your Home

For many Americans, our home is our most valuable asset and, notwithstanding the depressed real estate market in the last several years, many of us live in a residence that has appreciated significantly over the years. Should you decide to move when you retire, odds are that you will want to sell your residence as part of the move. Although the tax treatment of gains on the sale of a principal residence have changed over the years, the current law allows singles to exclude a gain of up to $250,000 on the sale of your principal residence. To qualify for this exclusion, you must have used your residence as your principal residence for at least two years in the five-year period preceding the date of the sale.

A definition of a "principal residence" is a fairly straightforward concept if you only have one residence. Should you have more than one residence, however, you will need to be able to demonstrate that the residence sold, and for which you plan to exclude the gain, is your principal residence. In general, your principal residence is usually located in the state in which you reside for most of the year and where you vote. Generally, your driver's license and automobile registration are in the state of your principal residence. Your principal residence is usually a home, including a single-family residence, a condominium, townhouse, cooperative apartment, or mobile home, but can also be a yacht or houseboat.

If your residence was rented or used for business at any time on or after January 1, 2009, a portion of the gain on its sale will be taxed. The taxable gain will include any depreciation deductions claimed for the rental or business use, and a portion of the remaining gain will be attributed to the rental or business use on the basis of the period of time of the rental or business use (on or after January 1, 2009) to the total period of ownership of the residence.

As is the case with most tax rules, there are many exceptions to the general rules, including exceptions to the requirement to have used the residence as your principal residence for two out of the five years preceding the date of the sale and exceptions to the allocation of gain to rental or business use for periods after the date you last used the residence as your principal residence. Should these exceptions possibly apply to you, it would be best to seek the counsel of a CPA or lawyer specializing in tax matters.

Other Considerations When Selling Your Residence

The real estate taxes for the year of sale will be apportioned between the seller and the buyer based on the number of days of ownership during the property tax year. Depending on whether property taxes in your state are paid in advance or in arrears, this may result in a cash charge or credit at closing as well as an increased or reduced property tax deduction for you. The proration of property taxes will show on your settlement sheet.

The payoff of your old mortgage will also be a line item on your settlement sheet, and it includes the unpaid principal balance of your mortgage as well as interest to the date of sale. You should be sure this interest included in the payoff amount is also included in the tax reporting form you receive from the bank. To verify this, you may end up having to call the bank and ask.

If you refinanced your home (and who hasn't) and paid points on the new loan, the points are usually amortized and deducted over the period of your new loan. Upon the payoff of this loan at closing, the unamortized points become fully deductible.

Usually there are a lot of household items that you no longer want when moving to a new residence. For example, the old furniture may not fit with the new residence, or it may not be worth the cost of moving it there. Usually such a move also entails getting rid of lots of stuff accumulated over the years. Yes, a yard sale may be in order, but an alternative is to contribute the unwanted items to a charity and claim a tax deduction for their fair market value. Be sure you get a receipt for the contribution and, in the event the fair market value is $5,000 or more, you will generally need to have the items appraised by a qualified appraiser and attach Form 8283 to your income tax return.

Will Uncle Sam Help Pay Your Moving Expenses?

Moving expenses are generally deductible only when they are incurred in connection with full-time employment in your new location or retirees moving back to the United States from overseas jobs. So, as a general rule, most retirees will not be able to deduct the costs of moving to a new retirement home. But wait—why not consider working for a while after your move? Perhaps this is your plan anyway. A job can provide a current income, help you meet people in your new location, and allow you to grab a moving-expense deduction. What are the requirements?

First, your new principal place of employment must be at least 50 miles farther from your old residence than your old residence was from your old job or, if there was no old job, at least 50 miles from your old residence. So, if your daily commute used to be 15 miles, your new job must be at least 65 miles away from your old residence to qualify under this test. (Confused? The IRS has an easy worksheet to figure this out at www.irs.gov/publications/p521/ar02.html#en_US_2010_publink1000203454.) Second, you must be employed full time for at least 39 weeks during the 12-month period immediately after the move. If you are self-employed, the requirement changes to working full time for at least 78 weeks in the first 24-month period after your move. Importantly, you do not have to have a job before you move, as long as you meet the time test.

If you qualify for the moving-expense deduction, your deduction includes all the costs of packing, shipping, and unpacking your household goods and personal effects, including the cost of shipping your car and your pets, plus the transportation costs to move you to your new location. If you drive, you are allowed to claim a transportation cost (23 cents per mile in 2012). You can also deduct the cost of disconnecting and reconnecting your appliances, as well as your meals and lodging during the move.

Even if you don't plan on working, keep track of those moving expenses; you may fall into a full-time position soon after you move. This tip can take some of the sting out of the hassle of moving.

Did You Know?

Generally, women receive much more in Social Security and Medicare benefits than they pay in taxes, according to the Urban Institute. Bankrate. com gives this example: Assuming an average lifetime wage of $43,100 a year, a woman who retired at age 65 in 2010 paid $345,000 in total Social Security and Medicare taxes and will receive $464,000 in total benefits over her life expectancy.

A Dollar Saved Is as Good as a Dollar Earned

Our focus in this chapter has been on saving for retirement, estimating your retirement expenses, and determining how to fund them. But another important part of your planning should be on reducing your expenses, both before and in retirement. Earlier in the chapter we discussed moving to a lower cost-of-living area as a strategy to reduce your expenses. The following are additional ideas for you to consider:

Monitor Your Spending. This may be one of the most important ways to reduce costs. Consider using a free site such as Mint (www.mint.com) or Pageonce (www.pageonce.com) to help you do this. As Suze Orman noted, "Hope is not a financial plan."

Reduce Your Property Tax. We have gone through a wrenching decline in the values of our homes. While that can be bad news if you are planning to sell soon (although largely negated by the reduced cost of the replacement home you might buy), it can be good news if you take the time to review your property tax assessment and appeal for a lower value if the assessment is too high, as they often are. This is a gift that keeps giving, as a successful appeal will likely result in lower property taxes for years to come. Often, an appeal can be no more complicated than comparing your assessment to the sales prices of comparable homes in your neighborhood and discussing the overassessment with the property tax appraiser. Although a more formal appeal may be necessary, I have successfully appealed the property tax valuation on all four of the homes I have owned and only once had to make a formal appeal. The three other times, the reduced valuation was worked out with the appraiser either by telephone or by meeting and discussing my concerns, armed with the information I had gathered on the comparables selling for less than my assessed value.

Take a Look at the Cost to Insure Your Home. Insurance companies like to have inflation-guard features in their homeowner policies. This feature results in annual increases in coverage, without regard to whether your home has actually gone up or down in value. As we all know, home values as well as construction costs have decreased significantly in almost every area of the United States over the past several years. You probably have too much coverage and are paying dearly for it. Contact your insurance company and have your home reappraised to determine the appropriate coverage amount. Also, contact several other companies and get their recommended coverage amount, as well as their estimated premium for coverage. Internet sites like www.insure .com can help you in this process. In addition, price homeowner coverage at the company that covers your automobile, as there are often discounts for carrying both policies with the same company.

When Rosemary T. got her most recent renewal notice for her homeowner's insurance, she noticed a 4 percent inflation coverage increase in the insured value. After further review, she realized this had been going on for quite a few years and her home was now covered for 21 percent more than it was worth. Additionally, living in a hurricane-prone area, her coverage for wind damage had a 5 percent deductible, meaning that the excess insured value of the homeowner policy not only increased the annual premium but also increased the amount of the 5 percent deductible. She was effectively paying a higher premium, and could end up paying substantially more if there was a wind-damage loss.

Accelerate Your Mortgage. Contact your mortgage company about changing your monthly payment to the same payment every four weeks or half the monthly payment every two weeks. This not only helps coordinate your payments with your paycheck but will save thousands in interest on your mortgage and will result in paying it off years early.

Get a Housemate. We mentioned this before: Why not get a roommate to share the living costs? Not only will you live more cheaply, but maybe you'll also like having the company or the help when you get older. More than a million women over 45 have a nonrelative roommate, according to the 2010 Census.

Pay Off Those High-Cost Credit Cards. It generally makes no sense to make minimum payments on credit card debt while you have other funds in low-earning bank accounts. For example, have you noticed the bills show you how much you'll pay if you make only the minimum payments? Take my Delta American Express bill. I have a balance of $5,599 and my minimum payment is $112. If I make only the minimum payments each month, it would take me 16 years to pay off this one bill, and I would have paid a total of $11,268. If I paid $193 a month, it would take me three years to pay it off, and I'd pay a total of $6,939 (a savings of $4,329 compared to the minimum payment amount). Pay off those that you can and, for the others, call the credit card company and try to negotiate a lower interest rate. This can often be successful, particularly if you have been a good customer over the years and have a good credit rating. And from now on, skip the credit card and only buy what you can pay for in cash.

Use Credit Cards That Pay You. A number of credit cards pay you to use them—although recent changes in the law that reduce the fees these card companies can charge merchants may reduce the availability of such cards. Compare cards such as Blue Cash from American Express, Capital One No Hassle Cash Rewards, Chase Freedom, and Discover More. These cards currently pay rebates from 1 percent to as much as 5 percent on certain purchases.

Don't Pay Foreign Transaction Fees. Although most credit cards charge up to 3 percent extra for charges in foreign countries, some do not. Examples of cards not imposing this fee are the Capital One Venture Card and the Citibank Thankyou Premier Card. Although these cards do have an annual fee (currently waived for the first year), they also give you incentives worth one to two cents or more for each dollar charged on the card. On a recent trip to Europe that cost about $5,000 for food, hotels, rental cars, trains, and foreign airfares, I saved about $150 in foreign exchange fees and earned $100 in rewards. Bon voyage.

Review Your Credit Card Bills Closely. Over the years you may have signed up for a number of services that automatically bill your credit card. Often you end up not needing or using the service, but you did not bother to cancel it. Month after month you are billed for services you don't want, and they can add up when you multiply them by 12 to get the annual cost. Examples are charges for old e-mail accounts you no longer use, magazine subscriptions, and credit monitoring services that provide little benefit. Call and cancel them.

Stop Paying ATM Fees. Whenever you withdraw money from an ATM not operated by your own bank, you are probably paying a fee to get your own money, often to both the bank that owns the ATM as well as to your own bank. The total fee could be as much as $5. That can run you more than

$500 a year, if you withdraw money twice a week. Instead, consider withdrawing funds from your own bank and stop using other banks' ATMs. If your bank is not convenient or charges a fee for ATM withdrawals, change banks. You might also use your debit card to get cash back from your grocery or big box store when you check out.

Tip

Bank fees have risen to record amounts, according to Bankrate.com. The highest ATM fees were in Denver, and the lowest in Cleveland. Bounced-check fees averaged a high of $33 in Dallas and a low of $28 in San Francisco. Ouch.

Reduce Your Telephone Bills. Do you have a home telephone and a cell phone? Consider joining the younger generation and getting rid of your landline. Not only will you save the annual cost of the home phone, but you will probably also miss fewer calls. Before canceling your home phone, be sure its cost is not bundled in a discounted package with TV or Internet service. And while you are reviewing your telephone costs, check to be sure you are not paying for more minutes on your cell phone plan than you need.

Reduce Your Television Costs. Are you paying for programming you really don't watch? Premium content means premium costs. Go back and look at what is available in the basic cable or satellite package and compare its cost to what you are currently paying. Maybe there is "gold in them thar hills" just waiting for you to mine. Some of you may be able to get adequate programming the old way, with just a free antenna on your roof or rabbit ears on your TV.

Ask. (This sounds so much nicer than haggling.) It's surprising what people and companies are willing to do if you just ask. Remember, the worst they can say is no. For example, Monica P. noticed her cable television provider was advertising a discount of $30 a month for a year for new subscribers. After she called them to discuss the unequal treatment of new customers and existing customers, the company agreed to reduce her monthly bill by the same $360 over the next year. When she called the *New York Times* to cancel her subscription because of its high cost, she was offered a 50 percent discount for six months, saving her almost $200.

Take Your Vacation at Home. Consider spending an occasional vacation at home instead of paying huge amounts to travel afar. Most of us have interesting things to do and see close to where we live, and often we have not bothered to do them or see them.

Travel on the Cheap. When you travel out of town, check out discount sites to reduce your travel costs. Travel costs can be priced and booked at Web sites like www.expedia.com, www.kayak.com, and www.priceline.com. Cruise fares lower than those offered by the cruise lines are often available at sites like www.cruise.com and www.vacationstogo.com. Be wary of paying nonrefundable amounts for a better deal; if you don't end up going, you'll have wasted money, not saved it.

Use Discount Services. Social buying sites, such as Groupon (www.groupon.com), LivingSocial (www.livingsocial.com), and kgbdeals (www.kgbdeals.com), offer sizable discounts on deals in specific cities, with up to 50 percent to 90 percent off for such things as dining, spa services, teeth-whitening, plastic surgery, vacations, and entertainment. For example, Angela K. got a $20 gift card for Amazon for $10, and Jill B. got a one-hour $70 facial in Chicago for $35. But beware of the trap of purchasing things you wouldn't normally buy just because they're a good deal. That would totally defeat the purpose.

Free/Inexpensive Drugs. Ask your doctor if a generic drug will work for you. Janine M. has diabetes and pays $4 a month for Metformin (a generic) through Walgreens. A comparable brand-name drug, such as Actos, would cost closer to $300 a month. Certain oral antibiotics, including amoxicillin and Penicillin VK, are free through stores such as Publix and Meijer. You'll still need a prescription.

Shop Your Pantry. Inventory what is in your pantry and use it up over the next week, instead of shopping for more at the store. We waste lots of food, according to the National Institutes of Health, as much as 1,400 calories worth per day per person.

Drop Your Unused Gym Membership. Do you have a gym membership that you rarely use? Maybe you signed up as part of a New Year's resolution to get fit but found out it just wasn't you. Consider buying a workout video and exercising at home in front of your TV instead. It is a lot more convenient and could save you tons (pun intended) of money.

Set Up a 529 Plan for Yourself. You can set up a Qualified Tuition Program (generally known as Section 529 plans) to help fund your education in retirement. Although the contributions to the plan that you make are not deductible, the earnings are not taxable as long as distributions from the plan are used for your qualified educational expenses. Distributions of earnings from Section 529 plans not used for qualified educational expenses are subject to income tax and a 10 percent penalty. If you decide later on that you don't need some or all of the funds in your Section 529 plan, you can designate another family member as the beneficiary. In addition, if you set up a Section 529 plan in the past for a family member but now find you need the money, as the account owner you can distribute the funds to yourself, being taxed only on the accumulated earnings and the additional 10 percent penalty. Yes, you hate to pay a penalty, but this is a potential source of funds that you might not want to ignore. You can set up a 529 plan through most major brokerages, such as Fidelity Investments, Merrill Lynch, and TD Ameritrade.

Reduce the Insurance Premiums on Your Car. Consider increasing the deductibles for collision and comprehensive coverage to as much as $1,000. In fact, if you are driving an old, fairly valueless vehicle, you might consider dropping the collision and comprehensive coverage completely because the premiums may not be worth the value of a potential claim. Yes, you will be assuming more risk if there is a claim, but your premiums will go down significantly, paying you for this risk. Put the savings aside in a "self-insurance" pool in case you do have a claim.

Save on Car Bills. And, speaking of cars, purchasing a used car or one that gets great gas mileage (or keeping yours if it's running fine—mine now has more than 110,000 miles) is also a cost-saver. Best time to buy a new car? December. Better yet, if you move to a community that is walkable, ditch the car, buy a bike, and save all kinds of money while you get healthier.

Refinance Your Car. Most of us are familiar with refinancing our homes to get a lower interest rate. Another possibility is to refinance your car. Check this out with your bank or credit union, and ask about the fees and costs. Just a 1 percent reduction in the rate could save you hundreds of dollars in interest costs.

Stop the Insurance on Your Car When You're Not Driving. Patricia F. did a home exchange for half a year, swapping her place in Denver for a place in Sitges, Spain. Because the visiting couple from Spain did not want to use her car, Patricia suspended the coverage on her car for six months and saved 70 percent off her insurance, as long as the car was driven fewer than 25 miles over six months as part of a maintenance plan.

Extend Your Time Between "Maintenance Visits." By adding an extra week between manicure/pedicure and hair appointments, Vivian K. saved about $200 over the course of a year. Of course, she could have done her own nails and let her hair go natural, but she wasn't ready to take that plunge.

Use Loyalty/Membership Cards. There are lots of possibilities here. Jenny G. gets a gas discount at Kroger (a grocer that also sells gas at certain locations) by using her Kroger loyalty card. I use my Epic card at the movie theater—free popcorn or drinks and free movie tickets after a certain amount is purchased at the box office. If you're like Belinda F. and shop at Chico's clothing, you'll get an additional 5 percent discount on every purchase if you register for Chico's "passport program" and reach a total of $500 in purchases. Of course, you need to make sure that you feel you're getting a good deal even without the added perks, or you're defeating the purpose. Save money on hotels, attractions, and other perks with your AARP or AAA card. If you're 62 or older, get an "America the Beautiful" senior pass at a national park for $10, which is a lifetime pass that gets you into more than 2,000 recreation sites.

Search For Missing Money. Most states have property laws under which unclaimed property must be turned over to the state. According to the National Association of Unclaimed Property Administrators, 117 million accounts totaling $33 billion are held by state treasurers and other agencies available to be returned to their owners. Examples of unclaimed property are dormant bank accounts, utility deposits, uncashed money orders or traveler's checks, unclaimed stock dividends, and even unclaimed inheritances. Many states have specific Web sites that you can use to search for these missing funds, or you can find missing money in most of the states by searching at www.missingmoney.com. Or, what about old treasury bonds that you may have purchased many years ago, or even received as a gift? You can search for them at www.treasurydirect.gov.

Eat, Drink, and Save Money. If you're working, make your own lunch instead of eating out; it not only saves money, but you also can more easily control what is going down the hatch. Brew your own coffee and bypass those expensive cups of joe on your way to the office. Drink free water instead of bottled water or sodas, and monitor how and what kind of alcohol you drink; this can really make a difference in cost as well as calories.

Write Your Own Will. Many of us have simple estates. Consider drafting your own will using software costing about $50. Check out Quicken WillMaker Plus 2012 (www.nolo.com /products/) and LegacyWriter (www.legacywriter.com).

If you have any concerns about the adequacy of what you drafted, have it reviewed by an estate lawyer for a much lower fee than if you paid her to draft it from scratch. Once you have finalized your will, including having your signature witnessed and in some states notarized, put it in a safe place like a safe deposit box or a fireproof safe in your home. Destroy any old versions of your will. Um . . . and be sure to tell the appropriate people the location of your will.

Invest Any Refunds. A tax refund is not "free money," although psychologically it might seem that way. If you are owed a refund, consider adjusting your withholding so you don't overwithhold in the future.

"Someday" is a disease that will take your dreams to the grave with you. So said author Timothy Ferriss, and I think most of us would agree with him. Let's make "someday" today, and start planning for this exciting phase of our life called retirement: Plan financially, psychologically, geographically, spiritually, emotionally, and physically.

More 411

www.aarp.org (useful information on all aspects of retirement).

www.aarp.org/work/social-security/ (useful information on Social Security).

www.dailyworth.com and www.learnvest.com (financial info for women; sign up for free newsletters delivered to your inbox).

Belsky, Gary. *Why Smart People Make Big Money Mistakes and How to Correct Them.* New York: Simon & Schuster, 2010.

Blayney, Eleanor. *Women's Worth: Finding Your Financial Confidence.* McLean, Virginia: Direction$, 2010.

Breathnach, Sarah Ban. *Peace and Plenty: Finding Your Path to Financial Security.* New York: Grand Central Publishing, 2010.

Deloitte.com. *The 2012 Essential Tax and Wealth Planning Guide.* www.deloitte.com/assets/Dcom-UnitedStates/Local%20 Assets/Documents/Tax/us_tax_The_2012_Essential_Tax _and_Wealth_Planning_Guide_131011.pdf (free download-able book).

IRS Publications (www.irs.gov):

    IRS Publication 17 "Your Federal Income Tax"

    IRS Publication 521 "Moving Expenses"

    IRS Publication 523 "Selling Your Home"

    IRS Publication 554 "Older Americans' Tax Guide"

    IRS Publication 590 "Individual Retirement Arrangements (IRAs)"

    IRS Publication 915 "Social Security and Equivalent Railroad Retirement Benefits"

Peterson, Jonathan. *AARP's Social Security for Dummies.* Hoboken: John Wiley & Sons, 2012.

Quinn, Jane Bryant. *Making the Most of Your Money Now.* New York: Simon & Schuster, 2009.

Ramsey, Dave. *The Total Money Makeover: A Proven Plan for Financial Fitness.* Nashville, Tennessee: Thomas Nelson, 2009.

Social Security Publication 05-10127 "What Every Woman Should Know" (http://ssa.gov/pubs/10127.html).

Stovall, Jim. *The Ultimate Financial Plan: Balancing Your Money and Life.* New York: John Wiley & Sons, 2011.

Weston, Liz. *The 10 Commandments of Money: Survive and Thrive in the New Economy.* New York: Hudson Street Press, 2011.

Yeager, Jeff. *The Cheapskate Next Door: The Surprising Secrets of Americans Living Happily Below Their Means.* New York: Three Rivers Press, 2010.

Appendix 8: How the States Tax Singles—2012

State	Personal Income Tax Rate (%)	State and Local Sales Tax Range (%)	State Does NOT Tax Social Security Benefits	State Has an Estate Tax	State Has an Inheritance Tax
Alabama	2.0–5.0	4.0–12.0	X		
Alaska	None	0–7.5	X		
Arizona	2.59–4.54	6.6–12.7	X		
Arkansas	1.0–7.0	6.0–11.5	X		
California	1.0–9.3	6.25–9.75	X		
Colorado	4.63	2.9–9.9			
Connecticut	3.0–6.7	6.350		X	
Delaware	2.2–6.75	None	X	X	
District of Columbia	4.0–8.95	6.0	X	X	
Florida	None	6.0–7.5	X		
Georgia	1.0–6.0	4.0–8.0	X		
Hawaii	1.4–11.0	4.0–4.5	X	X	
Idaho	1.6–7.8	6.0–9.0	X		
Illinois	5.0	6.25–10.5	X	X	
Indiana	3.4	7.0	X		X
Iowa	0.36–8.98	6.0–8.0			X
Kansas	3.5–6.45	6.3–11.3	X		
Kentucky	2.0–6.0	6.0	X		X
Louisiana	2.0–6.0	4.0–10.75	X		
Maine	2.0–8.5	5.0	X	X	

State	Personal Income Tax Rate (%)	State and Local Sales Tax Range (%)	State Does NOT Tax Social Security Benefits	State Has an Estate Tax	State Has an Inheritance Tax
Maryland	2.0–5.5	6.0	X	X	X
Massachusetts	5.3	6.25	X	X	
Michigan	4.35	6.0	X		
Minnesota	5.35–7.85	6.875–7.875		X	
Mississippi	3.0–5.0	7.0–7.25	X		
Missouri	1.5–6.0	4.225–10.85			
Montana	1.0–6.9	None			
Nebraska	2.56–6.84	5.5–7.5			X
Nevada	None	6.85–8.1	X		
New Hampshire	5.0 on dividends and interest only	None	X		
New Jersey	1.4–8.97	7.0	X	X	X
New Mexico	1.7–4.9	5.125–10.75			
New York	4.0–8.82	4.0–9.0	X	X	
North Carolina	6.0–7.75	4.75–7.75	X	X	
North Dakota	1.51–3.99	5.0–8.0			
Ohio	0.587–5.925	5.5–7.75	X	X	
Oklahoma	0.5–5.25	4.5–10.85	X		
Oregon	5.0–9.9	None	X	X	
Pennsylvania	3.07	6.0–8.0	X		X
Rhode Island	3.75–5.99	7.0		X	
South Carolina	0–7.0	6.0–9.0	X		

State	Personal Income Tax Rate (%)	State and Local Sales Tax Range (%)	State Does NOT Tax Social Security Benefits	State Has an Estate Tax	State Has an Inheritance Tax
South Dakota	None	4.0–6.0	X		
Tennessee	6.0 on dividends and interest only	7.0–9.75	X	X	
Texas	None	6.25–8.25	X		
Utah	5.0	4.7–9.95			
Vermont	3.55–8.95	6.0–7.0		X	
Virginia	2.0–5.75	4.0–5.5	X		
Washington	None	6.5–9.5	X	X	
West Virginia	3.0–6.5	6.0–7.0			
Wisconsin	4.6–7.75	5.0–6.5	X		
Wyoming	None	4.0–8.0	X		

References

Aagaard-Tillery, Kjersti. "Developmental Origins of Disease and Determinants of Chromatin Structure: Maternal Diet Modifies the Primate Fetal Epigenome." *Journal of Molecular Endocrinology*, Volume 41, 2008, 91–102.

Accountemps Survey. "What You Don't Know Can Hurt You." 2011. (www.accountemps.rhi.mediaroom.com/interview_mistake).

Ajilon Professional Staffing. "Ten Best Cities for Finding Employment in the U.S," 2011. (www.ajilon.com/about-us/press-room/press-releases/Pages/ajilon-professional-staffing-announces-10-best-cities-to-find-a-job.aspx).

Allianz Survey. "Allianz Demographic Pulse," January 2011. (www.allianz.com/static-resources/en/economic_research/images_englisch/pdf_downloads/specials/v_1296472489000/demographicpulsejan11.pdf).

Ameriprise Financial. "The New Retirement Mindscape II" study, 2010. (www.newsroom.ameriprise.com/article_display.cfm?article_id=1439).

Associated Press. "Boomers Swelling the Ranks of Online Dating Sites." *USA Today*, June 3, 2011. (www.usatoday.com/news/health/wellness/dating/story/2011/06/Boomers-swelling-the-ranks-of-online-dating-sites—/48018456/1).

Babcock, Linda. *Women Don't Ask: The High Cost of Avoiding Negotiation—and Positive Strategies for Change.* New York: Bantam, 2007.

Baron, Kelly G. "Role of Sleep Timing in Caloric Intake and BMI." *Obesity*, Volume 19, 2011, 1374–1381.

Barry, Lisa. "Higher Burden of Depression Among Older Women." *Archives of General Psychiatry*, Volume 65, No. 2, 2008, 172–178.

Belsky, Gary and Gilovich, Thomas. "Struggling for Investment Answers? It Helps to Reframe the Question." *Time*, October 12, 2011.

Bluestone, Barry. "After the Recovery: Help Needed." MetLife Foundation, 2010. (www.encore.org/files/research/JobsBluestone Paper3-5-10.pdf).

Brady, John. "Our 2012 Best Places to Retire List," TopRetirements.com, 2012. (www.topretirements.com).

References

Brandon, Emily. "10 Bargain Retirement Spots." *U.S. News & World Report,* 2011. (www.money.usnews.com/money/retirement/slideshows/10-bargain -retirement -spots).

Brandon, Emily. "10 Best Places for Single Seniors to Retire," *U.S. News & World Report,* 2010. (www.money.usnews.com/money/retirement /articles/2010/11/01/the-10-best-places-for-single-seniors-to-retire).

Braun, Barry. "Effects of Exercise on Energy-Regulating Hormones and Appetite in Men and Women." *American Journal of Physiology,* Volume 296, No. 2, 2009, 233–242.

Carrns, Ann. "Fees, Fees, Everywhere Higher Bank Fees," *New York Times,* September 28, 2011. (www.bucks.blogs.nytimes.com/2011/09/28 /fees-fees-everywhere-higher-bank-fees/).

Chen, Wendy. "Moderate Alcohol Consumption During Adult Life, Drinking Patterns, and Breast Cancer Risk." *Journal of the American Medical Association,* Volume 306, No. 17, November 2011, 1884–1890.

Cherkas, Lynn. "The Association Between Physical Activity in Leisure Time and Leukocyte Telomere Length." *Archives of Internal Medicine,* Volume 168, No. 2, 2008, 154–158.

Cohen, Robin. "Health Insurance Coverage," National Center for Health Statistics, 2010. (www.cdc.gov/nchs/data/nhis/earlyrelease /insur201112.htm).

Consumers Union. "Reverse Mortgages Can Come with Big Risks & High Costs for Seniors," *Consumer Reports,* December 7, 2010. (www .consumersunion.org/pub/core_financial_services/017190.html).

Costanzo, Erin. "Psychosocial Factors and Interleukin-6 Among Women with Advanced Ovarian Cancer." *Cancer,* Volume 104, No. 2, 2005, 305–313.

DALBAR. "Quantitative Analysis of Investor Behavior 2011," March 2011. (www.qaib.com/public/default.aspx).

Davis, Susan. "America's Top 50 Courses for Women," *Golf Digest Woman,* 2011. (www.golfdigest.com/golf-courses/2011-06/top-50- courses- for-women).

Employee Benefit Research Institute. "The 2010 Retirement Confidence Survey," 2010. (www.ebri.org/pdf/briefspdf/EBRI_IB_03-2010_ No340 _ RCS.pdf).

Family Caregiver Alliance. Selected Caregiver Statistics, 2006. (www.care giver.org/caregiver/jsp/content_node.jsp?nodeid=1822&expandnod eid=384).

Farzaneh-Far, Ramin. "Association of Marine Omega-3 Fatty Acid Levels with Telomeric Aging in Patients with Coronary Heart Disease." *Journal of the American Medical Association,* Volume 303, No. 3, 2010, 250–257.

Finke, Michael. "Old Age and the Decline in Financial Literacy," *Finance,* Volume 14, 2011, 1–33.

References

Fleming, Michael. "Brief Physician Advice for Alcohol Problems in Older Adults: Randomized Community-Based Trial." *The Journal of Family Practice*, Volume 8, No. 5, 1999, 378–384.

Frasure-Smith, Nancy. "Social Support, Depression, and Mortality During the First Year After Myocardial Infarction." *Circulation*, Volume 101, No. 16, 2000, 1919–1924.

Fried, Carla. "Retirement Risk for Women: Oversold Immediate Annuities," CBS MoneyWatch, April 25, 2010. (www.cbsnews.com/8301-505146_162-39540558/ retirement- risk- for-women-oversold-immediate-annuities/).

Giles, Lynn. "Effect of Social Networks on 10-Year Survival in Very Old Australians." *Journal of Epidemiology and Community Health*, Volume 59, 2005, 574–579.

Golson, Barry. "Paradise Found," *AARP: The Magazine*, September/October 2010. (www.aarp.org/home-garden/livable-communities/info-07-2010/paradise_found.html)

Gopie, Nigel. "A Double Dissociation of Implicit and Explicit Memory in Younger and Older Adults." *Psychological Science*, Volume 22, No. 5, 2011, 634–640.

Gu, Jian. "Genetic Variation Linked to Longer Telomeres and Lower Risk of Bladder Cancer." *American Association for Cancer Research*, 2011.

Harris Interactive poll commissioned by Rocket Lawyer, March 9–13, 2011. (www.insider.rocketlawyer.com/2011-wills-estate-planning-survey-9524).

Harris Interactive. "The MainStay Investments Boomer Retirement Lifestyle Study," May 13, 2010. (www.prnewswire.com/news-rcleases/baby-boomers-willing-to-delay-gratification-now-for-a-better-lifestyle-in-their-golden-years-100024919.html).

Higgins, Janine. "Resistant Starch Consumption Promotes Lipid Oxidation." *Nutrition & Metabolism*, Volume 1, No. 8, 2004, 1–8.

Hill, Alison. "Infectious Disease Modeling of Social Contagion in Networks." *PLoS Computational Biology*, Volume 6, No. 11, 2010, 1–15.

Hollis, Jack. "Weight Loss During the Intensive Intervention Phase of the Weight-Loss Maintenance Trial." *American Journal of Preventive Medicine*, Volume 35, No. 2, 2008, 118–126.

Johnson, Rebecca. Human Companion Animal Attachment: Motivation for Adherence to a Walking Program. *Clinical Nursing Research*, Volume 19, No. 4, 2010, 387–402.

Kalata, Jean. "Looking at Act II of Women's Lives: Thriving and Striving from 45 On," The AARP Foundation Women's Leadership Circle Study, 2006. (http://assets.aarp.org/rgcenter/general/wlcresearch_1.pdf).

Kalish, Nancy. *Lost and Found Lovers: Facts and Fantasies of Rekindled Romances*. New York: William Morrow, 1997.

References

Korb, Brian. "Financial Planners and Baby Boomer Widows: Building a Trusting Relationship," *Journal of Financial Planning*, Volume 23, Issue 1, 48–61.

Lahey, Joanna. "Do Older Workers Face Discrimination?" Center for Retirement Research at Boston College, No. 33, 2005, 1–8.

Li, Jie. "Improvement in Chewing Activity Reduces Energy Intake in One Meal and Modulates Plasma Gut Hormone Concentrations in Obese and Lean Young Chinese Men." *The American Journal of Clinical Nutrition*, Volume 94, No. 3, 2011, 709–716.

Libert, Claude. "X Chromosome-Located MicroRNAs in Immunity: Might They Explain Male/Female Differences?" *BioEssays*, 2011. (www.ts-si .org/files/doi101002bies201100047.pdf).

Lindquist, Lee. "Cruise Ship Care: A Proposed Alternative to Assisted Living Facilities." *Journal of the American Geriatrics Society*, Volume 52, Issue 11, November 2004, 1951–1954.

Livermore, Gina. "The Role of Health Insurance in Successful Labor Force Entry and Employment Retention." U.S. Department of Health and Human Services, 2001. (www.aspe.hhs.gov/daltcp/reports/lfentry.htm).

Lowe, Dawn. "Mechanisms Behind Estrogen's Beneficial Effect on Muscle Strength in Females." *Exercise and Sport Sciences Reviews*, Volume 38, No. 2, 2010, 61–67.

Lucas, Richard E. "Reexaming Adaptation and the Set Point Model of Happiness: Reactions to Changes in Marital Status." *Journal of Personality and Social Psychology*, Volume 84, No. 3, 2003, 527–539.

Luscombe, Belinda. "Who Needs Marriage? A Changing Institution." *Time*, November 18, 2010. (www.time.com/time/magazine/article /0,9171,2032116,00.html).

MacLean, Paul. "Regular Exercise Attenuates the Metabolic Drive to Re-gain Weight After Long-Term Weight Loss." *American Journal of Physiology*, Volume 297, No. 3, 2009, 793–802.

Marttila Strategies. "The Retirement Abyss: America's Seniors' Search for Security," National Reverse Mortgage Lenders Association, October 2010. (https://services.nrmlaonline.org/NRMLA_Documents/NRMLA _Poll_Presentation.pdf).

Max, Sarah. "25 Best Places to Retire," CNN Money, 2010. (www.money .cnn.com/galleries/2011/real_estate/1109/gallery.best_places_retire .moneymag/index.html)

McSweeney, J. C., et al. "Women's Early Warning Symptoms of Acute Myocardial Infarction." *Circulation*, November 25, 2003, 108(21): 2619–23.

MetLife Mature Market Institute. "Housing for the 55+ Market: Trends and Insights on Boomers and Beyond," 2009. (www.metlife.com/assets /cao/mmi/publications/studies/mmi-55-housing-trends-study-.pdf).

References

MetLife Mature Market Institute. "The 2011 MetLife Market Survey of Nursing Home, Assisted Living, Adult Day Services, and Home Health Care Costs," October 2011. (www.metlife.com/assets/cao/mmi/pub lications/studies/2011/mmi-market-survey-nursing-home-assisted-living-adult-day-services-costs.pdf).

National Center for Health Statistics (CDC). "Marriage and Divorce," April 2010. (www.cdc.gov/nchs/mardiv.htm).

National Endowment for Financial Education Poll conducted by U.S. Harris Interactive, May 10–12, 2011. (www.nefe.org/press-room/news/parents-financially-supporting-adult-children.aspx).

Odean, Terrance. "Boys Will Be Boys: Gender, Overconfidence, and Common Stock Investment." *Quarterly Journal of Economics*, Volume 116, No. 1, 2001, 261–292.

Ortega, Francisco. "In Fitness and Health? A Prospective Study of Changes in Marital Status and Fitness in Men and Women." *American Journal of Epidemiology*, Volume 10, 2010, 337–334.

Painter, James. "The Pistachio Principle." American Dietetic Association Food & Nutrition Conference & Expo, 2010. Pennsylvania Convention Center, Philadelphia, Pennsylvania (www.businesswire .com/news/home/20101122005262/en/California-Pistachios-Calorie-Reduction-Restriction).

Patel, Alpha. "Leisure Time Spent Sitting in Relation to Total Mortality in a Prospective Cohort of US Adults." *American Journal of Epidemiology*, July 22, 2010.

Payne, Krista. "Household Financial Contributions by Adult Live-in Children Are Influenced by Family Structure," presentation at the American Sociological Association, San Francisco, August, 2009. (www.asanet.org/press/20090810_2.cfm).

Petersen, Ronald. "Prevalence of Mild Cognitive Impairment Is Higher in Men: The Mayo Clinic Study of Aging." *Neurology*, Volume 75, 2010, 889–897.

Puchalski, Christina. "The Role of Spirituality in Health Care." Baylor University Medical Center Proceedings, Volume 14, 2001, 352-357.

Puterman, Eli. "The Power of Exercise: Buffering the Effect of Chronic Stress on Telomere Length." *Public Library of Science*, Volume 5, No. 5, 2010, 1–6.

Reis, J. P., Loria, C. M., Sorlie, P. D., et al. Lifestyle Factors and Risk for New-Onset Diabetes. A Population-Based Cohort Study. *Annals of Internal Medicine*, 2011; 155:292–299.

References

Robert Charles Lesser & Co. "RCLCO Announces Top-Selling U.S. Master-Planned Communities for 2010," March 17, 2011. (www.marketwire.com/press-release/rclco-announces-top-selling-us-master-planned-communities-for-2010-1413642.htm).

Rogers, Todd. "The Artful Dodge: Answering the Wrong Question the Right Way." *Journal of Experimental Psychology*, Volume 17, No. 2, 2011, 139–147.

Simon, Robin. "The Joys of Parenthood, Reconsidered." *American Sociological Association*, Volume 7, No. 2, 2008, 40–45.

Sinclair, Kevin. "Housing 360 Survey," Hanley Wood, July 2011. (www.hanleywood.com/?page=prbmhousing360results).

Smith, Linell. "Gay Boomers are Wary of Homophobic Retirement Care," *Baltimore Sun*, April 6, 2007.

Society of Actuaries Online Survey, January 5, 2011. (www.soa.org/News-and-Publications/Newsroom/Press-Releases/Nearly-Half-of-Americans-Ages-45-70-Have-No-Plans-to-Protect-Themselves-Against-Outliving-Assets-or-the-Rising-Cost-of-Healthcare-in-Later-Life.aspx).

Soman, Dilip. "The Fewer the Better: Number of Goals and Savings Behavior," *Journal of Marketing Research*, Volume 48, No. 6, December 2011, i–vi.

St-Onge, Marie-Pierre. "Short Sleep Duration Increases Energy and Fat Intakes in Normal Weight Men and Women." American Heart Association Conference, 2011.

Straus, Jillian. "Lone Stars: Being Single." *Psychology Today*, May 1, 2006.

Sun, Qi. "Alcohol Consumption at Midlife and Successful Ageing in Women: a Prospective Cohort Analysis in the Nurses' Health Study." *PLoS Medicine*, Sept. 6, 2011. (www.plosmedicine.org/article/info%3Adoi%2F10.1371%2Fjournal.pmed.1001090).

Survey by BLR (Business and Legal Resources). "Weight Discrimination Still an Issue in the Workplace," 2010. (www.hr.blr.com/HR-news/Staffing-Training/Recruiting/Weight-Discrimination-Still-an-Issue-in-the-Workpl/).

Tarnopolsky, Mark. "Endurance Exercises Rescue Progeroid Aging and Induces System Mitochondrial Rejuvenation in mtDNA Mutator Mice." *Proceedings of the National Academy of Sciences of the United States of America*, Volume 108, No. 10, 2011, 4135–4140.

The Charles Schwab Q4 Retirement Omnibus Survey, 2009. (www.scrs.schwab.com/press_releases/20091201_RLRS_Q4_Pulse_Survey.pdf).

References

Transamerica Center for Retirement Studies. "Strengthening Retirement Savings in a Weak Economy." 10th annual Transamerica Retirement Survey, April 14, 2009. (www.transamericacenter.org/resources /TCRS%2010th%20Annual%20Survey%20-%20Strengthening%20 Savings.pdf).

Tumin, Dmitry. "Large Weight Gains Most Likely for Men After Divorce, Women After Marriage." Annual Meeting of the American Sociological Association, Las Vegas, August 22, 2011. (www .researchnews.osu.edu/archive/weightshock.htm).

Turek, Fred. "Circadian Timing of Food Intake Contributes to Weight Gain." *Obesity*, Volume 17, No. 11, 2009, 2100–2102.

Twentysomething, Inc. 2011 Poll of Graduates About Returning Home. (www.newsfeed.time.com/2011/05/10/survey-85-of-new-college-grads -moving-back-in-with-mom-and-dad/).

U.S. Census Bureau. "Families and Living Arrangements." 2011 March Current Population Survey, March 2011.

U.S. Government Accountability Office. "Income Security," GAO, October 2011.

Waite, Linda J. "Does Marriage Matter?" *Demography*, Volume 32, No. 4, 1995, 483–508.

Watkins, Wade. "Financial Fraud and the Elderly," *Deseret News*, October 6, 2011.

Wells Fargo and Harris Interactive. "Retirement Survey from Wells Fargo and Company (7th Annual)," August 9–September 23, 2011. (www .wellsfargo.com/press/2011/20111116_80IsTheNew65).

Whelehan, Barbara. "Social Security Benefits vs. Taxes," Bankrate .com, January 7, 2011. (www.bankrate.com/financing/retirement/ social-security-benefits-vs-taxes/).

Whitehouse, Mark. "Number of the Week: Class of 2011, Most Indebted Ever." *Wall Street Journal*, May 7, 2011. (www.finance.yahoo.com/news /class-2011-most-indebted-ever-070000924.html).

Yvonne, Michael. "Living Arrangements, Social Integration, and Change in Functional Health Status." *American Journal of Epidemiology*, Volume 153, No. 1, 2001, 123–131.

Zoosk's Online National Pet Peeve Week survey of October 2011. (www.reuters .com/article/2011/10/10/idUS114086+10-Oct-2011+PRN20111010).

About the Author

Jan Cullinane is the best-selling co-author of *The New Retirement: The Ultimate Guide to the Rest of Your Life* and *Retire Happy!* She has been featured on TV, on the radio, and in many newspapers and magazines. *The New Retirement* reached the number two rank on both Barnes and Noble's Web site and Amazon.com, and was chosen as a book club selection by *The Washington Post's* "The Color of Money" columnist Michelle Singletary. Cullinane is a speaker and consultant on retirement lifestyle issues; her clients include Ford Motor Company, Deloitte & Touche LLP, the federal government, the Smithsonian Institution, and Wells Fargo Advisors. Cullinane has a bachelor's and master's degree from the University of Maryland. She lives in Palm Coast, Florida and can speak backwards fluently!

Index

Index